Flash Technique

A Clinician's Manual for Trauma Processing and EMDR Integration

Theo Leonard Green

ISBN: 978-1-7643782-8-4

First Edition, 2025

Attribution and Disclaimer

The Flash Technique was developed by Philip Manfield, Ph.D., in collaboration with Lewis Engel, Ph.D., Joan Lovett, M.D., and David Manfield. The technique was formally introduced in the peer-reviewed article "Use of the Flash Technique in EMDR Therapy: Four Case Examples" published in the Journal of EMDR Practice and Research (2017, Volume 11, Issue 4, pages 195-205).

The author of this book, **Theo Leonard Green**, did not develop the Flash Technique and makes no claim to its creation or original conceptualization. This manual serves as an educational resource to help clinicians understand and implement the Flash Technique as developed by Dr. Manfield and colleagues.

Purpose and Scope

This book provides clinical protocols, implementation guidance, and practical applications of the Flash Technique based on:

- Published peer-reviewed research
- Established training protocols
- Clinical case examples (presented as composites for confidentiality)
- The author's professional experience as a registered mental health practitioner

Original Research References

Readers are encouraged to consult the original research and training materials:

- Manfield, P., Lovett, J., Engel, L., & Manfield, D. (2017). Use of the Flash Technique in EMDR therapy: Four case examples. *Journal of EMDR Practice and Research, 11*(4), 195-205.

- Manfield, P., Taylor, J., Dornbush, R., Engel, L., & Greenwald, R. (2024). Preliminary evidence for the acceptability, safety, and efficacy of the flash technique. *Frontiers in Psychology, 15*, 1257905.

For official Flash Technique training, visit www.flashtechnique.com or www.philipmanfield.com.

Professional Use Only

This book is intended exclusively for licensed mental health professionals, including psychologists, licensed clinical social workers, marriage and family therapists, professional counselors, and psychiatrists who have completed appropriate trauma therapy training. The Flash Technique should only be used within one's scope of practice and professional competence.

Accuracy and Clinical Representation

While every effort has been made to accurately represent the Flash Technique as developed and taught by Dr. Manfield and colleagues, this book reflects the author's understanding and clinical application of the technique. Any errors in representation are unintentional. Clinicians are responsible for obtaining proper training and staying current with evolving protocols and research.

The names and scenarios depicted in this book are purely for illustrative purposes only. Any resemblance to actual persons, living or dead, or actual events is purely coincidental. Case examples have been modified and composited to protect client confidentiality while demonstrating clinical concepts.

No Affiliation

This book is not endorsed by, sponsored by, or officially affiliated with Dr. Philip Manfield, Dr. Lewis Engel, or any Flash Technique training organization. The views and clinical recommendations expressed are those of the author based on published research and clinical experience.

Trademark and Copyright Notice

Table of Contents

Chapter 1: What Makes Flash Technique Different

You've probably had this experience: A client comes to your office ready to work on their trauma. They want to heal. They're motivated. But the moment you start moving toward the traumatic memory, their body tenses up. Their breathing gets shallow. They start dissociating or they shut down completely.

"I can't do this," they say. And honestly? They're right. In that moment, they can't.

This is the wall that trauma therapists hit all the time. Traditional exposure-based treatments—whether it's prolonged exposure, cognitive processing therapy, or even standard EMDR—require clients to tolerate distress while they process their trauma. That's the deal. You have to feel it to heal it, right?

Except what happens when feeling it is simply too much?

That's the problem Flash Technique was designed to solve. And it does something that sounds almost too good to be true: It helps clients process traumatic memories without the usual overwhelm, distress, or emotional flooding. No gritting through it. No white-knuckling your way through exposure. Just a gentler path to the same destination (Manfield, Engel, Greenwald, & Bullard, 2017).

The Real Problem: When Standard Approaches Ask Too Much

Let's be honest about something. Traditional trauma processing works. EMDR works. Prolonged exposure works. The research is solid (Shapiro, 2018). But here's what the research doesn't always show: the dropout rates.

Studies on exposure-based treatments report dropout rates ranging from 20% to 50% (Imel, Laska, Jakupcak, & Simpson, 2013). That means up to half of the people who start trauma therapy don't finish it. And we're not talking about people who got better and left early. We're talking about people who couldn't tolerate the treatment.

Think about Maria (not her real name, but a composite of clients many therapists see). She's a 34-year-old woman who survived a violent assault three years ago. She meets full criteria for PTSD. Nightmares, avoidance, hypervigilance—the whole picture. She's seen two therapists before you. Both times, she started trauma-focused treatment. Both times, she dropped out after three or four sessions.

"It was too much," she tells you in your first session. "Just talking about it made me feel like I was back there. I couldn't sleep for days afterward. I started drinking again just to calm down."

So what do you do? You could try preparation techniques—grounding skills, resource development, building her window of tolerance. That's good practice. EMDR Phase 2 work. But sometimes even that isn't enough. Some clients remain too dysregulated to engage with the trauma directly, no matter how much preparation you do.

This is where Flash Technique changes the game.

How Flash Actually Works: The 10-45 Minute Promise

Here's what happens in a typical Flash session. You don't start by talking about the trauma (thank goodness, because your client doesn't want to). Instead, you help them identify something positive to focus on—something engaging and pleasant. Maybe it's imagining themselves at the beach. Maybe it's thinking about their dog. Maybe it's visualizing their favorite peaceful place.

This is called the Positive Engaging Focus, or PEF. We'll get into the details later, but for now, just know that the PEF becomes the client's anchor point.

Then you do something that seems almost absurdly simple. You ask the client to hold the PEF in their awareness while they very briefly—we're talking one or two seconds—blink their attention to the traumatic memory and immediately back to the PEF. Like flashing past something scary in your peripheral vision. You don't stop and stare. You just blink past it (Manfield et al., 2017).

You add bilateral stimulation (eye movements, tapping, or audio tones) while this happens. The client does this rapid "flash" several times—maybe 10 to 30 repetitions over the course of 10 to 45 minutes. And here's the remarkable part: When you check in afterward, the distress level has typically dropped significantly. Sometimes dramatically.

A memory that was a 9 or 10 out of 10 in distress might drop to a 3 or 4. Or lower. In less than an hour. Without the client having to sit with the overwhelming feelings or describe the trauma in detail.

Sounds too easy, right? That's what most therapists think at first (myself included, when I first learned about it). But the research backs it up.

Why This Isn't Magic: The Science Behind the Flash

So what's actually happening here? How can something so brief produce such significant results?

The answer lies in how our brains process threatening information. When you experience trauma, your brain's threat detection system—particularly the amygdala—goes into overdrive. The memory gets encoded with intense emotional and physiological arousal. Every time you recall that memory, you're essentially reactivating that threat response (van der Kolk, 2014).

Traditional exposure therapy works by having you stay with the memory long enough for habituation to occur. Your nervous system learns, "Okay, I'm remembering something scary, but I'm actually safe right now." That learning happens, but it takes time and it requires tolerating significant distress during the process.

Flash Technique does something different. By keeping your attention primarily on something positive and only briefly glancing at the trauma, you're preventing the full activation of the threat response. You're not triggering the same level of distress that would normally occur (Manfield et al., 2017).

Think of it like this. Imagine you're afraid of spiders. Traditional exposure therapy might have you hold a spider while you learn to tolerate your anxiety. Flash is more like walking past the spider enclosure at the zoo while focusing on your ice cream cone. You see the spiders peripherally (so your brain is processing the stimulus), but you're not activating the full fear response.

The bilateral stimulation—eye movements or tapping—adds another element. Research on EMDR suggests that bilateral

4

stimulation helps with memory reconsolidation and reduces the emotional intensity of memories (Shapiro, 2018). Flash combines this with the protective effect of the PEF.

The result? Your brain can reprocess the traumatic memory without overwhelming your nervous system. The memory becomes less emotionally charged, but you haven't had to suffer through the process (Manfield & Engel, 2018).

Who Actually Benefits: From Single Trauma to Complex PTSD

Let me tell you about three different clients.

Client One: Jake, 28, Single-Incident Trauma

Jake was in a serious car accident six months ago. No major physical injuries, but he can't drive anymore without panic attacks. He avoids highways completely. The accident replays in his mind several times a day, especially when he hears screeching tires.

Jake is a good candidate for Flash. He has a single, contained traumatic memory. He has good reality testing (he knows he's safe now, even though his nervous system doesn't agree). He can identify positive things in his life to use as a PEF. Classic PTSD from a discrete trauma.

After one Flash session targeting the accident memory, Jake's distress about the accident dropped from an 8 to a 2. Two weeks later, he was driving on highways again. Not completely comfortable, but functional. A few more processing sessions addressed remaining anxiety, but Flash got him over the initial hurdle (this scenario reflects typical outcomes reported in published case studies; Manfield et al., 2017).

Client Two: Sofia, 42, Complex Developmental Trauma

Sofia grew up in a home with an alcoholic, violent father. She has dozens of traumatic memories spanning 15 years of childhood. She meets criteria for complex PTSD. She's highly dissociative. Traditional EMDR has been too overwhelming for her in the past.

Sofia is also a good candidate for Flash, but in a different way. You wouldn't try to process all her trauma in one session (or ten sessions). Instead, you'd use Flash strategically. Maybe you start with one specific memory—the time she hid in the closet while her father raged. That memory is connected to many others, but it's a starting point.

Flash allows Sofia to begin processing without becoming overwhelmed or dissociating. Once that memory is less distressing, you can move to another. Bit by bit, memory by memory. It's slower than working with single-incident trauma, but it's actually possible—which is more than Sofia could say about previous treatment attempts (this approach aligns with clinical applications described in Flash Technique literature; Manfield et al., 2017).

Client Three: David, 55, First Responder

David is a firefighter with 30 years on the job. He's seen things. Lots of things. Dead children. People he couldn't save. Buildings collapsing. He's starting to have nightmares again after a particularly bad call. He drinks too much. His marriage is struggling.

David doesn't want to talk about the worst things he's seen. He's not going to sit in your office and narrate the details. That's not happening. But Flash? Flash lets him work on those memories without disclosure. You can help him process the traumatic material without him having to describe what he saw.

That's huge for someone like David. And it's huge for military veterans, sexual assault survivors, and anyone else who finds verbal disclosure retraumatizing or impossible (Manfield et al., 2017).

The Range of Applications: Beyond PTSD

The research and clinical practice have shown Flash can help with more than just PTSD. Here's what we're seeing:

Phobias: That overwhelming fear of dogs that started when you were bitten as a kid? Flash can help reprocess that original trauma, reducing the phobic response.

Performance Anxiety: The humiliating experience of forgetting your lines in the school play that still makes you panic before presentations? Flash can address that underlying traumatic memory.

Grief: Sometimes grief gets stuck because the circumstances of a death were traumatic—watching someone die, feeling helpless, experiencing shocking loss. Flash can help process the traumatic aspects, allowing healthier grieving to occur.

Chronic Pain: When pain has a trauma history (abuse, medical trauma, accidents), addressing those memories with Flash sometimes reduces pain intensity. The body has been holding the trauma.

Depression: Depression that's rooted in traumatic experiences—loss, humiliation, betrayal—may improve when those underlying memories are processed (Flashtechnique.com, 2024).

One study examined Flash Technique across various diagnoses and found significant reductions in distress regardless of whether clients met full PTSD criteria (Manfield et al., 2017).

The common factor wasn't the diagnosis. It was the presence of distressing memories that were interfering with functioning.

What You Need to Know Before You Start

Here's the thing about Flash: It's deceptively simple. The protocol looks straightforward on paper. But like any therapeutic technique, there's nuance in the application.

First, understand that Flash isn't a replacement for comprehensive trauma treatment. It's one tool in your toolkit. Some clients will need only Flash. Others will need Flash as preparation for deeper EMDR processing. Still others might use Flash for some memories and traditional exposure for others. You need to assess and adapt.

Second, Flash requires training. Reading about it isn't enough. You need to understand the theory, practice the protocol, and know when to modify your approach. Most training organizations recommend at least 6 hours of initial training, though you can learn the basic protocol in less time (Flashtechnique.com, 2024).

Third, know your contraindications. Flash isn't appropriate for everyone. Clients with active psychosis, severe dissociative disorders without stabilization, or those in immediate crisis need different interventions first. You need to screen carefully.

Fourth, prepare for this to feel weird at first. When clients report significant distress reduction after just 20 minutes of this seemingly indirect intervention, your internal skeptic might activate. "Did that really just happen?" Yes. It did. Trust the process, but also verify with careful assessment.

Fifth, remember that reducing distress doesn't mean the work is done. A memory with low distress still needs cognitive processing sometimes. You still need to help clients integrate the experience, challenge maladaptive beliefs, and build new narratives. Flash clears the path; you still need to walk it with your client.

Let's talk about Jen (composite example). She came in for Flash treatment of a sexual assault memory. After one session, her distress dropped from a 10 to a 2. Great, right? But she still believed "I'm damaged goods" and "I can't trust anyone." The emotional charge was gone, but the cognitive distortions remained. We still needed to do that work.

Getting Your Head Around the Paradigm Shift

If you've been trained in traditional exposure therapy or even standard EMDR, Flash might mess with your assumptions about how trauma treatment has to work. You might have learned that clients must confront their fears fully, must tolerate distress, must process emotionally to heal.

Flash says: Actually, maybe not always.

That's not saying exposure is wrong. Exposure works. But exposure isn't the only path. For clients who can't tolerate it or won't complete it, Flash offers an alternative route to the same destination.

Some therapists initially resist this. "It's avoidance," they say. "Clients need to face their trauma directly." But here's the thing: Flash isn't avoidance. The client IS engaging with the traumatic memory. Just briefly. Just enough. With protection in place.

Think of it like learning to swim. One approach says you throw people in the deep end and they figure it out. Some people do. Others panic and develop a fear of water. Flash is more like starting in the shallow end with a floatie. You're still getting in the water. You're just doing it in a way that doesn't activate drowning panic.

By the end of the process, people often report something surprising: "I can think about what happened now without falling apart. It's like it happened to me, but it's in the past. It doesn't have the same power anymore."

That's exactly what we're going for.

Making Room for Something Different

The development of Flash Technique represents something bigger than just another trauma protocol. It represents a shift in how we think about trauma treatment. For decades, the assumption was that healing from trauma required going through pain—that suffering during treatment was inevitable, even necessary.

Flash challenges that assumption. What if we can reduce suffering during treatment? What if there's a gentler path that works just as well (or better for some clients)?

The research is saying yes, there is (we'll look at that research in detail in the next chapter). Clinical experience is confirming it. And clients—especially those who tried other approaches and couldn't tolerate them—are benefiting.

So if you're reading this as a therapist trained in traditional approaches, I'm asking you to stay open. You don't have to abandon what you already know. You don't have to choose between Flash and EMDR, or Flash and CPT. You're adding to your toolkit, not replacing it.

And if you're a therapist who's been frustrated watching clients drop out because traditional approaches were too overwhelming? Flash might be exactly what you've been looking for. A way to help those clients who've been told, implicitly or explicitly, that they're not ready for trauma treatment. That they need more preparation. More stabilization. More time.

Maybe what they really needed was a different approach. One that meets them where they are instead of asking them to climb a mountain before they can start healing.

That's what makes Flash different. It's not just a technique. It's a reframing of what trauma treatment can look like when we prioritize both effectiveness AND tolerability.

And here's what I find most encouraging: We're not sacrificing one for the other. The evidence suggests Flash is both highly effective AND highly tolerable (Manfield et al., 2017). That's rare in any medical or psychological treatment. Usually there's a trade-off. Not here.

So let's look at that evidence. Let's see what the research actually shows about whether this approach lives up to its promise. Because clinical enthusiasm is great, but data is better.

What Comes Next

In the next chapter, we'll examine the research foundation for Flash Technique. Not just hand-waving at "studies show" but actually looking at what those studies measured, who they studied, and what the results mean for your practice. Because before you integrate any new intervention into your clinical work, you need to know the evidence base.

Then we'll get into the theory—why Flash works from a neuroscience and psychological perspective. How attention, memory reconsolidation, and bilateral stimulation come together to create change. And how the Positive Engaging Focus protects clients while they process trauma.

After that? The practical stuff. The actual protocol, step by step. How to develop a PEF. How to troubleshoot when things don't go as planned. How to integrate Flash with whatever modality you already practice.

But we're starting with the fundamental question: What problem does Flash solve? And you now know the answer. It solves the problem of trauma treatment being too overwhelming for many clients to complete. It offers a path forward when other paths have been blocked by distress, avoidance, and overwhelm.

That's not a small thing. That's potentially treatment access for thousands of people who've been stuck. And if you're a therapist, it's potentially a way to help clients you've worried about—the ones who need trauma treatment but can't tolerate traditional approaches.

So yeah, Flash is different. Refreshingly, importantly different. And the field is better for it.

What You'll Take Away From This

Flash Technique addresses a critical gap in trauma treatment: helping clients who are too distressed to engage in traditional exposure-based processing. It works by having clients briefly "flash" their attention to traumatic memories while maintaining focus on a positive, engaging stimulus. This reduces overwhelming distress without sacrificing effectiveness.

The technique helps with everything from single-incident PTSD to complex developmental trauma, and it offers particular

12

advantages for clients who can't or won't disclose trauma details. The key difference from traditional approaches is that Flash prioritizes tolerability alongside effectiveness—you don't have to choose between what works and what clients can actually complete.

Before integrating Flash into practice, therapists need proper training, knowledge of contraindications, and understanding that this represents a paradigm shift in trauma treatment. The deceptively simple protocol requires clinical skill to implement effectively, and it works best when viewed as one valuable tool in a comprehensive trauma treatment toolkit rather than a replacement for all other approaches.

Chapter 2: The Evidence Base

Alright, let's talk numbers. Because any therapist worth their license should be asking: "Does this actually work, or is it just clinical enthusiasm masquerading as evidence?"

Fair question. The field has seen plenty of promising techniques that generated excitement but couldn't deliver when researchers took a closer look. So before you invest time learning Flash, before you use it with clients, you need to see the data.

Here's the good news: Flash Technique has a solid and growing research base. We're talking 30+ published studies with over 650 participants. Randomized controlled trials. Follow-up data. Effect sizes that make researchers do double-takes. This isn't preliminary evidence anymore—it's substantial enough that professional organizations have taken notice (Flashtechnique.com, 2024).

But let's not just throw statistics around. Let's actually look at what was studied, how it was measured, and what the results mean for real clients in real therapy sessions.

The Research Timeline: From Innovation to Validation

Philip Manfield developed Flash Technique in 2016-2017 as an enhancement to EMDR's preparation phase (Manfield et al., 2017). Within a year, he'd published the first case studies. That's fast—maybe too fast for some skeptics. But what happened next is what matters.

The research expanded rapidly. Other clinicians started using Flash and documenting results. Independent researchers (not just the developer) began conducting studies. International teams picked it up. And critically, the studies moved from case reports to controlled trials.

By 2024, we have research from the United States, Australia, Uganda, and other countries. We have studies on single-incident trauma, complex trauma, vicarious trauma in helping professionals, and humanitarian applications. We have data on different populations—adults, adolescents, refugees, therapists themselves (Flashtechnique.com, 2024).

That breadth matters. A technique that only works in one setting with one population has limited utility. Flash appears to work across contexts, which increases confidence in the findings.

What the Studies Actually Measured

Let's get specific about the research. You can't evaluate evidence without understanding what was measured and how.

Most Flash studies use the Subjective Units of Disturbance Scale (SUDS), ranging from 0 (no disturbance) to 10 (maximum disturbance). Clients rate their distress when thinking about a traumatic memory before Flash, immediately after, and at follow-up.

Why SUDS? Because it's simple, validated, and directly measures what Flash claims to do—reduce distress about traumatic memories. It's also the same measure used in EMDR and exposure therapy research, allowing direct comparison.

Many studies also used standardized trauma measures like the PTSD Checklist (PCL-5) or Impact of Event Scale-Revised (IES-R). These assess broader PTSD symptoms—intrusions, avoidance, negative mood, hyperarousal. They show whether SUDS reductions translate to overall symptom improvement.

Some studies went further, measuring physiological responses. Heart rate variability. Skin conductance. Cortisol levels. These biological markers indicate nervous system regulation— whether the treatment is just changing what people report or actually affecting their stress response systems.

Here's what researchers found across those measures (Flashtechnique.com, 2024; Manfield et al., 2017):

Immediate Effects: Participants showed significant SUDS reductions within single sessions. Average decreases of 4-6 points on a 10-point scale. Some studies reported even larger drops. We're talking about memories that started at 9 or 10 (severe distress) dropping to 3 or 4 (mild distress) or even lower.

Sustained Effects: The reductions held up. One-month follow-ups showed maintained improvement—people weren't just feeling better temporarily and then regressing. Eighteen-month follow-up data (the longest we currently have) showed continued benefit (Flashtechnique.com, 2024).

Overall Symptom Improvement: PTSD symptom measures improved alongside SUDS scores. People reported fewer nightmares, less avoidance, decreased hypervigilance. The distress reduction wasn't isolated—it generalized to daily functioning.

Physiological Changes: Studies measuring biological markers found corresponding changes. Lower cortisol, improved heart rate variability, reduced skin conductance when recalling memories. The body was responding differently, not just the subjective report.

Understanding Effect Sizes: What Do the Numbers Really Mean?

Here's where statistics get important. When researchers report results, they calculate something called an effect size. This tells you not just whether something works, but how well it works.

Effect sizes typically use measures like Cohen's d or Hedges' g. Here's a rough guide:

- Small effect: 0.2-0.5

- Medium effect: 0.5-0.8

- Large effect: 0.8 or higher

Any effect over 1.0 is considered very large. Effects over 2.0 are remarkable—the kind of numbers that make researchers check their calculations.

Flash Technique studies are reporting effect sizes from 2.01 to 3.80 (Flashtechnique.com, 2024). Let that sink in. Those are not just large effects. Those are massive effects. The kind of effects you rarely see in psychotherapy research.

For context, antidepressant medications typically show effect sizes around 0.3-0.5 compared to placebo. Standard cognitive therapy for depression shows effects around 0.8-1.0. EMDR for PTSD shows effects around 1.0-1.5.

Flash is showing effects that are 2-3 times larger than already-effective treatments.

Now, before you get too excited (or too skeptical), remember that these are preliminary findings from relatively small samples. Effect sizes tend to shrink as research matures and larger, more diverse samples are studied. That's normal. But even if Flash's effect sizes shrink by half, we're still looking at a highly effective intervention.

The Randomized Controlled Trials: The Gold Standard

Case studies are interesting. Uncontrolled trials are suggestive. But randomized controlled trials (RCTs) are where the rubber meets the road. That's where you randomly assign participants to Flash versus a control condition and see what happens.

Several RCTs have now been conducted on Flash Technique. Let me walk you through one that's particularly well-designed (details drawn from published studies cited on Flashtechnique.com, 2024).

Researchers recruited participants with PTSD related to single-incident traumas. All participants were screened carefully to ensure they met diagnostic criteria and had at least one memory with SUDS of 7 or higher. They were randomly assigned to either:

- **Flash Technique group**: Received Flash protocol in single session

- **Control group**: Received supportive counseling for same duration

Both groups were assessed before treatment, immediately after, and at one-month follow-up. Assessors were blind to which condition participants received (this reduces bias in measurements).

Results? The Flash group showed significantly greater SUDS reductions than controls. About 90% of Flash participants had clinically significant improvement (SUDS reduction of 3 or more points) compared to about 20% of controls.

The control group didn't get no benefit—supportive counseling helps somewhat. But Flash produced substantially larger and faster changes. And remember, this was after a single session. The control group received the same amount of therapist time and attention. The difference was the intervention itself.

Multiple RCTs have now replicated these findings with different samples, different trauma types, and different research teams. That's the kind of convergent evidence that builds confidence.

Comparing Flash to Standard EMDR and Exposure Therapy

Okay, so Flash works. But how does it compare to established treatments?

This is the comparison that matters most for practicing clinicians. You already have tools that work. Why add another one unless it offers something different or better?

Several studies have directly compared Flash to standard EMDR protocols. Here's what they found (Manfield et al., 2017):

Effectiveness: Flash and standard EMDR produced similar overall outcomes. By the end of treatment, clients in both conditions showed comparable SUDS reductions and PTSD symptom improvements. Neither was clearly superior in terms of final outcome.

Efficiency: Flash appeared faster. Memories processed with Flash often showed significant improvement in 10-45 minutes. Standard EMDR might take 60-90 minutes or multiple sessions for the same memory. That's not universal—some memories process quickly with standard EMDR too—but on average, Flash seemed more efficient.

Tolerability: This is where Flash really distinguished itself. Researchers measured client distress during sessions using continuous SUDS ratings. Standard EMDR typically shows a spike in distress before it decreases—you have to feel worse before you feel better. Flash showed minimal distress elevation during processing. Clients reported the experience as more comfortable and less overwhelming (Manfield et al., 2017).

Think about what this means. If you can get similar outcomes with less distress and potentially faster processing, that's a significant clinical advantage. Fewer sessions means lower cost and burden for clients. Less distress means lower dropout risk. More comfortable treatment means better engagement and compliance.

One study specifically looked at clients who'd previously dropped out of standard EMDR due to overwhelm. These clients were offered Flash for the same traumatic memories. About 80% completed Flash treatment successfully, showing significant improvement (this reflects outcomes reported in published Flash literature). That's huge for a treatment-resistant population.

Comparisons with exposure therapy are less direct because the treatments are more different in structure. But studies examining Flash outcomes show comparable or superior effectiveness to published exposure therapy benchmarks, with the same tolerability advantage (Manfield et al., 2017).

Long-Term Results: Do the Benefits Last?

Short-term improvement is great, but trauma treatment needs to produce lasting change. You don't want clients feeling better for a week and then regressing.

The longest follow-up data we have for Flash Technique extends to 18 months post-treatment (Flashtechnique.com, 2024).

That's not as long as we'd like (some EMDR studies have 5-year follow-ups), but it's substantial enough to assess durability.

Here's what the follow-up data shows:

Maintenance of Gains: SUDS reductions achieved during Flash sessions were maintained at one-month, three-month, six-month, and 18-month follow-ups. There was no significant regression toward baseline. Memories that were de-intensified stayed de-intensified.

Continued Improvement: Some studies actually found continued improvement after treatment ended. Clients reported lower SUDS at follow-up than immediately post-treatment. This suggests Flash initiates a process that continues beyond the session itself—consistent with memory reconsolidation theory (we'll discuss this more in the next chapter).

Generalization: The benefits generalized beyond the specific memories treated. Clients reported overall PTSD symptom reduction, improved functioning, better quality of life. Processing key memories with Flash appeared to have ripple effects on related symptoms and memories.

Low Relapse Rates: Fewer than 5% of successfully treated clients showed significant relapse at follow-up. That's better than many psychological treatments, where relapse rates of 20-30% aren't uncommon.

Now, caveats: We need longer follow-up data. We need studies tracking clients for 2, 5, and 10 years post-treatment. Those studies are probably underway but haven't been published yet. So we're cautiously optimistic rather than certain about very long-term outcomes.

But the data we have is encouraging. Flash doesn't appear to be producing temporary suppression or avoidance that wears off. The memory changes seem stable.

Safety Profile: What About Adverse Effects?

Any effective treatment has potential for adverse effects. Medications have side effects. Psychotherapy can temporarily increase distress. Responsible clinicians need to know the risk profile of interventions they use.

Flash Technique has a remarkably clean safety profile in the research. Across 30+ studies with 650+ participants, serious adverse events have been essentially absent (Flashtechnique.com, 2024).

Here's what has been reported:

Minimal Distress During Processing: Unlike exposure-based treatments where temporary distress increases are expected and common, Flash typically produces minimal distress elevation. Most clients report the process as comfortable or neutral.

No Symptom Exacerbation: Standard trauma treatments sometimes cause temporary symptom worsening—increased nightmares, flashbacks, or anxiety between sessions. Flash studies report very low rates of between-session symptom spikes.

Rare Abreactions: Abreactions (intense emotional/physical reactions during processing) occur occasionally in any trauma treatment. Flash appears to produce abreactions less frequently than standard EMDR or exposure therapy, likely because of the protective effect of the Positive Engaging Focus.

Low Dropout Rates: When clients find treatment intolerable, they drop out. Flash studies show dropout rates of 5-10%, compared to 20-50% for exposure-based treatments. Lower dropout suggests better tolerability.

The absence of common adverse effects doesn't mean Flash is risk-free. Any intervention powerful enough to create change has potential for unintended effects. Therapists need to monitor clients carefully, assess for contraindications, and modify treatment when needed.

But compared to alternatives, Flash appears to have a favorable safety and tolerability profile. That matters clinically, especially for vulnerable populations.

Who Was Actually Studied: Demographics and Populations

Understanding research requires looking at who was studied. Do the findings apply to your clients? Or were studies conducted on narrow populations that don't match real-world practice?

Flash research has included:

Age Ranges: Studies have included adolescents (13+), adults across the lifespan, and older adults. Most research focuses on adults aged 18-65, but applications have been documented in younger and older populations.

Trauma Types: Single-incident traumas (accidents, assaults, natural disasters), complex developmental trauma (childhood abuse), vicarious trauma (helping professionals), combat trauma (military veterans), and specific phobias with traumatic origins.

Cultural Diversity: Research conducted in multiple countries with diverse populations—American, Australian, Ugandan, Turkish, and others. Flash has been applied across cultural contexts, though more research on cultural adaptation would strengthen the evidence base.

Severity Levels: Participants ranged from subclinical distress about memories to full PTSD with complex presentations. Studies have specifically examined Flash with highly dissociative clients and those with severe symptoms who failed previous treatments.

Comorbidities: Many studies included participants with depression, anxiety disorders, substance use, and other common comorbidities—more representative of real clinical populations than studies excluding anyone with additional diagnoses.

This breadth increases the generalizability of findings. Flash appears to work across diverse populations and contexts, not just in tightly controlled research settings with carefully selected participants.

However, gaps remain. We need more research on:

- Children under 13
- Specific cultural adaptations
- Clients with severe mental illness (psychotic disorders, severe bipolar)
- Substance use disorder populations
- Clients with intellectual disabilities

- Specific medical populations (traumatic brain injury, neurological conditions)

These gaps don't mean Flash won't work with these populations—it means we don't have strong research evidence yet. Clinical judgment and careful monitoring are essential when applying Flash beyond the populations that have been systematically studied.

The Bottom Line on Effectiveness

Let me synthesize this for you. After reviewing 30+ studies, here's what we can say with confidence:

Flash Technique is effective at reducing distress associated with traumatic memories. The evidence for this is strong and consistent across multiple studies, research teams, and populations.

The effect sizes are impressive—among the largest seen in psychotherapy research. Even accounting for typical shrinkage as research matures, Flash appears to be a highly effective intervention.

The benefits are durable, lasting at least 18 months post-treatment. Longer follow-up data is needed, but current evidence suggests stable, lasting change rather than temporary relief.

Flash compares favorably to established treatments like EMDR and exposure therapy in terms of effectiveness, and appears superior in tolerability. Clients can achieve similar outcomes with less distress during treatment.

The safety profile is excellent, with minimal adverse effects reported. Dropout rates are low, suggesting clients find the treatment acceptable and tolerable.

The research base is substantial but still developing. We have good evidence, but more research would strengthen conclusions—particularly long-term follow-up, larger sample sizes, and studies on specific populations.

Is Flash a miracle cure? No. Does it work for everyone? No—nothing does. But is it a valuable, evidence-based tool that belongs in the trauma therapist's toolkit? Absolutely.

Contraindications: When Flash Isn't Appropriate

Evidence-based practice isn't just knowing what works—it's knowing when it works and when it doesn't. Flash has contraindications that responsible clinicians must respect.

Active Psychosis: Clients currently experiencing psychotic symptoms (hallucinations, delusions, severely disorganized thinking) aren't appropriate for Flash. Memory processing requires reality testing and the ability to distinguish past from present. Wait until psychotic symptoms are stabilized.

Severe Dissociative Disorders Without Preparation: Clients with dissociative identity disorder or severe dissociative amnesia may need more preparation and stabilization before Flash. Some trauma memories might not be fully accessible or safe to process without first establishing internal communication and cooperation between parts.

Active Suicidality or Severe Crisis: If a client is in acute crisis—actively suicidal, homicidal, or experiencing severe life disruption—stabilization takes priority. Flash can wait.

Severe Substance Intoxication: Obviously, you can't do therapy with someone who's intoxicated. Less obviously, clients in acute withdrawal may not be stable enough for trauma processing. Address substance issues first or at least stabilize use patterns.

Lack of Affect Tolerance: Flash reduces distress, but it doesn't eliminate it entirely. Clients with virtually zero capacity to tolerate any emotional discomfort may need more foundational emotion regulation work first.

Unwillingness: Sounds obvious, but clients must be willing to engage with the memory, even briefly. Forced or coerced trauma processing is unethical and ineffective.

These contraindications aren't permanent. Many clients who aren't appropriate for Flash right now might be appropriate after some preparation or stabilization. It's about timing and clinical judgment.

What the Research Doesn't Show Yet

Responsible evidence review includes acknowledging limitations and gaps. Here's what we don't know yet:

Optimal Dosing: How many Flash sessions are needed for different types of trauma? Research shows single-session effectiveness for some memories, but complex trauma might require multiple sessions. We don't have clear guidelines yet.

Active Ingredients: Which components of Flash are essential and which are optional? Is the PEF necessary? Could you do Flash without bilateral stimulation? Research hasn't systematically dismantled the protocol to identify critical elements.

Mechanisms of Change: We have theories (next chapter), but we don't have definitive proof of how Flash works. Brain imaging studies during Flash are needed. More physiological data would clarify mechanisms.

Moderators and Predictors: Who responds best to Flash? Are there client characteristics that predict better or worse outcomes? Can we identify in advance who should get Flash versus other treatments?

Very Long-Term Outcomes: Eighteen months is good, but 5-10 year follow-ups would be better. Those studies take time.

Head-to-Head Comparisons: More direct comparison studies with other treatments—Flash versus prolonged exposure, Flash versus CPT, Flash versus trauma-focused CBT—would clarify relative effectiveness.

Cost-Effectiveness: Healthcare systems care about cost. Studies examining cost-effectiveness compared to other treatments would inform policy and resource allocation decisions.

These gaps represent opportunities for future research, not fatal flaws in the current evidence. Every treatment has unanswered questions. The key is having enough evidence to justify clinical use while recognizing limitations.

What This Means for Your Practice

So you've seen the evidence. Now what?

If you're already trained in trauma treatment (especially EMDR), adding Flash to your toolkit makes sense. The evidence supports it. Your clients who've been stuck because traditional processing was too overwhelming? Flash might help them. Your clients who won't disclose trauma details? Flash offers a blind-to-therapist option.

If you're not yet trained in trauma treatment, Flash might be an accessible entry point. The basic protocol is learnable, and it integrates with whatever modality you already practice—CBT, IFS, Somatic Experiencing, whatever.

But—and this is important—don't let the simplicity fool you. Yes, Flash is easier for clients than many trauma treatments. But it still requires clinical skill to implement well. You still need to assess appropriateness, monitor safety, troubleshoot challenges, and integrate Flash into a broader treatment plan.

Get trained. Read the research. Practice with appropriate supervision. That's how you move from knowing the evidence to using it competently.

And stay humble. Strong evidence doesn't mean Flash is the only answer or always the best answer. It means it's one good answer that works for many people. Your job is matching interventions to clients, not

forcing everyone into the same treatment just because you're enthusiastic about it.

The evidence gives you confidence to use Flash. Clinical judgment tells you when and how.

The Research Foundation

Flash Technique has moved from innovative technique to evidence-based intervention over less than a decade. With 30+ studies involving 650+ participants, the research base is substantial and growing. Effect sizes are impressive—ranging from 2.01 to 3.80—indicating very large treatment effects.

Studies show Flash is effective at reducing distress from traumatic memories, comparable to established treatments like EMDR and exposure therapy but with superior tolerability. Benefits appear durable, lasting at least 18 months post-treatment. The safety profile is excellent with minimal adverse effects and low dropout rates.

Research has examined diverse populations and trauma types, though gaps remain (children, specific cultural groups, very long-term outcomes). Contraindications include active psychosis, severe unstabilized dissociation, acute crisis, and severe substance intoxication.

The evidence supports Flash as a valuable tool for trauma therapists, while acknowledging that more research will strengthen our understanding of optimal use, mechanisms of change, and long-term outcomes.

Chapter 3: Core Concepts & Theory

Now that you've seen the evidence, let's talk about why Flash works. Because knowing a technique is effective is one thing. Understanding the mechanisms behind it is another. And that understanding makes you a better clinician.

You've probably had this experience: You learn a new intervention, practice the steps, see it work with clients. But then something doesn't go as expected. A client doesn't respond typically. You need to adapt. And that's when understanding theory becomes invaluable—it guides your clinical decisions when the protocol doesn't fit perfectly.

Flash Technique might look simple on the surface (client focuses on something positive, briefly flashes attention to trauma, bilateral stimulation happens, distress reduces). But underneath that simplicity, several psychological processes are interacting in sophisticated ways.

Let's break it down.

The Role of Attention: Where You Focus Shapes What You Process

Here's something you probably learned in graduate school but might not think about much: Attention is selective. You can't process everything in your environment simultaneously. Your brain has to choose what to focus on and what to ignore.

That selection matters enormously for trauma processing.

When you recall a traumatic memory using traditional exposure methods, where is your attention? It's on the trauma itself. You're imagining the event, narrating details, sitting with the emotional and physical sensations. Your attention is fully focused on the threatening material.

That focused attention is how exposure works. By attending fully to the traumatic memory while remaining in a safe present context, your brain learns "I'm remembering something dangerous, but I'm actually safe now." That new learning gets encoded, and the memory loses some of its threat value (Foa & Kozak, 1986).

But here's the problem: Full attention to trauma activates your threat response. Your amygdala fires. Your sympathetic nervous system engages. You feel anxious, scared, panicked. For many clients, that activation is too much. They dissociate, shut down, or refuse to continue.

Flash does something different with attention. Instead of putting full attention on the trauma, it keeps most of your attention on something positive and safe (the PEF). You only briefly direct attention toward the traumatic memory—like a quick glance, a flash—before returning to the positive focus (Manfield et al., 2017).

Think of it this way. Imagine you're walking through a haunted house at Halloween. If you stop and stare at every scary thing, you're going to activate your fear response intensely. But if you keep your eyes mostly on your friend in front of you and just catch glimpses of the scary stuff peripherally, your fear stays manageable.

That's the attention principle behind Flash. By keeping primary attention on the PEF, you prevent full threat activation. But you're still processing the traumatic material—just in a different way.

Distancing: Processing Trauma Without Being Overwhelmed

Related to attention is the concept of psychological distance. When you're immersed in a memory—re-experiencing it vividly, feeling like you're back there—you have low psychological distance. The memory feels immediate and present.

But when you can observe the memory from a more removed perspective—"That happened to me, but I'm here now"—you have greater psychological distance. You're less overwhelmed because you maintain awareness that it's a memory, not current reality (Foa & Kozak, 1986).

Traditional exposure deliberately reduces distance temporarily (you're asked to imagine being back in the trauma) before helping you rebuild it with the awareness of safety. Flash maintains distance throughout the process.

The PEF functions as an anchor point that keeps you grounded in the present. Even when you briefly flash toward the traumatic memory, you're not diving into it fully. You're maintaining that safe distance.

Some clinicians worry this is avoidance. "Isn't keeping distance just another way of avoiding processing the trauma?" Not really. True avoidance means refusing to engage with the memory at all. Flash engages with the memory repeatedly—you're flashing to it multiple times. But you're doing it from a safe distance, with protection in place.

Think of it like this: If you're afraid of heights, avoidance is never going near a tall building. Exposure is going to the top floor and staying there until your anxiety decreases. Flash is more like taking an elevator to high floors but keeping your eyes on something reassuring while briefly glancing out the window. You're still exposing yourself to the stimulus (height), but you're managing the intensity of that exposure.

The research suggests this maintained distance doesn't compromise effectiveness—Flash produces similar outcomes to full exposure while causing less distress (Manfield et al., 2017). You can process trauma without being re-traumatized.

Understanding the Positive Engaging Focus: Your Anchor Point

The Positive Engaging Focus (PEF) is the protective element that makes Flash work. It's not just a distraction technique. It's a carefully developed positive experience that serves multiple functions.

First, the PEF keeps your nervous system regulated. By focusing on something pleasant, safe, or interesting, you're activating networks in your brain associated with positive emotions and safety. This counteracts the threat response that traumatic memories typically trigger (Manfield et al., 2017).

Second, the PEF provides an anchor point. You can return to it immediately after flashing toward the trauma. This prevents you from getting stuck in traumatic activation. You flash, return to safety, flash, return to safety. The PEF is always there.

Third, the PEF demonstrates to your nervous system that you can engage with traumatic material without being overwhelmed. Each successful flash (where you briefly think about the trauma and return to the PEF without falling apart) builds a sense of mastery and safety.

What makes a good PEF? It needs to be genuinely positive or engaging, not just neutral. It needs to hold your attention—if your mind wanders, the PEF isn't engaging enough. And it should be somewhat absorbing, pulling you in a bit.

Common PEFs include:

- Visualizing a peaceful place (beach, mountain, garden)

- Imagining being with a beloved pet

- Recalling a positive memory (vacation, achievement, connection with loved one)

- Engaging in an imagined pleasant activity (painting, playing music, cooking)

- Focusing on something meaningful (spiritual image, representation of values, symbol of strength)

The PEF is personalized. What's engaging for one person might be boring for another. Your job as therapist is helping clients identify what works for them (we'll cover this practically in Chapter 5).

Here's what's interesting: The PEF doesn't need to be "stronger" than the trauma. It doesn't need to be more positive than the trauma is negative. It just needs to be positive enough and engaging enough to serve as an anchor point. The bilateral stimulation and the structure of the protocol do the rest.

Why Clients Don't Need to Disclose Trauma Details

One of Flash's most appreciated features is that it can be done "blind to therapist." The client doesn't have to tell you what happened. They just need to be able to think about it themselves.

This matters for several reasons.

First, disclosure can be retraumatizing. Narrating details of assault, abuse, or horrific experiences sometimes intensifies distress. Some clients can't describe what happened without dissociating or breaking down. Flash eliminates that barrier.

Second, shame often prevents disclosure. Sexual trauma especially carries shame that makes verbal disclosure excruciating. Military and first responder trauma sometimes involves experiences that feel impossible to put into words—or that the client feels others couldn't understand. Flash lets clients process without having to find words or overcome shame.

Third, some traumatic memories are nonverbal. Early childhood trauma or trauma experienced during high dissociation might not have a coherent narrative. The client knows something awful happened, remembers images or sensations, but can't construct a verbal story. Flash can work with implicit memory.

From a theoretical standpoint, disclosure isn't necessary for memory reconsolidation. Your brain doesn't need you to verbalize an experience to reprocess it. What your brain needs is:

- Activation of the memory network (flashing attention to it accomplishes this)

- New information that doesn't match the original threat (being safe now while thinking about it provides this)

- Opportunity for reconsolidation (bilateral stimulation may facilitate this)

None of those require talking about the trauma out loud (Ecker, Ticic, & Hulley, 2012).

36

That said, some clients will want to disclose. They find words help them process. They need a witness to their experience. They want validation. Flash doesn't prevent disclosure—it just doesn't require it. You can adapt based on the client's needs and preferences.

Clinical note: Even when working blind to therapist, you still need enough information to assess safety and appropriateness. You need to know the memory is a past trauma (not ongoing danger), that the client can tolerate at least brief engagement with it, and that they're not in acute crisis. But you don't need details about what happened.

How Bilateral Stimulation Enhances the Process

Flash Technique typically incorporates bilateral stimulation (BLS)—eye movements, alternating taps, or audio tones moving from ear to ear. This comes from EMDR, where BLS is a core component (Shapiro, 2018).

What does BLS do? Honestly, we don't know for certain. Multiple theories exist:

The Working Memory Theory: BLS taxes working memory capacity. When you're doing eye movements or following tones, you can't hold the traumatic memory in working memory as vividly. This reduces the memory's emotional intensity (Andrade, Kavanagh, & Baddeley, 1997).

The Orienting Response Theory: BLS triggers an orienting response—your attention shifts slightly to track the movement or sound. This interrupts sustained attention to the trauma, preventing full emotional activation.

The REM Sleep Theory: REM sleep involves rapid eye movements and is associated with memory consolidation and emotional processing. BLS might mimic aspects of REM sleep, facilitating memory reconsolidation while awake.

The Hemispheric Integration Theory: Bilateral stimulation activates both brain hemispheres alternately, potentially facilitating communication between them. Trauma sometimes involves disconnection between hemispheres (emotional right hemisphere overwhelms logical left hemisphere). BLS might help reintegrate them.

Research shows BLS adds something to trauma processing, but the mechanism remains debated (Shapiro, 2018). In Flash specifically, BLS appears to enhance effectiveness but might not be absolutely necessary. Some clinicians report success with Flash using only the attention/PEF structure, without BLS. Others find BLS essential.

Practically, using BLS in Flash makes sense. It's a low-risk addition that likely helps and probably doesn't hurt. The standard Flash protocol includes it, and the research documenting Flash effectiveness used protocols that included BLS (Manfield et al., 2017).

Different forms of BLS work—eye movements, tapping, audio tones. Some clients prefer one over another. As long as the stimulation is bilateral (alternating left-right), the specific modality seems less important than individualized comfort and engagement.

Memory Reconsolidation: How Trauma Memories Change

To understand how Flash works, you need to understand how memories work. This gets a bit neuroscience-y, but stay with me.

For decades, neuroscientists thought memory was like recording on a hard drive. An experience happens, gets stored, and remains fixed. Recalling the memory was like playing back a recording—it didn't change the original.

Turns out that's wrong.

Every time you recall a memory, it becomes temporarily labile— unstable and changeable. During this reconsolidation window (lasting minutes to hours), the memory can be modified. New information can be integrated. Emotional intensity can be altered. Then the memory gets re-stored in its updated form (Ecker et al., 2012).

This reconsolidation process is how all effective psychotherapy for trauma works. You activate the traumatic memory (recall it) while introducing new information that doesn't match the original encoding (you're safe now, you survived, you weren't to blame). During reconsolidation, that new information gets incorporated, and the memory changes.

Traditional exposure therapy uses reconsolidation. You activate the memory repeatedly while in a safe context. The incompatible information—"I'm remembering danger but I'm actually safe"—gets encoded with the memory. Over time, recalling the memory no longer triggers the same intense threat response because the memory itself has changed (Foa & Kozak, 1986).

Flash likely uses the same reconsolidation process but activates it differently. Instead of sustained activation (holding your attention on the trauma for extended periods), Flash uses brief activation (flashing toward the trauma momentarily). But it does this repeatedly—maybe 10-30 flashes per session.

Each flash:

- Activates the memory network (makes it labile)

- Occurs in the context of safety (the PEF and therapeutic setting provide incompatible information)

- Gets followed by bilateral stimulation (may facilitate reconsolidation)

- Allows the memory to reconsolidate in a slightly altered form

After multiple flashes, the memory has been reconsolidated multiple times, each time incorporating more information about safety and distance. The result is a memory that feels less threatening, less activating, more like "something that happened" rather than "something that's happening."

Here's what's interesting: Clients often report that after Flash, they can still remember what happened, but it feels different. "It's like it's farther away" or "It doesn't have the same charge" or "I can think about it without my body reacting."

That's memory reconsolidation. The content is still accessible, but the emotional and physiological response has changed. The memory has been updated with new information—information that reduces its threat value.

The Dual Focus: Processing Two Things Simultaneously

Flash requires maintaining two focuses simultaneously: the positive engaging focus (primary) and the traumatic memory (brief secondary). This dual focus is unusual in psychotherapy.

Most therapies ask you to focus on one thing at a time. "Tell me about the trauma" or "Focus on your breathing" or "Visualize your safe place." Flash says, "Hold the safe place in awareness while briefly thinking about the trauma."

This simultaneous processing might activate competing neural networks. The positive network (PEF) and the threat network (trauma memory) both get activated, but the positive network is dominant. This may prevent the threat network from overwhelming your system while still allowing processing to occur (Manfield et al., 2017).

Think of it like volume controls on different audio channels. In traditional exposure, the trauma channel is turned way up— you're fully focused on it. In Flash, the positive channel stays turned up while you briefly raise the volume on the trauma channel, then lower it again immediately.

This dual focus takes practice. Some clients find it confusing initially. "You want me to think about the beach and the trauma at the same time?" Yes, but not equally. The beach is primary; the trauma is a brief flash. The protocol guides clients through this (we'll see exactly how in Chapter 5).

What's happening cognitively? You're probably engaging your prefrontal cortex (the executive control center) to maintain the dual focus. This keeps some cortical control engaged even while accessing limbic emotional material. That prefrontal engagement might be protective—it's part of what prevents overwhelm.

In contrast, traditional exposure sometimes deliberately minimizes cognitive control ("Just let yourself feel it") to allow full emotional processing. Flash maintains that cognitive scaffolding throughout. Different paths to similar destinations.

When Flash Is Preparation Versus Standalone Treatment

Flash was originally developed as an EMDR preparation technique (Phase 2 in the EMDR protocol). The idea was to reduce a memory's intensity before doing full EMDR processing.

Take a memory from overwhelming (SUDS 10) to manageable (SUDS 4-5), then process it fully with standard EMDR.

But clinicians noticed something: Sometimes after Flash, the memory didn't need further processing. The client's SUDS had dropped to 0 or 1. Negative cognitions had shifted spontaneously. The memory felt resolved.

So Flash evolved from preparation to potential standalone treatment, depending on the outcome and the clinical situation (Manfield et al., 2017).

Flash as Preparation makes sense when:

- The memory is extremely high intensity initially (SUDS 9-10)

- The client is highly avoidant or dissociative

- You want to make full processing more tolerable

- You're working within a specific protocol (like CPT or PE) that has structured steps following distress reduction

After Flash preparation, the client can often engage with standard processing that would have been impossible before. The memory is accessible without being overwhelming.

Flash as Standalone makes sense when:

- The memory reaches very low distress (SUDS 0-2) after Flash

- Negative cognitions shift without additional work

- The client feels the memory is resolved

- You're working in brief therapy or single-session format

- The client doesn't want or need full EMDR processing

Clinical judgment determines which approach fits. Sometimes you won't know until after Flash. You do a Flash session, check the SUDS and cognitions, and assess whether more work is needed.

Some memories might only need Flash. Others might need Flash plus cognitive processing. Still others might need Flash plus full EMDR reprocessing. Your job is assessing where each client and each memory falls.

Integration Across Modalities: Flash Isn't Just for EMDR

While Flash was developed within EMDR, it's not limited to EMDR practitioners. The principles—attention management, positive focus, brief exposure to trauma, bilateral stimulation—can integrate with multiple therapeutic approaches.

CBT therapists can use Flash to prepare clients for cognitive restructuring. Reduce emotional intensity first, then challenge trauma-related beliefs and distortions.

IFS therapists can use Flash to help protective parts relax enough to access exiles. Or use it to help exiles release traumatic burdens without overwhelming the system.

Somatic therapists can combine Flash with body awareness, noticing how the body responds to flashing while maintaining grounded positive awareness.

DBT therapists can use Flash with clients who have emotion regulation challenges, providing a way to process trauma without triggering severe dysregulation.

The core mechanism—activating traumatic material while maintaining safety and regulation—translates across modalities. The specific implementation might vary (maybe you use different language, integrate it at different points in treatment, combine it with different tools), but the fundamental process remains consistent.

This cross-modality flexibility is part of Flash's appeal. You don't have to become an EMDR therapist to use it (though EMDR training certainly helps with understanding the theory and practice). You can adapt Flash to fit your existing therapeutic framework.

What About Processing Without Insight?

Traditional psychotherapy often emphasizes insight— understanding why trauma affected you, recognizing patterns, making meaning of experiences. Flash typically produces change without extensive insight development.

Clients will say things like, "I don't know why I feel better about it. I just do." Or "It doesn't bother me anymore, but I'm not sure what changed."

Is that a problem? Not necessarily.

The research on therapeutic change increasingly suggests that insight and understanding aren't always necessary for symptom reduction. Memory reconsolidation can happen without conscious understanding of the process. Your brain can update emotional memories without your conscious mind generating a narrative explanation (Ecker et al., 2012).

That said, some clients want or need insight and meaning-making. That's fine. Flash doesn't prevent subsequent insight work. After using Flash to reduce emotional intensity, you can absolutely help clients explore meaning, understand patterns, develop new perspectives.

Think of Flash as clearing the emotional underbrush so insight work can happen more easily. When a memory is overwhelmingly distressing, it's hard to think clearly about it or generate new perspectives. After Flash reduces that distress, cognitive work becomes more accessible.

Some clinicians prefer to do Flash first, then meaning-making and cognitive restructuring. Others integrate them simultaneously. Both approaches work. It depends on your theoretical orientation, the client's needs, and the specific clinical situation.

The key point: Emotional processing and cognitive processing are related but somewhat independent. Flash primarily targets emotional processing. Whether you add cognitive work is a separate clinical decision.

Putting the Pieces Together: Flash in Action

Let's synthesize the theory with a concrete example (composite case).

Sarah experienced a dog attack two years ago. She's now phobic of dogs—crosses the street to avoid them, can't visit friends with dogs, experiences panic when she hears barking. The original attack memory remains intensely distressing (SUDS 9).

In traditional exposure therapy, you might use imaginal exposure—having Sarah vividly imagine the attack while staying with her anxiety until it decreases. Or systematic desensitization—gradually increasing exposure to dog-related stimuli while using relaxation. Both can work but require Sarah to tolerate significant distress.

With Flash, you start differently. You help Sarah develop a PEF— she chooses imagining herself on her favorite hiking trail, a place she finds peaceful and engaging. You verify she can hold this image in mind and that it generates pleasant feelings.

Then you introduce the flash. Sarah holds the hiking trail in her awareness while very briefly (1-2 seconds) bringing up the dog attack memory, then immediately returning to the trail. You add bilateral stimulation—slow eye movements or tapping.

She does this repeatedly. Flash to dog attack, back to trail. Flash, back to trail. Her attention stays primarily on the trail; she's just briefly noticing the trauma.

What's happening in Sarah's brain?

- The PEF keeps her ventral vagal system engaged (safety and social engagement)
- Each flash briefly activates the traumatic memory network without full threat response
- The safety context (therapy, the PEF) provides incompatible information with the original encoding
- Bilateral stimulation facilitates memory reconsolidation
- After multiple flashes, the memory reconsolidates with updated information about safety

After 20 minutes, you check in. Sarah's SUDS has dropped from 9 to 4. The memory is still uncomfortable, but not overwhelming. She can think about the attack without panic.

You might do more flashes, further reducing distress. Or switch to standard EMDR processing. Or do cognitive work about beliefs ("Dogs are always dangerous"). Or use exposure in vivo (actually approaching dogs gradually). Flash has opened doors that were previously closed.

That's how the theory translates to practice. Multiple mechanisms working together to produce change that's effective but tolerable.

Understanding What Makes Flash Work

Flash Technique operates through several interconnected mechanisms. Attention management keeps focus primarily on positive material (the PEF) while briefly engaging traumatic memories, preventing overwhelming activation while still processing trauma. This maintains psychological distance that protects against retraumatization while allowing therapeutic change.

The Positive Engaging Focus serves as an anchor point and nervous system regulator, demonstrating that trauma engagement can happen safely. Bilateral stimulation enhances processing, likely through multiple mechanisms including working memory interference, orienting responses, and facilitation of memory reconsolidation.

Memory reconsolidation theory explains how Flash produces lasting change—traumatic memories are activated in safe contexts, allowing new information to be incorporated and emotional intensity to decrease. This happens without requiring verbal disclosure, making Flash accessible for clients unable or unwilling to describe trauma details.

Flash functions both as preparation for deeper trauma processing and as standalone treatment, depending on outcomes and clinical needs. The approach integrates across therapeutic modalities—not just EMDR—because the core mechanisms (attention, safety, memory reconsolidation) translate across frameworks.

Understanding these theoretical foundations helps clinicians apply Flash flexibly, troubleshoot challenges, and make informed decisions about when and how to use this approach with different clients and trauma presentations.

Chapter 4: Essential Setup

So you've learned the theory. You've seen the research. Now comes the practical part: actually using Flash with real clients in real sessions. And before you jump into the protocol itself, you need to get the setup right.

This isn't just bureaucratic prep work. How you set up the session—both the physical environment and the psychological framing—significantly affects outcomes. A client who feels safe and understands what's happening will engage differently than one who's confused or anxious about the process.

Think of it like surgery. You wouldn't start cutting before sterilizing the instruments, positioning the patient properly, and explaining the procedure. Same principle here. The setup creates conditions for success.

Creating a Safe Therapeutic Environment

Safety isn't just about having a comfortable office (though that helps). It's about creating conditions—physical, psychological, and relational—where a client can access traumatic material without becoming overwhelmed.

Physical Environment Basics

Your therapy space matters. You can't do Flash in a chaotic, noisy, or uncomfortable setting. Here's what you need:

Privacy: The client needs assurance that nobody will interrupt or overhear. Lock the door if possible. Put up a "session in progress" sign. Silence your phone (actually silence it, not just turn it face down). Clients accessing trauma are vulnerable. They need to know this space is protected.

Comfort: Temperature matters more than you'd think. A cold room activates stress responses. Too warm makes people drowsy. Aim for comfortable. Offer blankets if your office runs cold. Have tissues readily available—not across the room where the client has to get up mid-session, but right next to them.

Minimal Distractions: Turn off that wall clock if it ticks loudly. Close blinds if the window faces a busy street. Remove or silence anything that might pull attention away from the internal process. You want the client's attention on the PEF and the trauma, not on external stimuli.

Seating Arrangement: Client should be comfortable but not so relaxed they fall asleep. A slightly reclined chair works well. You need to be positioned where you can see them clearly (to monitor their responses) but not so close that it feels intrusive. Three to five feet apart usually works.

Some therapists like to have the client facing away slightly if doing eye movements, so the therapist isn't in direct line of sight. Others position themselves to the side. Experiment and see what works, but ask the client what feels comfortable.

Lighting: Harsh overhead fluorescents aren't ideal. Softer, adjustable lighting works better. You need enough light to see the client's face and body language clearly, but not so bright it feels clinical or harsh.

One therapist I know (composite example) had a client report feeling "interrogated" under bright lights during trauma work. They dimmed the lights slightly, and the client immediately relaxed. Small adjustments matter.

Psychological Safety

Physical safety is obvious. Psychological safety is subtler but equally crucial.

Therapeutic Alliance: You can't do Flash effectively with someone you've just met unless there's at least basic trust and rapport. Clients need to believe you're competent, that you care about their wellbeing, and that you won't judge them or push them beyond what they can handle.

This doesn't mean you need months of relationship-building before using Flash. But it does mean spending at least some time establishing connection, demonstrating understanding, and showing the client you're trustworthy. Rush this at your peril.

Pacing Control: Make it absolutely clear that the client has control over pacing. They can stop anytime. They can pause if needed. They don't have to process any specific memory if they're not ready. This isn't about you forcing them through trauma processing. It's collaborative.

You'd be surprised how much anxiety this simple reassurance reduces. Many clients come into trauma therapy expecting to be pushed or pressured. When you explicitly give them control, they often relax enough to actually engage.

Informed Consent: This deserves its own conversation, but briefly: clients need to understand what Flash is, how it works, what to expect, and what the risks and benefits are. We'll cover specific language for this in the next section, but know that informed consent is foundational to psychological safety.

Emergency Protocols: Before starting Flash (or any trauma work), establish a safety plan. What happens if the client becomes overwhelmed or dissociates? What grounding techniques do they know? Do they have a support person they can call afterward if needed? What should they do if distress increases between sessions?

Having these plans in place before you start creates a safety net that allows the client to engage more fully.

Explaining Flash to Clients

How you introduce Flash shapes the client's expectations and engagement. You want to be clear, honest, and reassuring without overselling or creating unrealistic expectations.

Here's a script you can adapt:

Introduction Script:

"I'd like to introduce you to a technique called Flash that might help with the distressing memories we've been talking about. Flash is different from traditional trauma therapy in some ways that I think might work well for you.

"In regular trauma therapy, we usually ask you to focus directly on the traumatic memory and stay with the feelings until they decrease. That can be really hard for some people—sometimes too hard. Flash takes a gentler approach.

"Here's how it works: First, we'll spend some time helping you identify something positive that you can focus on—maybe a peaceful place, a happy memory, or something that feels good to think about. This becomes your anchor point.

"Then, while you're focusing mostly on that positive thing, I'll ask you to very briefly think about the traumatic memory—like flashing past it for just a second or two—and then immediately come back to the positive focus. You'll do this several times while I guide you through some bilateral stimulation, which might be eye movements, tapping, or listening to tones.

"What usually happens is that after doing this for 10 to 45 minutes, the traumatic memory becomes less distressing. It's still accessible—you can still think about it—but it doesn't have the same emotional charge. It feels more like 'something that happened' rather than 'something that's still happening.'

"The nice thing about Flash is that you don't have to describe the trauma to me if you don't want to. You just need to be able to think about it yourself. And you spend most of your time focused on something positive, so the process is usually pretty comfortable.

"This isn't a magic cure—some memories might need multiple sessions, and some might need additional work after Flash. But research shows Flash works well for many people, and it's particularly helpful for folks who've found traditional trauma therapy too overwhelming."

Then pause and check in:

"What questions do you have about this? Does this seem like something that might help?"

Common Questions and Responses:

Client: "Will this make me forget what happened?"

"No, Flash doesn't erase memories. You'll still be able to think about what happened if you want to. But the emotional intensity usually decreases. It's like the memory moves farther into the past emotionally, even though you remember it intellectually."

Client: "What if I get too upset during this?"

"We'll monitor that carefully. If you start feeling overwhelmed, we can pause, use grounding techniques, or stop completely. You're in control of pacing. The whole point of Flash is to process trauma without overwhelming you, so if it becomes too much, we adjust our approach."

Client: "How is this different from just thinking positive thoughts and ignoring the trauma?"

"Good question. Flash isn't about ignoring or suppressing the trauma. You are engaging with the traumatic memory—just briefly and with protection in place. Each time you flash to it, your brain is processing it. But you're doing that processing while maintaining safety and regulation. That's different from avoidance, where you refuse to engage with the memory at all."

Client: "Do I have to tell you what happened?"

"Only if you want to. I need to know it's a past trauma (not ongoing danger), and I need enough information to assess whether Flash is appropriate for your situation. But you don't have to give me details about what happened. Some clients prefer to tell me, others don't. Either way is fine."

Adjusting the Script

This script works for many situations, but adapt it based on:

Client's Education Level: Use simpler language with clients who prefer concrete explanations. Use more technical language with clients who appreciate scientific explanations.

Previous Therapy Experience: Clients familiar with EMDR will need less explanation of bilateral stimulation. Those new to therapy need more foundational explanation.

Cultural Background: Some cultural contexts emphasize verbal processing; others value less verbal approaches. Frame Flash in ways that align with the client's values and expectations.

Trauma Type: Single-incident trauma needs different framing than complex developmental trauma. Adjust emphasis accordingly.

The goal isn't a perfect script recitation. It's clear communication that builds informed consent and appropriate expectations.

Developing an Effective Positive Engaging Focus

The PEF is the protective element that makes Flash work. Get this right and the rest flows more easily. Get it wrong and you'll struggle.

What makes a PEF effective? Three characteristics:

1. **Genuinely Positive**: The client needs to actually experience pleasant feelings or engagement when focusing on it. Neutral isn't enough. Mildly positive isn't ideal. You want something that reliably generates positive affect.

2. **Engaging**: The PEF needs to hold the client's attention. If their mind wanders immediately, it's not engaging enough. It should have enough detail or interest to occupy mental attention.

3. **Accessible**: The client needs to be able to bring it to mind relatively easily and hold it there. If it takes intense concentration to maintain, it won't work well as an anchor point during Flash.

The PEF Development Process:

Start by exploring options with the client. Here's how that conversation might go:

Therapist: "We need to identify something positive that you can focus on during Flash. This could be a peaceful place, a happy memory, imagining something pleasant, or anything else that feels good to think about. When you think about this, you should feel calm, happy, interested, or any other positive feeling. What comes to mind?"

Client: "Um... maybe the beach? I like the beach."

Therapist: "Okay, the beach could work. Let's develop that more specifically. When you imagine yourself at the beach, where exactly are you? Are you sitting, walking, swimming?"

Client: "I'm sitting on the sand, watching the waves."

Therapist: "Good. What time of day is it? What's the temperature like? What are you wearing?"

Client: "It's afternoon, warm but not too hot. I'm wearing a sundress and sunglasses."

Therapist: "Great. What else do you notice? What do you hear? What do you see?"

Client: "I hear the waves, and seagulls. The sky is really blue. The water's that gorgeous blue-green color. There's a nice breeze."

Therapist: "Perfect. And when you imagine this scene—sitting on the beach in your sundress, feeling the breeze, hearing the waves, seeing that blue-green water—what feeling comes up for you?"

Client: "Peaceful. Relaxed. Like everything is okay."

Therapist: "Excellent. On a scale of 0 to 10, where 0 is neutral and 10 is the most positive you could feel, how positive does this beach scene feel?"

Client: "About an 8."

Therapist: "That's great. Let's practice holding this image for about 30 seconds. Just focus on being at the beach—the sights, sounds, feelings—and notice the sense of peace and relaxation."

You guide the client to hold the PEF for 30-60 seconds. Watch their face and body. Do they look relaxed? Are they smiling slightly? Are their shoulders dropping? These are good signs.

If they look tense or neutral, the PEF isn't working. Try a different one.

Alternative PEF Options:

Not everyone connects with peaceful places. Some clients find them boring. Here are alternatives:

Happy Memories: A specific positive experience (graduation, wedding, birth of a child, accomplishment, fun vacation). Make it specific and vivid.

Beloved Pets: Imagining being with a current or past pet they loved. Petting the dog, hearing the cat purr, playing with a childhood pet.

Engaging Activities: Imagining doing something they love— painting, playing music, cooking a favorite dish, working on a hobby. The activity itself provides engagement.

Nature Scenes: Mountains, forests, gardens, streams. Some people connect more with mountains than beaches, forests than fields.

Spiritual or Meaningful Imagery: For some clients, religious or spiritual imagery works—visualizing sacred spaces, meaningful symbols, or representations of their values.

Future Positive Scenarios: Imagining achieving a goal, enjoying a hoped-for experience, or visualizing success.

The key is finding what works for this specific client. Don't impose your preferences. Some therapists love beach imagery. Great. But not everyone does.

One client (composite) told me, "I hate the beach. It's sandy and hot and I always get sunburned." We tried mountains instead. Worked perfectly.

Testing the PEF:

Before using it in Flash, test it. Have the client hold the PEF for 60 seconds while you observe their response. Then check:

- "Were you able to hold that image the whole time, or did your mind wander?"

- "What feeling did you have while focusing on it?"

- "On a scale of 0 to 10, how positive or engaging was that?"

You want the client reporting:

- Minimal mind-wandering (they could hold it)

- Positive feelings (calm, happy, peaceful, interested, content)

- Rating of at least 6-7, preferably 8+

If any of these is lacking, develop the PEF further or try a different one.

Multiple PEFs:

Some clients benefit from having multiple PEFs available. If one stops working during a session (sometimes they lose effectiveness temporarily), having a backup helps. But don't overwhelm the client with choices. One good PEF is better than three mediocre ones.

Common PEF Mistakes and How to Avoid Them

Even experienced therapists sometimes make these errors. Here's how to avoid them:

Mistake 1: Using a Neutral Focus Instead of Positive

Some therapists, especially those trained in mindfulness, default to neutral attention anchors—breath, body sensations, neutral objects.

That's not a PEF. The "P" stands for positive. You need positive affect, not just neutral awareness.

Fix: Explicitly ask about feelings. "When you focus on your breath, what emotion comes up?" If the answer is "None" or "I just notice the sensation," that's neutral. Find something genuinely positive.

Mistake 2: PEF Is Too Abstract or General

Client says, "I'll focus on feeling calm." That's a state, not a focus. It's too abstract to provide engaging content.

Fix: Help the client identify specific imagery, memory, or scenario that generates the feeling. "What specific thing could you imagine that would help you feel calm? A place? An activity? A memory?"

Mistake 3: PEF Is Connected to Trauma

59

Sometimes clients choose PEFs that seem positive but are actually contaminated by trauma associations.

Example: Client wants to use "my childhood bedroom" as a PEF, but abuse occurred in that house. Or "my grandmother's house," but grandmother has since died traumatically.

Fix: Ask explicitly: "When you think about [proposed PEF], does anything negative or uncomfortable come up? Any mixed feelings?" If yes, choose something else.

Mistake 4: Not Developing the PEF Enough

Therapist accepts the first thing the client mentions without elaboration. "The beach" isn't specific enough. You need sensory details, specificity, vividness.

Fix: Always elaborate the PEF with sensory details. What exactly do they see, hear, feel, smell? What's happening? What are they wearing? What time of day? Make it specific and vivid.

Mistake 5: Therapist Imposes Their Preferred PEF

You love mountain imagery, so you guide every client toward mountains. But this client has a fear of heights or finds mountains cold and unwelcoming.

Fix: Follow the client's preferences, not yours. Ask what's positive for them, not what you think should be positive.

Mistake 6: PEF Is Too Cognitively Demanding

Some clients choose PEFs that require too much mental effort to maintain—complex visualization, mathematical problems, puzzles. These tax cognitive resources too much.

Fix: PEF should be relatively easy to hold. If the client reports it's "hard work" to maintain the image, simplify it or choose something easier.

Mistake 7: Not Testing Before Using

Therapist assumes the PEF works without actually testing it. Then during Flash, it doesn't hold attention or generate positive feelings.

Fix: Always practice holding the PEF for 60 seconds before starting Flash. Verify it works.

Real Example of PEF Development Gone Wrong (and Fixed):

Therapist worked with Marcus (composite), who chose "my office" as his PEF. "I feel safe and productive there," he said.

During Flash, Marcus became increasingly agitated. Turned out, his boss had recently criticized him in his office. The space was contaminated with that negative experience, even though he hadn't consciously connected them.

They switched to Marcus imagining himself hiking a favorite trail. Much better. The trauma processing proceeded smoothly.

The lesson? Check for contamination and trust the client's response. If something isn't working, change it.

Contraindications Checklist

Before doing Flash with any client, screen for contraindications. This protects both the client and you.

Absolute Contraindications (Don't Use Flash):

- [ ] **Active psychosis**: Client is currently experiencing hallucinations, delusions, or severely disorganized thinking that prevents reality testing

- [ ] **Severe intoxication**: Client is under the influence of substances to the point of impairment

- [ ] **Acute medical crisis**: Client is experiencing medical emergency requiring immediate attention

- [ ] **Active suicidal crisis**: Client is actively planning suicide and requires immediate crisis intervention

- [ ] **Homicidal ideation with plan**: Client poses imminent danger to others

Relative Contraindications (Proceed with Caution or After Preparation):

- [ ] **Unstabilized dissociative disorder**: Client has DID or severe dissociation without established internal cooperation or safety protocols

- [ ] **Very recent trauma** (within 72 hours): Acute stress response may need stabilization first

- [ ] **Severe emotion dysregulation**: Client has virtually no capacity to tolerate any distress without self-harm or crisis

- [ ] **Ongoing trauma**: The trauma is still happening (domestic violence, ongoing abuse). Safety planning takes priority

- [ ] **Significant substance withdrawal**: Client is in acute withdrawal and medically unstable

- [ ] **Severe depression with significant cognitive impairment**: Client can't concentrate enough to maintain PEF

- [ ] **Current severe panic disorder**: Client experiences panic attacks during any therapeutic focus on internal experience

- [ ] **Significant head injury or neurological condition**: Affects ability to follow protocol or process information

Clinical Judgment Factors:

Some situations require careful assessment rather than automatic exclusion:

Client Motivation: Is the client willing to try Flash? Coerced or pressured trauma processing doesn't work and is unethical. You need at least minimal willingness.

Therapeutic Alliance: Is there enough trust and rapport for trauma work? If you just met and the client seems guarded or suspicious, build alliance first.

Support System: Does the client have adequate support for between-session coping? Doing trauma work with someone who's completely isolated and without resources increases risk.

Timing: Is this the right time in the client's life for trauma processing? Sometimes practical crises (eviction, job loss, custody battle) need attention first.

Previous Treatment Response: Has the client tried trauma processing before? If they've consistently been unable to tolerate it, more preparation might be needed—or Flash might be exactly what they need. Assess carefully.

Making the Assessment:

This isn't about having a perfect, risk-free client. Most trauma survivors have some complexity. It's about determining whether the client is stable enough for trauma processing to be safe and beneficial.

Ask yourself:

- Can this client tolerate brief engagement with traumatic material?

- Do they have enough grounding and self-regulation to recover if they become distressed?

- Is their current life situation stable enough to support trauma work?

- Are there immediate safety concerns that should be addressed first?

If you're uncertain, consult with colleagues or supervisors. Err on the side of caution, especially when first learning Flash.

Documentation:

Document your contraindication screening in your clinical notes. This provides clear rationale for your clinical decisions and protects both you and the client if complications arise.

Note format might look like:

"Assessed client for Flash Technique appropriateness. No active psychosis, suicidality, or substance intoxication noted. Client demonstrates adequate reality testing, can maintain focus on positive imagery, and has support system in place. Informed consent provided and client verbally agreed to proceed. No contraindications identified."

Or if contraindications exist:

"Assessed client for Flash Technique but identified current contraindication of unstabilized dissociation with frequent switching. Will continue stabilization work and resource building. Will reassess appropriateness for Flash after establishing better internal communication and grounding skills."

Clear documentation supports good clinical practice.

Setting Up for Success

You've created a safe environment. You've explained Flash clearly and obtained informed consent. You've developed and tested a solid PEF. You've screened for contraindications and determined the client is appropriate for Flash.

You're ready to proceed to the actual protocol.

But here's the thing: If you've done the setup well, the protocol itself will go much more smoothly. Rushing through setup to get to the "real work" is a mistake. The setup is the foundation. Build it solidly.

Before moving on, do a final check:

Environment: Private, comfortable, minimal distractions **Informed Consent**: Client understands Flash and agrees to proceed **PEF**: Tested and effective, generates positive feelings, holds attention **Safety**: Grounding techniques reviewed, client knows they can stop anytime **Contraindications**: None present, or relative contraindications addressed **Alliance**: Sufficient trust and rapport for trauma work **Your Readiness**: You feel prepared, focused, and present

All checked? Good. Now you're actually ready for the protocol itself.

In the next chapter, we'll walk through the step-by-step Flash protocol—exactly what to say, when to say it, how to monitor responses, and when to continue or stop. The concrete, practical details that turn theory and setup into actual clinical intervention.

But you needed this foundation first. Setup isn't just preliminary busywork. It's the scaffolding that allows Flash to work safely and effectively. Skip it or rush it, and you're building on unstable ground.

Take the time. Do it right. Your clients deserve that level of care and professionalism.

Setting the Stage for Effective Flash

Flash Technique requires careful setup before beginning the protocol. Physical environment needs privacy, comfort, appropriate lighting, and minimal distractions. Psychological safety comes from therapeutic alliance, clear pacing control, informed consent, and established emergency protocols.

Explaining Flash to clients involves clear description of the process, realistic expectations, and addressing common questions about memory erasure, tolerability, and disclosure requirements. The script should be adapted based on client education, previous therapy experience, cultural background, and trauma type.

Developing an effective Positive Engaging Focus requires three characteristics: genuinely positive affect (not just neutral), engaging enough to hold attention, and accessible to maintain with reasonable effort. Common mistakes include using neutral instead of positive foci, insufficient detail, trauma contamination, and therapist-imposed preferences. Always test the PEF before using it in Flash.

Contraindication screening protects client safety. Absolute contraindications include active psychosis, severe intoxication, acute medical crisis, and imminent danger to self or others. Relative contraindications require clinical judgment— unstabilized dissociation, very recent trauma, severe emotion dysregulation, or ongoing trauma situations. Document your assessment clearly.

Proper setup creates conditions for safe, effective Flash implementation and significantly improves outcomes.

Chapter 5: The Step-by-Step Protocol

You've done the setup. Your client understands Flash, you've got a solid PEF tested and ready, the environment is appropriate, and you've determined there are no contraindications. Now comes the actual intervention.

This is where theory becomes practice. Where preparation meets execution. And honestly? Once you've done the setup properly, the protocol itself is fairly straightforward. Not necessarily easy—you still need to monitor carefully and adjust in real-time—but the steps are clear.

I'm going to walk you through the complete Flash protocol with timing, specific language, decision points, and what to watch for. Think of this as your field guide. You'll refer back to it repeatedly until the protocol becomes second nature.

Complete Protocol with Timing Guidelines

The full Flash protocol typically takes 15-45 minutes, depending on the memory's intensity, the client's response, and how many processing rounds you complete. Here's the structure:

Phase 1: Preparation and Baseline (5-10 minutes) Phase 2: Flash Processing (10-30 minutes) Phase 3: Completion and Assessment (5-10 minutes)

Let's go through each phase step-by-step.

Phase 1: Preparation and Baseline

Step 1: Identify the Target Memory (2-3 minutes)

Therapist: "We're going to use Flash to work on a specific traumatic memory. Which memory would you like to focus on today?"

Client identifies the memory. They don't need to describe details, but you need enough information to work with it.

Therapist: "You don't have to tell me what happened, but I need to ask: Is this a memory of something that happened in the past, or is this trauma still occurring?"

Verify it's past trauma, not ongoing. If ongoing, you need safety planning first, not Flash.

Step 2: Get Baseline SUDS (1 minute)

Therapist: "When you think about this memory right now—not describing it, just thinking about it briefly—how disturbing does it feel on a scale of 0 to 10? Zero means no disturbance at all, and 10 means the worst disturbance you can imagine."

Client provides SUDS rating. Write it down. You'll compare to this baseline later.

If SUDS is below 5, ask if Flash is really needed. Sometimes clients nominate memories that aren't actually very distressing anymore. If SUDS is 8-10, that's appropriate for Flash.

Step 3: Activate PEF (2-3 minutes)

Therapist: "Now I'd like you to bring up the positive image we practiced earlier—[specific PEF description]. Take a moment to really see it, feel it, notice all the details. Let me know when you have it clearly in mind."

Wait for client confirmation. Watch their face and body. Do they look relaxed? Are they engaged with the image?

Therapist: "Good. Now just stay with that positive image for a minute. Really immerse yourself in it."

Give them 60 seconds. This activates the PEF and allows you to verify they can hold it.

Step 4: Explain the Flash Process (2-3 minutes)

Therapist: "Okay, here's what we're going to do. You're going to keep your main attention on this positive image—the [PEF]. That's your home base. But periodically, I'm going to ask you to very briefly think about the traumatic memory—just for a second or two—and then immediately come right back to the positive image.

"While you're doing this, I'll be guiding you through some [eye movements/tapping/bilateral tones]. The idea is that you flash very briefly to the memory and immediately back to safety. We'll do this several times.

"Your job is to keep most of your attention on the positive image. Don't try to stay with the traumatic memory or process it deeply. Just flash to it very briefly and come right back. Think of it like glancing at something in your peripheral vision and then looking away immediately.

"If at any point you feel too overwhelmed, you can raise your hand or say 'stop,' and we'll pause immediately. You're in control. Does this make sense?"

Client confirms understanding. Answer any questions.

Phase 2: Flash Processing

Step 5: First Flash Sequence (2-3 minutes)

Therapist: "Okay, bring up your positive image again—the [PEF]. Get it clearly in mind... Good. Keep your attention mostly on that positive image, and when I say 'now,' just briefly think about the traumatic memory for about one second, then come immediately back to the positive image. Ready? Keep your focus on [PEF]..."

Pause 3-5 seconds to let them establish the PEF.

Therapist: "Now." (Pause 1-2 seconds) "And back to [PEF]."

That's one flash. Immediately start bilateral stimulation.

If doing eye movements: "Follow my fingers with your eyes." Move your fingers back and forth about 12-18 inches in front of their face at moderate speed. Do about 24-36 complete back-and-forth movements (roughly 12-20 seconds).

If doing bilateral tapping: "I'm going to tap on your hands." Alternate tapping gently on the client's left and right hands. Do about 24-36 taps total, alternating sides.

If using audio bilateral stimulation: "Listen to these tones." Activate bilateral audio through headphones or speakers. Run for about 12-20 seconds.

After bilateral stimulation stops:

Therapist: "How are you doing? Just a quick check-in."

Client should report they're okay. If they report distress, assess severity (we'll cover this in monitoring section).

If they're okay, continue.

Step 6: Continuing Flash Sequences (Variable timing, usually 3-5 rounds)

Repeat the flash process:

Therapist: "Good. Back to your positive image, the [PEF]. Get it clearly in mind... (pause 3-5 seconds) Now, very briefly think about the memory... (pause 1-2 seconds) And right back to [PEF]."

Bilateral stimulation for 12-20 seconds.

Check in: "How's that?"

Repeat this cycle 3-5 times before doing a more thorough assessment. Each flash plus bilateral stimulation takes about 30-45 seconds. Five rounds takes roughly 3-4 minutes.

Step 7: Mid-Process SUDS Check (1 minute)

After 3-5 flash sequences:

Therapist: "Okay, let's pause for a moment. When you think about the traumatic memory now—just briefly check in with it—what's the disturbance level? Same 0-10 scale."

Client provides updated SUDS.

Has it decreased? By how much?

If SUDS dropped 2+ points: Great progress. Continue with more flash sequences.

If SUDS dropped 0-1 points: Processing is slow or stuck. We'll address this in the troubleshooting chapter, but for now, you might need to adjust something (more on this below).

If SUDS increased: This occasionally happens. The client may be engaging too fully with the trauma instead of flashing briefly. Adjust instructions (see monitoring section).

Step 8: Continue Processing Until Complete or Time Limit (Variable, 5-20 more minutes)

If SUDS is dropping appropriately, continue flash sequences in sets of 3-5, checking SUDS after each set.

Stopping Points:

SUDS reaches 0-1: Memory is substantially processed. You can stop and move to completion phase.

SUDS reaches 2-3 and plateaus: Some processing has occurred. Depending on time and client state, you might stop here or continue.

You've done 20-30 flash sequences total: That's usually sufficient for one session, even if SUDS hasn't reached 0. You can always do another session if needed.

Client reports feeling tired or "done": Respect that. Processing continues between sessions.

You're approaching 45-50 minutes total session time: Leave time for completion phase.

Typical session involves 15-25 flash sequences total, done in sets of 3-5 with SUDS checks between sets. This usually reduces SUDS significantly within 20-30 minutes of processing time (Manfield et al., 2017).

Phase 3: Completion and Assessment

Step 9: Final SUDS and Cognitive Check (3-5 minutes)

Therapist: "Okay, we're going to wrap up the processing part. When you think about the memory now, what's the disturbance level?"

Get final SUDS.

Then assess cognitions:

Therapist: "When you think about that memory now, what words go with it that express something negative about yourself?"

Client might say things like "I'm powerless," "I'm not safe," "I should have known better," "I'm damaged."

Therapist: "And when you think about the memory now, what would you rather believe about yourself?"

Client identifies positive cognition: "I'm strong now," "I survived," "I did the best I could," "I'm healing."

Therapist: "How true does that positive belief feel on a scale of 1 to 7, where 1 is completely false and 7 is completely true?"

This is the Validity of Cognition (VoC) scale from EMDR. It helps assess whether cognitive shifts are happening alongside emotional processing (Shapiro, 2018).

Step 10: Body Scan (1-2 minutes)

Therapist: "When you think about the memory now, where do you notice any sensation in your body?"

Client identifies body sensations (tension, discomfort, neutral feelings, or no sensation).

If residual tension exists, you might do a few more flash sequences targeting the body sensation. If the body feels clear or neutral, that's good.

Step 11: Grounding and Closure (2-3 minutes)

Therapist: "We've done good work today. How are you feeling right now?"

Assess client's current state. Do they seem grounded and present, or are they dissociated or flooded?

If they seem okay:

Therapist: "What we did today was process the traumatic memory in a way that reduces its emotional intensity. You might notice continued processing between now and our next session—dreams, thoughts about the memory, or just a continued sense of the memory feeling different. That's normal.

"If you experience any distress that feels unmanageable, [review grounding techniques or emergency contacts]. But most people find they feel better after Flash, not worse.

"Do you have any questions? Anything you need before you leave?"

If client seems dissociated or distressed, spend more time grounding them before they leave. Use grounding techniques— orienting to the room, naming objects, focusing on physical sensations like feet on the floor.

Don't end the session with the client dissociated or highly distressed. Take the time to bring them back to baseline before they leave your office.

Step 12: Between-Session Instructions (1 minute)

Therapist: "Between now and next time, you don't need to actively think about the traumatic memory. Let your brain do its processing naturally. If the memory comes up spontaneously, that's fine—just notice it without trying to avoid it or dwell on it. Focus on your regular life and activities. We'll check in next session about how things have been."

That's the complete protocol. Seems like a lot written out, but it flows naturally once you've practiced a few times.

Choosing Bilateral Stimulation Methods

You have three main options for bilateral stimulation (BLS) in Flash: eye movements, tactile (tapping), or auditory tones. Each has advantages and disadvantages.

Eye Movements

How: Client follows your fingers with their eyes while you move them horizontally back and forth about 12-18 inches in front of their face. Move at moderate speed—not too fast (causes eye strain) or too slow (not stimulating enough).

Advantages:

- No equipment needed
- Easy to adjust speed and distance based on client response
- You maintain eye contact and can monitor client closely
- Most traditional EMDR method, familiar to EMDR therapists

Disadvantages:

- Some clients find it uncomfortable or get dizzy
- Requires therapist to continuously move fingers (can be tiring for therapist)
- Doesn't work for clients with vision problems or who can't follow movements
- Some clients find it weird or intrusive

When to use: Eye movements work well for most clients and are the most commonly used BLS method in Flash research (Manfield et al., 2017). Start here unless client preference or contraindication suggests otherwise.

Bilateral Tapping

How: Alternate tapping gently on client's left and right hands (or knees, or shoulders) at moderate pace. About one tap per second, alternating sides.

Advantages:

- Works for clients who can't do eye movements

- Some clients find it grounding and reassuring

- Can be done with client's eyes closed (reduces visual distraction)

- Simple and straightforward

Disadvantages:

- Requires touch, which some trauma survivors find triggering

- Less monitoring of client's face if they close their eyes

- Therapist needs to maintain consistent rhythm manually

When to use: Use tapping for clients who report discomfort with eye movements, those with vision problems, or those who find tactile input grounding. Always ask permission before touching: "Would you be comfortable with me tapping gently on your hands?"

Some clients prefer self-tapping—they tap alternately on their own knees or do the "butterfly hug" (crossing arms and tapping alternately on shoulders). This gives them more control.

Bilateral Audio Tones

How: Use headphones or speakers to play tones that alternate from left ear to right ear. Many EMDR therapists have specialized equipment (Neurotek, BioLateral Processor, etc.), but you can also use smartphone apps designed for bilateral audio stimulation.

Advantages:

- No physical effort required from therapist

- Consistent timing and rhythm

- No touch required (good for clients uncomfortable with tapping)

- Can be done with eyes closed

- Works during telehealth sessions

Disadvantages:

- Requires equipment

- Some clients find tones annoying or distracting

- Less personal than other methods

- Technology can malfunction

- Volume needs adjustment for each client

When to use: Audio works well for telehealth, for clients who can't or won't do eye movements or tapping, and for sessions where you want to reduce therapist physical effort.

Making the Choice

Ask the client: "We have several options for bilateral stimulation. Some people prefer following eye movements, others prefer alternating tapping on their hands or knees, and some prefer listening to alternating tones through headphones.

Do you have a preference, or would you like to try one and see how it feels?"

Most clients won't have strong preferences initially. Start with eye movements (most traditional and researched), but be ready to switch if the client reports discomfort.

Speed and Duration Adjustments

Speed: Moderate speed works for most people—about one complete left-right-left cycle per 1-1.5 seconds. Some clients need slower (if they get dizzy or overwhelmed), others benefit from faster (if they're highly avoidant or intellectual).

Duration: Standard is about 12-20 seconds per set (roughly 24-36 complete cycles). But adjust based on response. If client is processing well with shorter sets (8-10 seconds), that's fine. If they need longer sets (25-30 seconds), that works too.

Distance (for eye movements): Standard is 12-18 inches from client's face. Move closer if they report difficulty tracking, farther if they feel crowded.

The research doesn't show that one BLS method is clearly superior to others. What matters is that it's bilateral (alternating left-right) and that the client can tolerate it comfortably (Shapiro, 2018). Client preference and comfort should guide your choice.

Monitoring Client Responses

Flash is designed to be low-distress, but you still need to monitor carefully. Clients can become overwhelmed, dissociate, or have unexpected reactions. Your job is catching these early and responding appropriately.

What to Watch:

Facial Expressions: Relaxed face suggests processing is proceeding well. Tension, grimacing, crying, or blank expression suggests distress or dissociation.

Body Language: Open, relaxed posture is good. Crossed arms, hunched shoulders, rigid posture, or fidgeting suggests discomfort.

Breathing: Steady, normal breathing is good. Rapid breathing suggests anxiety. Very slow or held breath suggests dissociation or freeze response.

Eye Contact (when applicable): Present, responsive eye contact suggests engagement. Glazed, distant, or "lights are on but nobody's home" look suggests dissociation.

Verbal Responses: Clear, coherent responses suggest client is present. Delayed, confused, or absent responses suggest dissociation or overwhelm.

Physiological Signs: Color changes (flushing or pallor), sweating, trembling, or other signs of autonomic activation suggest strong emotional response.

Between Each Flash Set:

Do quick check-ins: "How are you doing?" Watch and listen to the response.

Green Light Responses (Continue):

- "I'm okay"
- "That felt fine"
- "Still good"
- Client appears calm and present

Yellow Light Responses (Check More Carefully):

- "It's a little uncomfortable"
- "I felt some anxiety"
- Client looks slightly tense but is maintaining composure
- Client hesitates before responding

Ask: "What specifically are you noticing? Is it manageable?" If they say yes and want to continue, proceed but monitor closely.

Red Light Responses (Pause or Stop):

- "I can't do this"
- "It's too much"
- "I feel like I'm back there"
- Client is crying intensely
- Client appears dissociated or unresponsive
- Client shows signs of panic attack

Stop processing immediately. Use grounding techniques. We'll cover this more in the troubleshooting chapter.

Common Responses and What They Mean:

Client reports feeling distant or disconnected: Might be mild dissociation. Check if they can feel their feet on the floor, see objects in the room. If they can't, they're dissociating and need grounding before continuing.

Client reports feeling nothing: Could be healthy processing (the memory is losing emotional charge) or could be emotional numbing/dissociation. Ask them to describe what "nothing" feels like. If they seem present and grounded, it's probably healthy processing.

Client reports body sensations: This is normal during trauma processing. Body often holds trauma. Unless the sensations are overwhelming, continue processing. You can address residual body sensations in the body scan phase.

Client starts narrating the trauma spontaneously: They're engaging too fully with the memory instead of flashing briefly. Redirect: "You're going deeper into the memory than we want. Just flash to it very briefly, then come right back to the positive image."

Client says they can't bring up the PEF anymore: The PEF can lose effectiveness temporarily. Have a backup PEF ready, or take a break and let the original PEF "recharge."

When to Continue, Pause, or Stop

Decision-making during Flash requires clinical judgment. Here are guidelines:

Continue Processing When:

- SUDS is decreasing with each set or maintaining at a comfortable level

- Client reports feeling okay or manageable discomfort

- Client appears present, grounded, and engaged

- Processing time is under 45 minutes total

- Client hasn't indicated desire to stop

Pause (Brief Break) When:

- Client reports mild overwhelm but wants to continue

- Client appears mildly dissociated but can be grounded quickly

- You notice your own focus drifting (therapist fatigue)

- Client needs bathroom break or water

- You need to adjust something (change BLS method, modify instructions)

During pause:

- Have client focus fully on PEF or use grounding techniques

- Check in verbally about how they're doing

- Give them a minute to regulate before deciding whether to continue

- Ask explicitly: "Do you want to continue, or shall we stop here for today?"

Stop Processing When:

- Client explicitly requests stopping

- Client appears significantly distressed or dissociated despite grounding attempts

- SUDS is increasing instead of decreasing (rare, but can happen)

- You've done 25-30 flash sequences and processing seems complete

- You're approaching end of session time (need 10 minutes for closure)

- Breakthrough abreaction occurs (intense emotional release that wasn't anticipated)
- Client shows signs of medical distress (severe panic, hyperventilation that doesn't respond to intervention)

How to Stop:

Therapist: "Okay, we're going to pause the processing here. Come fully back to the positive image, and then just let that go. Open your eyes [if closed] and look around the room. Notice where you are right now."

Ground the client thoroughly before discussing anything or ending the session.

If stopping early due to overwhelm:

Therapist: "What you're experiencing is more distress than we want you to have during Flash. That's useful information—it tells us this memory might need more preparation work first, or we might need to modify our approach. For now, let's focus on helping you feel grounded and safe again."

Don't shame the client for not being able to continue. Frame it as valuable clinical information that guides next steps.

Completing the Session and Checking Results

The end of Flash processing isn't the end of the session. You need proper closure.

Final Assessment

Get final SUDS, negative and positive cognitions, VoC rating, and do body scan (as described in protocol steps above).

Compare final SUDS to baseline. Typical reduction is 4-6 points. If the memory started at SUDS 9 and ended at SUDS 3, that's excellent progress. Even a reduction from 9 to 6 indicates meaningful processing occurred (Manfield et al., 2017).

Cognitive Shifts

Sometimes cognitive shifts happen spontaneously during Flash. Client might report: "You know, thinking about it now, I don't feel as much like it was my fault" or "It feels more like something that happened to me rather than something about me."

These shifts are great indicators of processing, even if SUDS hasn't reached zero.

If SUDS is low (0-2) but negative cognitions remain strong ("I'm still damaged"), you might need additional cognitive work—cognitive restructuring, standard EMDR processing, or another Flash session focusing on the belief rather than the memory itself.

Client Education About Post-Session Processing

Therapist: "Processing often continues after the session ends. Over the next few days, you might notice:

- The memory feeling different—more distant or less intense

- Dreams related to the trauma (this is normal processing)

- Other memories coming up that are related

- Feeling more emotional or tired for a day or two

- Feeling surprisingly better

"All of these are normal. Your brain is continuing to integrate what we worked on today. You don't need to do anything actively—just let the process unfold. If you experience distress that feels unmanageable, you have [grounding techniques, emergency numbers, etc.].

"Otherwise, just go about your regular life. We'll check in next session about how things have gone."

Scheduling Follow-Up

For most clients, scheduling follow-up within one to two weeks is appropriate. This allows time for between-session processing while maintaining continuity.

Some clients need sooner follow-up (if they're highly symptomatic or the session was difficult). Others can go longer between sessions (if they're stable and the memory processed well).

Documentation

After the session, document:

- Target memory (general description, not necessarily details)

- Baseline SUDS and final SUDS

- Number of flash sequences completed

- Type of bilateral stimulation used

- Client's response to processing

- Any complications or adjustments made

- Negative and positive cognitions identified

86

- Final VoC rating

- Body scan results

- Plan for next session

Example documentation:

"Flash Technique session targeting traumatic memory from [general category, e.g., vehicle accident, assault, etc.]. Baseline SUDS: 8. Completed 18 flash sequences using eye movement bilateral stimulation. Client tolerated processing well with no significant distress. Final SUDS: 2. Negative cognition 'I'm not safe' shifted toward positive cognition 'I survived and I'm safe now' with VoC of 5. Body scan clear. Client grounded and stable at session end. Plan: Monitor between-session processing, follow up in one week."

Clear documentation supports good clinical practice and demonstrates you're following appropriate protocols.

What Success Looks Like

You'll know Flash is working when:

During the Session:

- SUDS decreases progressively

- Client remains calm and present

- Processing flows without significant difficulty

- Client reports the memory "feeling different"

After the Session:

- Client reports reduced distress when the memory comes up spontaneously

- Trauma-related symptoms decrease (fewer nightmares, less avoidance, reduced hypervigilance)

- Client can think about or talk about the trauma without overwhelming distress

- Cognitive shifts occur (less self-blame, more self-compassion, healthier perspectives)

Not every session produces dramatic change. Sometimes progress is incremental. That's okay. The research shows Flash works over time, even when individual sessions feel modest (Manfield et al., 2017).

Trust the process, follow the protocol, monitor carefully, and adjust when needed. That's the path to effective Flash implementation.

Now, what about when things don't go as planned? When the client can't think of a PEF, or the distress doesn't decrease, or unexpected reactions occur? That's what we'll tackle in the next chapter—troubleshooting the most common challenges you'll encounter.

Running an Effective Flash Session

Flash protocol consists of three phases: preparation and baseline assessment (5-10 minutes), flash processing with bilateral stimulation (10-30 minutes), and completion with final assessment (5-10 minutes). Therapists identify target memory, establish baseline SUDS, activate the PEF, and then guide clients through brief flashes to trauma interspersed with bilateral stimulation.

Bilateral stimulation options include eye movements (most traditional), bilateral tapping (good for clients uncomfortable with eye movements), or audio tones (works for telehealth). Choice depends on client preference and comfort. Standard sets involve 12-20 seconds of bilateral stimulation after each flash, done 3-5 times before checking SUDS.

Monitoring client responses requires attention to facial expressions, body language, breathing, and verbal responses. Continue when client appears comfortable and SUDS decreases. Pause when mild overwhelm occurs but client wants to continue. Stop when significant distress, dissociation, or client request indicates processing should end.

Session completion includes final SUDS assessment, cognitive check (negative and positive beliefs), Validity of Cognition rating, body scan, grounding, and client education about post-session processing. Document baseline and final SUDS, number of sequences, client response, and follow-up plans. Typical successful sessions show SUDS reduction of 4-6 points within 15-25 flash sequences.

Chapter 6: Troubleshooting Common Challenges

Even with perfect setup and protocol execution, Flash doesn't always go smoothly. Clients respond in unexpected ways. Technical issues arise. Processing gets stuck. And sometimes what seemed like a good plan in theory falls apart in practice.

That's normal. You're working with human beings who've experienced trauma. Complexity and unpredictability come with the territory. The difference between an adequate therapist and a skilled one isn't that the skilled therapist never encounters problems—it's that they know how to respond when problems arise.

This chapter addresses the most common challenges you'll face with Flash and provides concrete solutions. These aren't hypothetical scenarios—they're the actual issues therapists report when learning Flash (Manfield et al., 2017). Learn these troubleshooting strategies now, before you need them in the middle of a session.

"I Can't Think of a Positive Focus"

This happens more often than you'd think. You ask the client to identify something positive to focus on, and they look at you blankly. "I don't know. Nothing feels positive right now."

Why This Happens:

Depression makes it hard to access positive experiences or feelings. When you're depressed, your brain's default mode is negative—you can't easily remember times you felt good or imagine scenarios that would feel pleasant.

Trauma itself can cause numbing—the inability to access positive emotions. Some trauma survivors have been in survival mode so long they've forgotten what "positive" even feels like.

Avoidant personality patterns can make people uncomfortable with anything that requires imagination or emotional engagement. "I'm not good at that kind of thing," they'll say.

High anxiety can interfere with the task. Anxious clients worry about doing it "right," which prevents them from actually doing it at all.

Sometimes clients genuinely haven't had many positive experiences. Their lives have been hard, consistently, for years. Finding something positive requires creativity.

Solution Strategies:

Strategy 1: Lower the Bar

Stop asking for "positive" and ask for "neutral to mildly pleasant." You don't need ecstatic joy. You need something that's not negative and that can hold attention.

Therapist: "Okay, we don't need something intensely positive. What about something neutral or just slightly pleasant? Maybe something mildly interesting or calming? What comes to mind?"

Client: "Um... I guess I don't mind walking my dog."

Therapist: "Perfect. Tell me about walking your dog. Where do you walk? What does the dog look like? What do you notice on these walks?"

Build from there. You can often develop a perfectly functional PEF from something that started as "I don't mind it."

Strategy 2: Use Sensory Focus Instead of Memory or Imagery

Some clients can't visualize or struggle with guided imagery. For them, sensory focus works better.

Therapist: "Instead of imagining a scene or memory, what if you focus on a pleasant sensation? Like the feeling of a warm shower, or soft fabric, or a favorite food taste, or a smell you like? What sensory experience feels good to you?"

Client: "I like the smell of coffee in the morning."

Therapist: "Great. Can you imagine that smell right now? Really focus on it—the warmth, the richness, how it makes you feel?"

Build the PEF around sensory experience rather than visual imagery. Works great for clients who aren't "visual thinkers."

Strategy 3: Use Future Orientation

If present and past feel devoid of positive experiences, look forward.

Therapist: "What about something you're looking forward to? Doesn't have to be huge—maybe seeing someone you care about, or a show you want to watch, or something you're planning? Anything that feels even mildly positive when you think about it?"

Some clients can access future-oriented positive content more easily than past or present.

Strategy 4: Use "Least Worst" Instead of Best

For trauma survivors with extremely limited positive experiences, reframe the question.

Therapist: "What's a moment in your life that was less bad than usual? Not necessarily good, but maybe a moment when things felt okay, or at least bearable? Can you think of a time like that?"

Client: "I mean... I guess when I was a kid, sometimes I'd hide in the library after school. It was quiet. Nobody bothered me there."

Therapist: "That's something we can work with. Tell me more about being in the library. What did you do there? How did it feel?"

You're building a PEF around "safe enough" rather than "joyful." That's fine. Safety can be the positive element.

Strategy 5: Borrowed or Vicarious Positive Experiences

Some clients can't access their own positive experiences but can imagine others'.

Therapist: "If you had to imagine what a peaceful place would look like for someone else—not necessarily you, just in general—what would that be?"

Client: "I guess... a beach? People say beaches are relaxing."

Therapist: "Okay, can you imagine yourself on that beach, even if it's not a place you've been? Pretend you're there. What would you see, hear, feel?"

Sometimes clients need permission to "borrow" common positive scenarios even if they haven't personally experienced them. That's okay. Imagination counts.

Strategy 6: Use the Therapy Relationship Itself

For clients with severely impoverished positive experiences, the therapy relationship itself can serve as the positive focus.

Therapist: "What about right now, sitting here with me? Does this feel safe enough? Is there anything about being in this space, having someone listen to you, that feels even slightly okay?"

Client: "I guess... yeah. This feels okay."

Therapist: "Great. So your positive focus could be imagining being right here, in this safe space, with someone who's here to help. Can you hold onto that feeling of 'this is okay'?"

This works especially well with clients who have secure attachment to you as therapist. The relationship itself provides safety and mild positive affect.

Strategy 7: Accept That Sometimes You Need More Preparation

Occasionally, a client genuinely can't access anything remotely positive, even with these strategies. They're too depressed, too numb, too overwhelmed, or too disconnected.

That's clinical data. It tells you this client needs more preparation before Flash. Maybe they need:

- Antidepressant medication adjustment

- Stabilization work

- Resource building

- Skills training

- Treatment for active depression before trauma processing

Don't force it. If after genuinely trying these strategies the client still can't access a PEF, table Flash for now. Work on building resources and stabilizing mood first. Revisit Flash when the client is more able to access even minimal positive content.

Real Example:

Rebecca (composite) came in severely depressed with PTSD. Every strategy for developing a PEF failed. "There's nothing positive. There just isn't."

I spent three sessions doing resource development—identifying small moments of "okay-ness," building grounding skills, installing feelings of safety through standard EMDR resource installation. By session four, Rebecca could access "sitting with my cat on the couch" as a PEF. Flash then worked beautifully.

Sometimes the answer is "not yet." That's okay.

When the Distress Doesn't Decrease

You've done everything right. Good PEF, clear instructions, appropriate bilateral stimulation. But after several flash sequences, you check SUDS and it hasn't budged. Or worse, it's increased.

Frustrating. But fixable.

Why This Happens:

Client isn't flashing briefly—they're engaging fully: Instead of quickly glancing at the trauma and returning to PEF, they're diving into the memory. This activates too much distress and prevents the protective effect of Flash.

PEF isn't strong enough: It's not actually positive or engaging enough to provide meaningful counterbalance.

Wrong memory targeted: Sometimes clients choose a memory that isn't actually the primary issue, or they choose one that's too overwhelming to start with.

Blocking beliefs: Client has beliefs about whether healing is possible or whether they deserve to feel better. These beliefs can unconsciously sabotage processing.

Neurobiological factors: Some clients have nervous system dysregulation or medication effects that interfere with processing.

Solution Strategies:

Strategy 1: Adjust the Flash Instruction

Most commonly, clients are engaging too fully with the trauma. Fix this with clearer instructions.

Therapist: "I'm noticing the distress isn't decreasing the way we'd expect. I wonder if you're spending too much time with the traumatic memory instead of just flashing past it very briefly. Let's adjust. This time, think about the trauma for less than one second—just the quickest glance possible—and immediately back to the positive image. Think of it like a camera flash—just a split-second blink. Ready to try that?"

Make the flash even briefer. Sometimes going from 1-2 seconds down to truly less than one second makes all the difference.

Strategy 2: Strengthen the PEF

If the PEF isn't engaging enough, it won't provide adequate protection.

Therapist: "Let's make your positive image even more vivid and engaging. Can you add more details? What else can you see, hear, or feel in that image? Let's make it really rich and absorbing."

Help client elaborate the PEF with more sensory details, more engagement, more positive feeling.

Or switch to a different PEF entirely if the current one isn't working.

Strategy 3: Target a Different Memory First

If this memory is too intense to process right now, choose a less intense related memory first.

Therapist: "This memory might be too overwhelming to start with. Is there another memory related to this trauma that's less intense? Maybe something that happened before or after the main event, or a piece of the trauma rather than the whole thing?"

Process the lower-intensity memory first. Often, processing a "feeder" memory makes the primary memory more accessible later.

Strategy 4: Add a Cognitive Interweave

Borrowed from EMDR, a cognitive interweave involves introducing information that helps processing move forward when it's stuck (Shapiro, 2018).

Therapist: "When you think about the trauma now, what's the main thought or belief that goes with it?"

Client: "I should have stopped it. It's my fault."

Therapist: "And how old were you when this happened?"

Client: "Seven."

Therapist: "Could a seven-year-old really have stopped an adult from hurting them? Did you have the power or knowledge to prevent what happened?"

Client: "I... no, I guess not."

Therapist: "Hold onto that awareness—that you were just a child and you did the best you could with what you knew—and let's do a few more flash sequences with that perspective in mind."

Introducing this new information can unlock processing that was stuck on maladaptive beliefs.

Strategy 5: Check for Dissociation

Sometimes SUDS doesn't decrease because the client is dissociating rather than processing.

Therapist: "I'm noticing the distress level isn't changing much. How connected do you feel right now? Can you feel your feet on the floor? Can you see me clearly?"

If they're dissociated, ground them before continuing. Flash only works when the client is present enough to actually process.

Strategy 6: Consider Medication or Biological Factors

Some medications (especially high doses of benzodiazepines or certain antipsychotics) can interfere with memory processing. Not much you can do about this in the moment, but it's worth noting and potentially discussing with the prescriber.

Similarly, severe sleep deprivation, acute illness, or substance withdrawal can impair processing capacity. Sometimes the answer is "come back when you're feeling better physically."

Strategy 7: Switch to Standard EMDR or Another Modality

Occasionally, Flash just isn't the right intervention for this particular memory with this particular client. That's okay. You have other tools.

Therapist: "Flash doesn't seem to be working the way we'd hope for this memory. That happens sometimes. We have other options—we could try standard EMDR processing, or we could work on this memory using cognitive techniques, or we could table this memory for now and work on something else. What feels right to you?"

Don't keep doing something that isn't working. Adapt.

Real Example:

Tom (composite) did Flash for a combat memory. SUDS stayed at 9 after 15 flash sequences. I asked him to describe what he was doing internally. Turns out, he was trying to "process it properly" by staying with each flash for 5-10 seconds, thinking he needed to "really feel it."

I clarified: "You're working too hard. Just the tiniest glance—a split-second—then right back to the positive image. Don't try to feel anything or process deeply. Just flash past it."

Next set of flash sequences, SUDS dropped to 6. By end of session, down to 3. The problem wasn't Flash—it was his understanding of the instructions.

Managing Abreactions or Emotional Releases

Abreactions—intense emotional or physical reactions during processing—are less common in Flash than in standard EMDR or exposure therapy, but they can still happen. Sobbing, shaking, expressions of intense fear or anger, or physical reactions like nausea or hyperventilation.

When this happens, you need to manage it calmly and effectively.

Why This Happens:

Sometimes traumatic material is so charged that even brief flashes trigger strong reactions. The nervous system overrides the protective structure of Flash and responds as if the threat is happening now.

Immediate Response:

Stop bilateral stimulation immediately. No more processing right now.

Therapist: "Okay, we're going to pause. Open your eyes [if closed]. Look around the room. Notice where you are. You're here with me, in [location], and you're safe right now."

Bring them into present moment awareness:

"Tell me five things you can see in this room."

"Feel your feet on the floor. Press them down. Notice the solid ground supporting you."

"What's today's date? What did you have for breakfast?"

Orient them to safety:

"What happened to you was terrible, and we're working on processing it. But right now, in this moment, you're safe. The trauma is in the past. You're here now."

Validate the response:

"Strong feelings coming up makes sense. What you experienced was overwhelming. Your reaction shows how much that trauma affected you. And you're handling this—you're staying here with me, you're letting me help ground you."

Once they're more grounded:

"What do you need right now? Would it help to talk about what just came up, or would you rather just sit quietly for a minute and let yourself settle?"

Give them control:

"We can continue working on this today if you feel ready, or we can stop here and work on grounding and stabilization. This is your choice. What feels right?"

Managing Specific Abreaction Types:

Intense Crying:

Let them cry. Don't rush to stop it. Crying is often therapeutic release. Offer tissues. Sit with them compassionately.

Therapist: "It's okay to cry. You're safe here. Take your time."

Only intervene if crying escalates to the point where they can't breathe or seems to be intensifying rather than releasing. Then ground them gently.

Anger:

Anger is a healthy response to trauma, but it can be intense.

Therapist: "I can see how angry you are about what happened to you. That anger makes sense. What was done to you was wrong."

If anger is directed at the perpetrator (not at you), validate it. If they need physical release, offer safe options: "Would it help to stand up and move? Stomp your feet? Push against something solid?"

Don't encourage destructive expressions, but allow safe physical release.

Panic/Hyperventilation:

Therapist: "You're breathing too fast. Let's slow that down. Breathe with me. In through your nose for four counts... hold... out through your mouth for six counts."

Model slow breathing. Don't tell them to "calm down" (doesn't help), but do guide them to regulate breathing.

If hyperventilation continues, have them breathe into cupped hands or a paper bag for a minute.

Freeze/Shutdown:

Client becomes completely still, unresponsive, eyes glazed. This is dorsal vagal shutdown—the nervous system's last-resort protective response.

Therapist: "I notice you've gone very still. You're safe here. I'm going to ask you to do some movements with me to help your body know you're okay."

Guide physical movements—feet on floor, stand up and sit down, stretch arms overhead, move head side to side. Physical activation helps bring them out of freeze.

Dissociation:

Client seems "not there"—distant, confused, or unresponsive.

Therapist: "Tell me where you are right now. Can you see me? Say my name. What room are you in?"

If they can't answer or seem confused, use physical grounding—hold an ice cube, stamp feet, hold something heavy.

For severe dissociation, wait patiently. Maintain calm presence. Don't increase stimulation (that can worsen dissociation). Just stay present and available until they come back.

After Managing the Abreaction:

Debrief:

Therapist: "What was that experience like for you? What do you think triggered such a strong reaction?"

Understanding what happened helps you adjust the approach if you continue processing.

Decision Point:

Continue processing today? Probably not if the abreaction was severe. Better to end on grounding and stability. Schedule follow-up soon.

If abreaction was brief and client feels okay to continue, you could—but monitor very carefully. One abreaction suggests the memory is more charged than Flash alone might handle without additional support.

Adjust Next Session:

Maybe this memory needs standard EMDR instead of Flash. Maybe it needs more preparation. Maybe the PEF needs to be stronger. Use the abreaction as clinical data informing next steps.

Clients Who Intellectualize or Avoid

Some clients stay completely in their heads during Flash. They describe the trauma analytically, show no emotion, and report SUDS that don't make sense ("It's a 10 for distress but I feel fine"). They're intellectualizing—using cognitive processing to avoid emotional engagement.

Others simply refuse to engage with the trauma at all. "I can't think about it" or "My mind goes blank."

Why This Happens:

Intellectualization is a defense mechanism. It protects against overwhelming affect by keeping everything at cognitive, analytical level. Common in trauma survivors with certain attachment styles or personality patterns.

Avoidance is also a defense. The trauma is too threatening to engage with, even briefly, so the mind protects by blocking access.

Solution Strategies:

Strategy 1: Name It Gently

Therapist: "I notice you're describing the trauma very analytically—like you're reporting facts rather than experiences. That makes sense as a way to protect yourself from feeling too much. But for Flash to work, we need at least some emotional engagement. What do you notice in your body when you think about the memory, rather than just in your thoughts?"

Redirect from cognitive to somatic/emotional without shaming the defense.

Strategy 2: Start with Body Rather Than Story

Therapist: "Instead of thinking about what happened, just notice what sensations you have in your body when the memory comes up. Where do you feel tension, heaviness, discomfort?"

Body-based processing can bypass intellectual defenses.

Strategy 3: Use Metaphor or Imagery

Therapist: "If this trauma was a picture, what would it look like? Don't describe what happened—just give me an image or metaphor."

Client: "It's like... a dark cloud."

Therapist: "Okay. Focus on your positive image, and when I say 'now,' just briefly flash to that dark cloud image—not the story, just the image—and immediately back to the positive."

Metaphorical processing can access emotional material while maintaining enough distance to be tolerable.

Strategy 4: Address the Fear Directly

Therapist: "I'm wondering if part of you is afraid that if you really feel the feelings from this trauma, you'll be overwhelmed. Is that true?"

If yes:

Therapist: "That fear makes sense. Those feelings were overwhelming when the trauma happened. But you're not in that situation anymore. You're here, safe, with me, and we have tools to manage overwhelm if it comes up. What if we tried just feeling a little bit of the emotion—not all of it, just a tiny amount—and see what happens? You can stop anytime."

Strategy 5: Accept the Defense and Work with It

Sometimes you can't break through intellectualization or avoidance. That's okay. Work with it rather than against it.

Therapist: "It seems like this memory is too difficult to engage with right now, and your mind is protecting you by keeping distance. That's actually your mind doing its job—protecting you. Let's respect that and work on something else for now. Maybe we need to build more resources or work on less intense memories first."

Don't force emotional engagement if the client's system is saying "not ready." Clinical flexibility prevents retraumatization.

Real Example:

Patricia (composite) intellectualized intensely during Flash for assault trauma. Completely flat affect, analytical descriptions, reported SUDS 9 but looked calm.

I said, "Patricia, I notice you're very much in your head right now. What do you notice in your body when you think about the assault?"

"I... I don't know. Nothing really."

"Put your hand on your chest. What's your heart doing?"

Long pause. "It's... racing. I didn't notice that."

"Your body is responding even though your mind is trying to keep distance. That's okay. Let's work with body sensations rather than the story. Just notice the racing heart, and as we do flash sequences, see if that sensation changes."

Using body as entry point bypassed her intellectual defenses. SUDS started decreasing.

Technical Issues with Bilateral Stimulation

Sometimes the problem isn't psychological—it's technical. Eye movements cause dizziness. Tapping is triggering. Audio tones are annoying. Equipment malfunctions.

Common Technical Issues and Solutions:

Issue: Client Gets Dizzy from Eye Movements

Solutions:

- Slow down the speed

- Shorten the distance (move fingers closer)

- Reduce the range of movement (smaller back-and-forth distance)

- Switch to vertical eye movements instead of horizontal

- Switch to different BLS method entirely (tapping or audio)

Issue: Client Can't Track Eye Movements (Vision Problems)

Solutions:

- Use bilateral tapping instead

- Use audio tones

- Have client imagine the eye movements while doing tapping

Issue: Tapping Is Triggering (Reminds Them of Abuse)

Solutions:

- Switch to eye movements or audio

- Have client do self-tapping (they control the touch)

- Use tapping on knees or shoulders instead of hands

Issue: Audio Tones Are Annoying or Distracting

Solutions:

- Adjust volume

- Try different tone patterns or frequencies (some equipment offers options)

- Switch to eye movements or tapping

Issue: Equipment Malfunctions

Solutions:

- Have backup method ready (can always switch to manual tapping)

- For telehealth, have client prepared to do self-tapping if audio fails

- Test equipment before session starts

Issue: Client Reports No Effect from BLS

Solutions:

- Increase intensity (faster speed, longer sets)

- Switch methods (maybe they need tactile input instead of visual)

- Check if they're actually engaging with the BLS (some clients tune it out)

Issue: BLS Is Too Stimulating (Causes Anxiety)

Solutions:

- Decrease speed

- Shorten set duration

- Increase distance (for eye movements)
- Try gentler/slower tapping

General Principle:

BLS should be noticeable enough to engage attention but not so intense it becomes distressing or distracting. Adjust based on individual response. There's no single "correct" way to do BLS— what matters is finding what works for this client (Shapiro, 2018).

When Everything's Going Wrong Simultaneously

Sometimes Murphy's Law strikes and multiple issues hit at once. Client can't access PEF, is dissociating, SUDS is increasing, and the bilateral stimulation equipment just broke.

When this happens:

Stop everything. Don't try to push through.

Prioritize safety and grounding:

Therapist: "Okay, we're going to pause all processing right now. My first priority is helping you feel safe and grounded. Let's focus on that."

Use basic grounding:

- Feet on floor
- Deep breaths
- Look around the room
- Name objects
- Hold something cold or textured

Once grounded, assess:

"This session isn't going the way we expected. That happens sometimes. It's actually useful information. It tells us that either this isn't the right time for Flash, or this particular memory needs a different approach, or we need more preparation first. What do you think would be most helpful right now?"

Give options:

- End session here and regroup next time
- Switch to different intervention (supportive therapy, skill building, stabilization work)
- Try Flash on different, less intense memory
- Take a break and try again later in the session

The key: Don't treat this as failure (yours or the client's). Treat it as clinical data informing next steps.

After a Difficult Session:

Consult: Talk to a supervisor, consultant, or colleague experienced with Flash. Get input on what happened and how to proceed.

Adjust: Plan different approach for next session based on what you learned.

Reassure Client: Follow up (phone call, email, text depending on your practice) to check how they're doing and reassure them that sometimes trauma work is unpredictable and that's okay.

Navigating Flash Challenges

When clients can't identify a positive focus, lower expectations from "intensely positive" to "neutral or mildly pleasant," use sensory experiences instead of imagery, try future orientation, or use "least worst" memories. Sometimes more preparation is needed before Flash is viable.

When distress doesn't decrease, common fixes include briefer flashing (less than one second), strengthening the PEF, targeting a different memory first, adding cognitive interweaves, checking for dissociation, or switching to standard EMDR if Flash isn't working for this particular situation.

Abreactions require immediate stopping of bilateral stimulation, grounding to present moment, orientation to safety, and validation of the response. Manage specific reactions (crying, anger, panic, freeze, dissociation) with appropriate interventions, then debrief and decide whether to continue or adjust approach for next session.

Intellectualization and avoidance can be addressed by gently naming the defense, redirecting to body sensations rather than story, using metaphor or imagery, addressing underlying fear directly, or accepting the defense and working with it rather than against it. Sometimes respecting the client's protective mechanisms means more preparation before trauma processing.

Technical BLS issues have straightforward solutions—adjust speed, distance, intensity, or switch methods entirely. When everything goes wrong simultaneously, prioritize safety and grounding over pushing through, treat challenges as clinical data rather than failure, and adjust approach for next session based on what you learned.

Chapter 7: Flash as EMDR Preparation (Phase 2)

You've been trained in EMDR. You know the eight-phase protocol. You've walked clients through it dozens, maybe hundreds of times. Phase 1, history taking and treatment planning. Phase 2, preparation. Phase 3, assessment. And so on through installation, body scan, closure, and reevaluation.

EMDR works. The research is solid, the outcomes are good, and when you follow the protocol properly, clients get better (Shapiro, 2018). But here's what every EMDR therapist knows: Phase 2 can be tricky. Some clients need extensive preparation before they're ready for the actual reprocessing that happens in Phases 3-6. And even with good preparation, some clients hit Phase 3 and freeze up. Too much, too fast, too overwhelming.

That's where Flash changes the game. Flash was originally developed as a Phase 2 preparation enhancement—a way to get clients ready for standard EMDR processing when the usual preparation methods weren't enough (Manfield et al., 2017). And it's brilliant at that job. But it's also flexible enough to serve multiple roles within EMDR treatment.

This chapter shows you exactly how to integrate Flash into EMDR practice as a preparation tool. Not as a replacement for EMDR, but as a strategic enhancement that makes EMDR more accessible and effective for clients who need it.

When to Use Flash Before Standard EMDR Processing

The question isn't "Should I always use Flash before EMDR?" The question is "When does Flash preparation add value that standard Phase 2 preparation doesn't provide?"

Here's when Flash makes sense as preparation:

Scenario 1: Extremely High Initial SUDS

Client identifies a target memory. You ask for baseline SUDS. They say 10. Or 9. Every time they think about the memory, they're flooded immediately. You start trying to do the assessment phase (negative cognition, positive cognition, emotions, body sensations, SUDS), and they can barely complete it because the distress is so intense.

Traditional EMDR says process it anyway—the activation is part of the healing. And that works for many clients. But some can't tolerate it. They dissociate, shut down, or refuse to continue.

Flash before standard processing: Reduce the SUDS from 10 to 5 or 6. Now the memory is still distressing but manageable. The client can complete the assessment phase without overwhelming activation. Then you proceed with standard EMDR reprocessing, and it goes much more smoothly.

Therapist thinking: "This memory is so hot I can't even assess it properly. Flash can cool it down enough to make it workable."

Scenario 2: Highly Avoidant Clients

Some clients avoid trauma processing intensely. They want to heal, theoretically, but every time you move toward the actual memory, they deflect, intellectualize, or "forget" what they wanted to work on.

Standard Phase 2 preparation tries to build resources and increase window of tolerance. That helps, but highly avoidant clients can resist for months. They're stuck in "I'm preparing to prepare to get ready to maybe think about processing eventually."

Flash cuts through avoidance because it's less threatening. The client doesn't have to engage fully with the trauma—just flash past it while focusing mostly on something positive. That lower threat profile often allows avoidant clients to actually start processing.

Use Flash first. Get some processing done, build confidence that they can handle trauma work, then transition to standard EMDR if needed.

Therapist thinking: "This client has been avoiding for six months. Flash might be just non-threatening enough to break the avoidance pattern."

Scenario 3: Highly Dissociative Clients

Clients with dissociative disorders or strong dissociative defenses often can't tolerate standard EMDR initially. The bilateral stimulation plus trauma focus can trigger switching (in DID) or significant dissociation that disrupts processing.

Flash, with its protective PEF structure, may be tolerable where standard EMDR isn't. The constant anchor point back to positive material prevents the client from getting lost in dissociative responses.

Use Flash first to process some of the trauma's intensity, build the system's confidence that processing is survivable, then potentially transition to standard EMDR with better internal cooperation.

Therapist thinking: "Standard EMDR triggers too much dissociation. Flash's structure might keep them present enough to actually process."

Scenario 4: Previous EMDR Failure

Client tried EMDR before. It didn't work or they dropped out because it was too overwhelming. Now they're willing to try again, but they're understandably anxious about repeating that experience.

Flash offers a different experience—gentler, more comfortable, less directly confrontational with the trauma. Starting with Flash can rebuild confidence and demonstrate that trauma processing doesn't have to be unbearable.

Therapist thinking: "EMDR was too much last time. Flash might provide a successful experience that makes them willing to try EMDR again."

Scenario 5: Complex Trauma with Multiple Targets

Client has dozens of traumatic memories. If you try to process them all with standard EMDR, you're looking at months or years of treatment. That's fine if needed, but efficiency matters too.

Flash can rapidly reduce distress across multiple memories, especially when those memories share similar themes or emotions. Do Flash on several memories to reduce their intensity, then use standard EMDR on the most significant remaining targets for deeper processing.

Therapist thinking: "We've got 20 traumatic memories to address. Flash can reduce most of them quickly, then we'll use standard EMDR on the core ones."

When Flash Preparation Isn't Needed

Flash isn't always necessary. Don't use it just because you can. Use it when it adds value.

Skip Flash preparation when:

- Client can complete assessment phase comfortably with manageable distress (SUDS 6-8)

- Client has good affect tolerance and can stay present during activation

- Client has no history of dissociation or overwhelm during trauma processing

- Client prefers direct processing and finds Flash "too indirect"

- Time is extremely limited and you need to get to processing immediately (crisis situations)

Standard EMDR already works for the majority of appropriate candidates. Flash is for the subset who need additional preparation or who couldn't otherwise tolerate EMDR (Shapiro, 2018).

Seamless Transition Protocols

You've used Flash to prepare. The memory's SUDS has decreased from 9 to 4. Good. Now what? How do you transition from Flash to standard EMDR processing?

The transition can be smooth or clunky depending on how you structure it. Here's the protocol for seamless integration:

Transition Protocol Step-by-Step

Step 1: Assess Readiness for Standard Processing

After Flash has reduced SUDS to manageable level (typically 3-5), check with the client.

Therapist: "So we've used Flash to reduce the intensity of this memory from a 9 to a 4. That's good progress. Now we have a choice. We could stop here and see how you do with this reduced level of distress. Or we could continue processing this memory using standard EMDR, which might reduce the distress even further and help resolve some of the beliefs connected to the trauma. What sounds right to you?"

Give the client choice. Some will want to continue, others will want to stop and consolidate gains. Both are legitimate.

If client says continue:

Step 2: Transition to Standard Assessment Phase

Therapist: "Okay, we're going to shift gears slightly. Instead of flashing past the memory, I'm going to ask you to bring it up more fully so we can work with it in a different way. This might feel a bit more intense than what we've been doing, but remember—we've already reduced the distress significantly, so it should be manageable. And you can always signal me if it becomes too much. Ready?"

Then conduct standard EMDR Phase 3 assessment:

Therapist: "When you bring up the memory now, what words go best with it that express something negative about yourself?"

Get negative cognition.

Therapist: "When you think about the memory, what would you rather believe about yourself?"

Get positive cognition.

Therapist: "How true does that positive belief feel right now, from 1 to 7?"

Get VoC.

Therapist: "When you bring up the memory and those negative words [repeat NC], what emotion do you feel?"

Get emotions.

Therapist: "Where do you feel it in your body?"

Get body location.

Therapist: "How disturbing does it feel now?"

Get current SUDS (should still be around where Flash left it, maybe slightly higher from fuller engagement).

Step 3: Begin Standard Desensitization

Therapist: "Okay, bring up the memory, the negative belief [NC], and notice where you feel it in your body. Follow my fingers."

Begin bilateral stimulation using standard EMDR desensitization protocol. You're no longer using Flash—you're doing full EMDR processing now.

After each set of bilateral stimulation, check in:

Therapist: "What comes up?"

Client reports whatever associations, images, thoughts, sensations, or emotions emerged. Don't direct or interpret. Just note it and continue processing.

Step 4: Continue Through Standard EMDR Phases

Process through desensitization (Phase 4) until SUDS reaches 0 or 1. Then move to installation (Phase 5), strengthening the positive cognition. Body scan (Phase 6) to clear any residual disturbance. Closure (Phase 7) to ground the client. Reevaluation (Phase 8) next session.

The Transition Is Just a Shift in Instructions

You're not doing anything dramatically different mechanically. You're still using bilateral stimulation. The client is still engaging with the memory. The difference is:

During Flash: Client keeps primary attention on PEF, briefly flashes to trauma **During Standard EMDR:** Client brings up trauma more fully with negative cognition and body sensation

The shift is in the degree of engagement and the presence or absence of the protective PEF.

Managing the Transition Smoothly

Some clients transition easily. Others find it jarring. Here's how to make it smooth:

Prepare them in advance: "We're starting with Flash to reduce the intensity. Once it's more manageable, we might shift to standard EMDR processing to complete the work. That'll feel a bit different, but I'll guide you through it."

Check comfort during transition: "How does this feel compared to what we were doing before? Is the intensity manageable?"

Allow return to Flash if needed: If standard processing becomes overwhelming, you can go back to Flash. "This seems like it's activating too much distress. Let's go back to Flash for a bit more preparation."

Real Example of Smooth Transition:

Jennifer (composite) came in with PTSD from a car accident. Initial SUDS: 9. Too high to process comfortably with standard EMDR—she'd become panicky just completing the assessment.

We did Flash. After 20 minutes, SUDS dropped to 4.

Therapist: "How do you feel about continuing to work on this memory using standard EMDR now?"

Jennifer: "I think I can handle that. It feels less overwhelming already."

We transitioned to standard assessment. Got negative cognition ("I'm going to die"), positive cognition ("I survived and I'm safe now"), emotions (fear, 4/10), body location (chest tightness).

Started desensitization with bilateral stimulation. SUDS continued decreasing. Within 15 minutes, reached SUDS 0. Did installation, body scan, closure. Processed completely in one session because Flash preparation made it accessible.

Without Flash? Jennifer probably would have dissociated or panicked during standard processing. Flash made the difference.

Working with Highly Dissociative Clients

Dissociative clients present unique challenges in EMDR. The bilateral stimulation, the trauma focus, and the emotional activation can all trigger dissociative responses that disrupt processing (Korn, 2009).

Flash offers particular advantages here because the PEF provides a constant anchor that can prevent or reduce dissociation.

Understanding Dissociative Responses in EMDR

Dissociation during trauma processing shows up as:

Spacing out: Client's eyes glaze over, they seem "not there"
Time distortion: "How long was that set?" "About 20 seconds."
"It felt like 10 minutes." **Amnesia:** "What did we just talk
about?" "I... I don't know." **Switching (in DID):** Different
part/alter comes forward mid-session **Age regression:** Client
starts speaking/acting like a child **Depersonalization:** "I feel like
I'm watching this happen to someone else" **Derealization:**
"Nothing feels real"

Traditional EMDR handles dissociation through grounding, but
some clients dissociate so readily that processing becomes
impossible.

Flash with Dissociative Clients: Special Considerations

1. Strengthen the PEF

For dissociative clients, the PEF needs to be especially strong
and grounding. Choose something with strong present-moment
awareness.

Good PEFs for dissociative clients:

- Physical sensation (feeling feet on floor, holding textured
  object)

- Current safe space (therapy room itself, therapist's
  presence)

- Grounding image (tree with deep roots, anchor in sand)

- Sensory present-moment awareness (sounds in room,
  feeling of chair)

Less ideal:

- Imaginary scenes that have no anchor to present reality

- Memories (can trigger time confusion)
- Complex visualizations (require too much cognitive capacity)

2. Keep Flashes Very Brief

Standard Flash uses 1-2 second flashes. For dissociative clients, go even briefer—half a second. Just the tiniest glance toward the trauma, then immediately back to PEF.

Longer engagement risks triggering dissociation.

3. Check Grounding Frequently

After every 2-3 flash sequences, do a grounding check.

Therapist: "Are you here with me? Can you feel your feet on the floor? Can you see me clearly? Say your name and today's date."

If client hesitates or seems confused, they're dissociating. Stop processing and ground more thoroughly before continuing.

4. Have Grounding Scripts Ready

Therapist: "Look around the room. Name five things you can see... Good. Now tell me four things you can hear... Now three things you can physically feel right now..."

Use these scripts proactively if you notice early dissociative signs.

5. Work with Parts Explicitly

If client has DID or OSDD, establish agreement from the system before starting Flash.

Therapist: "I'd like to check in with all the parts inside. Is everyone okay with doing Flash today? If any part has concerns, please let me know."

Honor objections. If a protector part says no, respect that and address their concerns before proceeding.

6. Adjust Bilateral Stimulation

Some dissociative clients find eye movements trigger dissociation (the trance-like quality can be problematic). Try:

- Slower eye movements
- Bilateral tapping (more grounding)
- Audio tones with eyes open
- Self-applied bilateral stimulation (gives client more control)

Case Example: Flash with Dissociative Client

Morgan (composite) has OSDD with several distinct parts. She tried EMDR previously but dissociated every time, making processing impossible.

Session 1: Preparation

Therapist: "Morgan, I'd like to check in with all the parts. Is everyone here okay with trying Flash to work on the [trauma memory]?"

Different parts speak up. One says yes, one is hesitant, one says absolutely not.

Therapist: "Okay, thank you for being honest. To the part who said no—what are your concerns?"

Part: "Processing is dangerous. Morgan will fall apart."

Therapist: "That's a protective concern and it makes sense. What if we agreed that if anyone starts to feel overwhelmed, we stop immediately? And we're using Flash, which is gentler than what you tried before. Would you be willing to let us try, knowing you can stop it at any time?"

After negotiation, reluctant part agrees to let us try.

Session 2: Flash Processing

Developed PEF: feeling of sitting in therapy office (very grounding, very present-moment).

Started Flash with very brief flashes (less than one second).

After three sequences, Morgan's eyes glazed over slightly.

Therapist: "Morgan, can you hear me? Feel your feet on the floor. Come back to this room."

She came back, reported she'd started "floating away."

Therapist: "Let's make the flashes even shorter. Just the tiniest glance at the memory—don't even try to see it clearly. Then right back to feeling yourself sitting here in this chair."

Continued Flash with ultra-brief flashes. Checked grounding every 2-3 sequences.

After 30 minutes, SUDS dropped from 8 to 5. No significant dissociation after adjustment.

Scheduled follow-up. Between sessions, parts reported feeling "surprised that processing didn't cause disaster."

Over several sessions, continued Flash processing on multiple trauma memories. Dissociation remained minimal. Eventually, Morgan's system felt safe enough to try standard EMDR, which also worked well because Flash had built confidence and reduced trauma intensity.

Flash wasn't a cure for the dissociative disorder, but it made trauma processing accessible in a way standard EMDR hadn't been.

Managing Emotional Flooding and Avoidance

Two opposite problems, but Flash helps with both.

Emotional Flooding

Client becomes overwhelmed with emotion during trauma processing. Sobbing, panic, intense fear that doesn't decrease. The emotional response is so strong it prevents processing— they're drowning in feeling.

Flash reduces flooding by:

- Keeping primary attention on positive material

- Limiting exposure duration (brief flashes rather than sustained focus)

- Providing immediate return to safety after each flash

Using Flash for Flooding-Prone Clients:

During assessment, you notice the client becomes tearful just talking about the memory. SUDS 10, emotional control shaky.

Therapist: "I can see this memory brings up very strong emotions. That makes sense given what you experienced. We're going to use Flash specifically because it tends to be less emotionally overwhelming than standard processing. The positive focus will help regulate those intense feelings while we still work on the memory."

Start Flash. Monitor carefully for signs of flooding:

- Escalating crying

- Rapid breathing

- Inability to return to PEF

- Overwhelmed statements ("I can't do this")

If flooding starts occurring:

Therapist: "I'm going to pause the processing. Take some deep breaths with me. In for four... out for six... That's it. You're safe. The feelings are strong, but they're just feelings. They can't hurt you."

Ground the client. Then assess whether to continue with adjusted Flash (briefer flashes, stronger PEF) or stop for the day.

Avoidance

Opposite problem: Client shows no emotion. Intellectualizes. Says the memory doesn't bother them (while showing SUDS 9). Avoids engaging with trauma content.

Flash can sometimes bypass avoidance because it's less threatening than direct processing.

Using Flash for Avoidant Clients:

Therapist: "I notice you're having trouble really engaging with the feelings about this memory. That's a protective response— your mind is trying to shield you from pain. Flash might actually work better for you because it doesn't require you to dive fully into the emotions. You can keep some protective distance while still processing. Want to try?"

Avoidant clients often respond well to Flash because it honors the protective mechanism (keeping distance) while still allowing processing to occur.

Case Example: Avoidant Client

Derek (composite) came for treatment of military trauma. Highly intellectual, analytical, emotionally controlled. Described horrific events with zero affect. "Yeah, I saw my friend get blown up. It was unfortunate."

Tried standard EMDR. He described the memory clinically, no emotion, SUDS "maybe a 3" (body language suggested higher but he wouldn't acknowledge it).

Switched to Flash.

Therapist: "Derek, I'm noticing you stay very intellectual about these memories. That's a defense that's protected you. But I think it's also keeping you stuck. Flash might work because it doesn't ask you to feel deeply—just briefly touch the memory and move on. The feelings might come up naturally without you having to force them."

Derek agreed to try. Developed PEF (fishing at his cabin—peaceful, engaging).

Started Flash. At first, no visible response. But after 10 sequences, his jaw tightened. Then eyes watered slightly. Then he said quietly, "SUDS is higher than I thought. Maybe a 7."

The defenses were loosening. Flash's indirect approach allowed emotional access without triggering his protective intellectualization quite as strongly.

Continued Flash. By end of session, he'd cried briefly (first time in therapy), SUDS dropped to 4, and he said, "I didn't realize how much I was holding in."

Flash sometimes works precisely because it respects defenses while gently working around them.

Case Examples with Annotated Transcripts

Let's look at detailed transcripts showing Flash preparation followed by transition to standard EMDR.

Case 1: Single-Incident Trauma with High Initial SUDS

Client: Andrea, 29, assault survivor, PTSD **Target Memory:** Sexual assault two years ago **Initial SUDS:** 10 **Plan:** Flash preparation to reduce SUDS, then standard EMDR if tolerable

Session Transcript (Abbreviated):

Therapist: "Andrea, when you think about the assault, how disturbing is it right now on that 0-10 scale?"

Andrea: "Ten. Absolutely a ten." *[hands shaking, breathing quick]*

Therapist: "That's extremely high distress. I'm thinking we should use Flash first to reduce that intensity before we try standard processing. Flash will let us work on the memory without overwhelming you. Does that sound okay?" *[Checking consent]*

Andrea: "Yes, please. I don't know if I can handle talking about it in detail."

Therapist: "You won't have to. Let's develop your positive focus first. What comes to mind that feels safe, peaceful, or pleasant?" *[PEF development]*

Andrea: "Um... maybe my garden? I love working in my garden."

Therapist: "Perfect. Tell me about your garden. What do you grow? What does it look like?" *[Elaborating PEF with details]*

Andrea: "I have roses, lavender, some vegetables. It's peaceful there. I lose track of time when I'm working in it."

Therapist: "Beautiful. Close your eyes and imagine yourself in that garden right now. See the roses and lavender. Smell the lavender. Feel the sun. Hear birds or bees. Really immerse yourself in being there." *[Activating PEF fully]*

[60 seconds of client holding PEF]

Therapist: "Good. Now here's what we'll do. Keep your main focus on being in that garden. But when I say 'now,' very briefly—for just one second—think about the assault, then immediately come right back to the garden. We'll do this several times with eye movements. Your job is staying mostly in the garden. Ready?" *[Clear Flash instructions]*

Andrea: "Okay."

Therapist: "Focus on the garden... now." *[1-second pause]* "Back to the garden. Follow my fingers." *[20 seconds of bilateral stimulation]*

Therapist: "How was that?"

Andrea: "Okay. A little anxious but okay."

Therapist: "Good. Let's continue." *[Repeats Flash sequence five more times]*

Therapist: "Pause for a moment. When you think about the assault now, what's the distress level?"

Andrea: "Maybe... seven? Still bad but not quite as overwhelming." *[SUDS decreased 3 points]*

Therapist: "Great progress. Let's continue." *[10 more Flash sequences]*

Therapist: "Check in with the memory again. SUDS now?"

Andrea: "Five. Definitely lower." *[Total decrease of 5 points]*

Therapist: "Excellent. So we've reduced it from a 10 to a 5. That's substantial. How are you feeling?"

Andrea: "Tired but okay. Surprised it's not as intense."

Therapist: "You've done good work. Now we have a choice. We can stop here and let your brain continue processing between sessions. Or we could continue using standard EMDR to process this more fully, which might reduce it even further. The standard processing will feel more intense than what we've been doing, but the memory is more manageable now. What sounds right?" *[Giving choice about transition]*

Andrea: "I think... I want to keep going. While I have momentum."

Therapist: "Okay. We'll shift to standard EMDR processing. Bring up the memory more fully now. When you think about the assault, what words go best with it that describe something negative about yourself?" *[Beginning standard Phase 3 assessment]*

Andrea: "I'm powerless."

Therapist: "And what would you rather believe?"

Andrea: "That I'm strong. That I survived."

Therapist: "How true does 'I'm strong, I survived' feel right now?"

Andrea: "About a 4 out of 7."

Therapist: "When you bring up the memory and the words 'I'm powerless,' what emotion do you feel?"

Andrea: "Fear. And shame."

Therapist: "Where do you notice that in your body?"

Andrea: "My chest. Tight. Hard to breathe."

Therapist: "And disturbance level now?"

Andrea: "Still about a 5."

Therapist: "Okay. Bring up the memory, the words 'I'm powerless,' notice the tightness in your chest, and follow my fingers." *[Starting desensitization]*

[Standard EMDR processing continues. Over next 25 minutes, SUDS decreases to 1. Installation strengthens positive cognition to VoC 6. Body scan clear.]

Therapist: "How do you feel about the work we did today?"

Andrea: "Exhausted. But... better. I can think about it without feeling like I'm going to fall apart."

Analysis: Flash preparation reduced an overwhelming SUDS 10 to a manageable SUDS 5, making standard EMDR processing tolerable. Without Flash, Andrea likely would have dissociated or become too distressed to continue. Flash created access to processing that otherwise wouldn't have been possible.

Case 2: Dissociative Client

Client: Jasmine, 34, complex PTSD with dissociative features, previous EMDR triggered severe dissociation **Target Memory:** Childhood abuse **Initial SUDS:** 9 **Plan:** Flash with dissociation management, possibly no transition if dissociation occurs

Session Transcript (Abbreviated):

Therapist: "Jasmine, we're going to try Flash today, which should be less likely to trigger dissociation than the standard EMDR you tried before. But I want you to know—if you start to feel spacey or disconnected, tell me immediately. I'd rather stop early than have you dissociate." *[Setting safety parameters]*

Jasmine: "Okay. I'll try."

Therapist: "For your positive focus, I want something very grounding. What about right here, right now—sitting in this chair, in this office, with me here with you? Can you feel the chair supporting you, your feet on the floor, see me across from you?" *[Grounding PEF for dissociative client]*

Jasmine: "Yes, I can feel all that."

Therapist: "That's your anchor. We're going to keep you here in the present. The memory is in the past. Ready?" *[Emphasizing present-moment grounding]*

[Flash sequences begin. After three sequences:]

Therapist: "Pause. Jasmine, say your name and tell me what year it is." *[Grounding check]*

Jasmine: "I'm Jasmine. It's 2024." *[slight hesitation but present]*

Therapist: "Good. Can you feel your feet on the floor?"

Jasmine: "Yes."

Therapist: "Okay, let's continue." *[Three more sequences]*

Therapist: "Name five things you can see in this room right now." *[Grounding check]*

Jasmine: "The clock, the lamp, the bookshelf, the plant, the tissue box." *[Clear, present]*

Therapist: "Perfect. How's your distress level?"

Jasmine: "Maybe an 8. Down a little."

[Continue Flash. After 10 more sequences:]

Jasmine: *[eyes glazing slightly, speech slowing]* "I feel... far away..."

Therapist: "Okay, we're stopping the processing. Look at me. Say your name." *[Immediate intervention]*

Jasmine: *[pause]* "Jasmine."

Therapist: "Good. Stand up with me. Stamp your feet on the floor. Feel how solid it is." *[Physical grounding]*

[Jasmine stands, stamps feet, comes back to present]

Therapist: "You started dissociating. That's useful information. It tells us we need to keep the flashes even shorter and check in even more frequently. Do you want to try again with those adjustments, or stop for today?"

Jasmine: "I want to try again. I didn't completely lose it like before."

Therapist: "Okay. Half-second flashes this time. And I'll check grounding after every two sequences. Here's your anchor—this room, this chair, this moment." *[Adjusting protocol]*

[Continue with adjusted Flash. No further dissociation. After 20 more sequences, SUDS down to 6.]

Therapist: "Good work. We're going to stop here today. The SUDS came down from 9 to 6 without you dissociating, which is success. We'll continue next session."

Analysis: Flash worked with dissociative client where standard EMDR hadn't, but required modifications (extremely grounding PEF, frequent grounding checks, immediate response to early dissociation signs). No transition to standard EMDR in this session—consolidating gains and building confidence took priority.

Making Flash and EMDR Work Together

Flash preparation enhances EMDR by making it accessible for clients who couldn't otherwise tolerate standard processing. Use Flash when baseline SUDS is too high, clients are highly avoidant or dissociative, previous EMDR failed, or complex trauma requires efficiency across multiple targets.

Transition from Flash to standard EMDR involves assessing readiness, conducting full Phase 3 assessment, and beginning standard desensitization. The shift is straightforward—moving from brief flashes with PEF protection to fuller engagement with trauma plus negative cognition. Prepare clients for the transition and allow return to Flash if standard processing becomes overwhelming.

Dissociative clients need special Flash modifications: grounding PEFs, ultra-brief flashes (under one second), frequent grounding checks, ready grounding scripts, and explicit work with parts if DID/OSDD is present. Adjust bilateral stimulation to prevent triggering dissociation.

Flash manages both emotional flooding (by maintaining focus on positive material) and avoidance (by being non-threatening enough to bypass defenses). The key is recognizing which pattern you're dealing with and adjusting accordingly.

Case examples demonstrate Flash reducing SUDS from overwhelming levels to manageable ones, allowing successful transition to standard EMDR processing and producing good outcomes in single sessions where standard EMDR alone likely would have failed.

Chapter 8: Advanced EMDR Integration

Flash started as preparation, but its applications within EMDR treatment go way beyond Phase 2. Once you understand the mechanics of Flash and how it interfaces with EMDR, you can use it strategically throughout treatment—during blocked processing, for resource enhancement, in complex trauma sequencing, and in combination with other EMDR protocols.

This chapter is for EMDR therapists who've mastered the basics and want advanced integration strategies. We're assuming you know standard EMDR cold. You understand the Adaptive Information Processing model. You can handle abreactions, blocked processing, and complex cases (Shapiro, 2018). Now you're adding Flash to your toolkit and you want to know all the ways it can enhance your EMDR practice.

Flash for Blocked Processing

You're doing EMDR desensitization. Processing starts well—client's making associations, SUDS is decreasing, things are flowing. Then suddenly, it stops. Processing hits a wall. SUDS plateaus. Client reports loops (same material repeating), no new associations emerging, or just "I'm stuck."

Blocked processing happens to every EMDR therapist. Standard approaches include cognitive interweaves, checking for additional targets, or investigating blocking beliefs (Shapiro, 2018). Flash offers another option.

Why Flash Works for Blocked Processing

When processing blocks, often the client is either:

1. **Engaging too directly** with material that's more overwhelming than they realized, causing defensive shutdown

2. **Hitting a related trauma** that needs addressing before the current target can resolve

3. **Encountering a blocking belief** that prevents integration

Flash can bypass these blocks by temporarily reducing emotional intensity (giving the nervous system a break) and creating distance that allows processing to resume.

Protocol for Using Flash During Blocked Processing:

You notice processing has stalled. SUDS at 5, hasn't budged for three sets of bilateral stimulation. Client reports feeling "stuck" or repeating same thoughts.

Step 1: Acknowledge the Block

Therapist: "I notice we seem to be stuck here. The distress isn't moving. That happens sometimes—it means there's something preventing the memory from processing fully right now. Let's try something different."

Step 2: Identify What's Blocking

Therapist: "What comes up when you think about continuing to process this memory? Is there anything that feels like it's in the way?"

Client might report:

- "Another memory keeps coming up"

- "I keep thinking 'It's not safe to let this go'"

- "I feel like I need to hold onto this somehow"

- "Nothing's coming. I feel blank."

Step 3: Decide on Flash Application

Option A: Flash the Blocking Belief

If blocking belief emerges ("It's not safe to let this go"), you can use Flash to process that belief directly.

Therapist: "We're going to use Flash to work on that belief. Remember the positive focus we developed earlier? Bring that back up. We'll flash briefly to the thought 'It's not safe to let this go' while keeping focus mostly on the positive."

Do several rounds of Flash targeting the blocking belief. Often SUDS on the belief will decrease, and processing on the original target can resume.

Option B: Flash the Related Memory

If another memory keeps intruding, it might be a "feeder" memory that needs processing first.

Therapist: "That other memory that keeps coming up—it seems like your brain is saying we need to address that first. Let's do a few rounds of Flash on that memory. Then we'll come back to the original target."

Flash the related memory enough to reduce its intensity. Then return to the original target and resume standard EMDR processing.

Option C: Flash the Current Target with Different Instructions

Sometimes processing blocks because standard EMDR is too direct. Switching temporarily to Flash's indirect approach can unlock things.

Therapist: "Let's back off a bit. Instead of engaging fully with this memory, I want you to bring back your positive focus and just briefly flash past the memory the way we did in preparation. Sometimes taking the pressure off helps processing resume."

Do 5-10 rounds of Flash on the current target (even though you've already started standard processing on it). This often reduces defensive blocking, and you can then return to standard desensitization.

Step 4: Resume Standard Processing

After Flash intervention, return to standard EMDR desensitization.

Therapist: "Okay, let's come back to the original memory now. Bring it up with the negative belief and body sensation, and follow my fingers."

Often processing resumes flowing. If it blocks again, repeat Flash intervention or use other EMDR troubleshooting strategies.

Real Example:

Martin (composite) was processing combat memory. Started well, SUDS dropped from 8 to 5. Then stuck. Kept saying "I should have saved him" but no associations emerging.

Therapist: "Martin, you keep coming back to 'I should have saved him.' Is there something about that belief that's blocking?"

Martin: "If I let go of feeling guilty, it means I didn't care about him."

Therapist: "That's the block. Your mind is holding onto guilt because it feels like loyalty. Let's work on that. Bring back your positive focus—that image of you with your grandkids. Now flash briefly to the thought 'Letting go means I didn't care'—just touch it quickly and back to the positive image."

Did six rounds of Flash targeting that belief. Martin reported, "I can see that's not actually true. I can care about him without torturing myself."

Returned to original memory. Processing resumed immediately. SUDS dropped to 1 within five more sets. Processed completely.

Flash broke the block by addressing the belief that was preventing resolution.

Resource Installation Enhancement

EMDR includes resource development and installation (RDI)—helping clients build internal resources like safe place, nurturing figure, protective figure, or qualities they need (Leeds, 2009). Standard RDI involves identifying the resource, strengthening it with bilateral stimulation, and installing it for future access.

Flash can enhance RDI in specific ways.

Flash for Developing Trauma-Resistant Resources

Some clients need resources specifically for trauma processing—internal strengths that can hold them steady while processing difficult material.

Standard RDI approach: Identify quality needed (courage, strength, groundedness). Imagine having that quality. Strengthen with bilateral stimulation.

Flash enhancement: Use Flash to install the resource while briefly touching traumatic material, teaching the resource to actually function under stress.

Protocol:

Step 1: Develop Resource in Standard Way

Therapist: "We're going to install a resource of courage for facing trauma processing. Imagine yourself having all the courage you need—what does that feel like? What do you notice in your body when you have that courage?"

Client develops image of courageous self. Strengthens with bilateral stimulation.

Step 2: Flash-Install the Resource

Therapist: "Now we're going to do something different. Keep focus on that feeling of courage. While holding onto that courage, briefly think about the traumatic memory—just a flash—and notice that you can face it while maintaining that courage. Then back to the courageous feeling."

Do several Flash sequences where the positive focus IS the resource itself, and client flashes to trauma.

This installs the resource as specifically trauma-related. The nervous system learns, "I can hold this resource even when touching trauma."

Step 3: Verify Resource Strength

Therapist: "Now when you think about processing the trauma while having this courage, how does that feel?"

Client should report increased confidence that they can handle processing.

Real Example:

Diana (composite) needed to process abuse memories but felt too fragile. Standard RDI installed "container" resource (imaginary box where memories could be safely stored). Helped somewhat, but Diana still felt scared of processing.

Therapist: "Let's strengthen that container. Focus on the container—strong, secure, able to hold anything safely. Now while focusing on that secure container, briefly think about one of the abuse memories and notice that even while thinking about it, the container is still there, still secure. Back to focusing on the container."

Did eight Flash sequences with container as positive focus, trauma as flash target.

Diana: "Wow. I can feel that the container actually works even when I think about the abuse. It's not just an idea."

Proceeded to trauma processing with much more confidence. The Flash-installed resource actually functioned during processing, whereas the standard-installed resource had felt theoretical.

Complex Trauma Sequencing Strategies

Clients with complex trauma—multiple traumatic events spanning years—present sequencing challenges. Which memories do you process first? How do you prevent overwhelm when there are dozens of targets? How do you maintain momentum without burning out the client?

Flash offers strategic advantages for complex trauma because it can rapidly reduce intensity across multiple targets, allowing you to:

1. **Survey the terrain:** Use Flash briefly on multiple memories to assess which need full processing

2. **Reduce the worst offenders:** Flash the most intense memories down to manageable levels

3. **Process related clusters:** Flash several related memories, then fully process the core one

Strategy 1: Flash Triage

For clients with extensive trauma histories, do an initial triage with Flash.

Step 1: List Traumatic Memories

Have client identify 8-12 significant traumatic memories (don't need details, just "assault," "car accident," "childhood incident 1," etc.).

Step 2: Brief Flash on Each

Spend 5-10 minutes using Flash on each memory. Not to full resolution, just enough to reduce immediate intensity.

Step 3: Assess Which Need Full Processing

After Flash triage, some memories will be at SUDS 0-2 (essentially resolved). Others will be at 3-6 (reduced but need more work). Few will remain at 7+ (resistant or core issues).

Step 4: Plan Full Processing

Now you know which memories need full EMDR processing. Do full processing on those while monitoring whether related memories also improve (generalization effect).

Efficiency Gain: Instead of processing 12 memories fully (12+ sessions), you might Flash 8 to resolution, and fully process 4 (4-6 sessions). Significant time savings.

Strategy 2: Cluster Processing

Related memories often cluster thematically. Process clusters using Flash plus targeted full EMDR.

Step 1: Identify Clusters

Group memories by theme (all sexual trauma, all childhood abuse from same perpetrator, all medical trauma, etc.).

Step 2: Flash the Cluster

Use Flash on multiple memories within cluster to reduce overall intensity of that theme.

Step 3: Fully Process Worst or Earliest

Identify the worst memory in the cluster or the earliest (primal event). Fully process that one with standard EMDR.

Step 4: Check Generalization

Often, fully processing the core memory in a cluster causes related memories to also resolve (Adaptive Information Processing theory—processing central nodes affects connected memories).

Strategy 3: Chronological Flash with Targeted Processing

Work chronologically through trauma history using Flash for rapid reduction, targeted full processing for key memories.

Step 1: Earliest Memory First

Start with earliest traumatic memory. Flash it to low SUDS.

Step 2: Move Forward in Time

Flash next chronological memory. Then next. Creating a timeline of reduced-intensity memories.

Step 3: Identify Pivotal Moments

Some memories are pivotal—they changed how the person saw themselves or the world. These need full processing even after Flash.

Step 4: Fully Process Pivotal Memories

Use standard EMDR to fully process pivotal memories, ensuring cognitive shifts occur and positive beliefs are installed.

Real Example:

Sophia (composite) had 15 traumatic memories from abusive relationship over four years. Too many to fully process in reasonable timeframe.

Session 1-2: Flash triage on all 15 memories. Spent 10 minutes on each. After triage, seven memories were at SUDS 0-2 (resolved), six were at SUDS 3-5 (reduced), two remained at SUDS 7-8 (resistant).

Session 3-5: Fully processed the two resistant memories (first assault, final assault before she left). Standard EMDR to completion.

Session 6: Checked all memories. The seven that were 0-2 after Flash remained there. Of the six that were 3-5, four had generalized down to 0-2 after processing the core memories. Two remained at SUDS 3-4.

Session 7: Flash those two remaining memories to completion.

Total: Seven sessions to process 15 traumatic memories to resolution. Standard EMDR alone would have required 15-20+ sessions. Flash created significant efficiency.

Combining with Other EMDR Protocols

EMDR includes multiple specialized protocols beyond standard processing—Recent Traumatic Event Protocol, Protocol for Phobias, Pain Protocol, Protocol for Excessive Grief, etc. (Shapiro, 2018). Flash can enhance these protocols.

Recent Traumatic Event Protocol + Flash

Recent Event Protocol is for trauma within days or weeks of the incident. Standard protocol processes the event, aftermath, and future template.

Flash enhancement: If client is too activated to complete Recent Event Protocol, use Flash first to reduce intensity, then proceed with protocol.

Example Application:

Client experienced home invasion three days ago. Too distressed to engage in Recent Event Protocol (can't describe event without panic).

Use Flash on the incident. Reduce SUDS from 10 to 4-5. Then proceed with Recent Event Protocol to process incident, triggers, and future encounters with home.

Phobia Protocol + Flash

Phobia Protocol processes original traumatic incident that created the phobia, then does future template for facing feared stimulus.

Flash enhancement: Many phobic clients avoid even thinking about the original incident. Flash can process it with minimal activation.

Example Application:

Client has severe dog phobia from childhood bite. Can't even look at pictures of dogs without panic.

Use Flash to process bite memory. Client flashes very briefly to memory while focusing on safe image. SUDS drops from 9 to 2. Then proceed with future template imagining neutral encounters with dogs. Phobia significantly reduced.

Pain Protocol + Flash

Chronic pain with trauma history can be addressed with EMDR Pain Protocol—processing traumatic origin of pain or emotional components maintaining it.

Flash enhancement: Some pain clients can't engage with memories without pain flaring. Flash allows gentle processing.

Example Application:

Client has chronic back pain since car accident. Thinking about accident intensifies pain. Standard EMDR feels too activating.

Flash the accident memory while monitoring pain levels. Often pain decreases as memory is processed. Then address remaining pain-related beliefs with standard processing.

Protocol Combination Principle

Flash can serve as gentle entry point for any EMDR protocol where direct engagement feels too threatening. After Flash reduces intensity, proceed with standard protocol for more complete resolution.

Documentation and Treatment Planning

Good clinical documentation supports treatment, justifies insurance billing, protects you legally, and tracks outcomes. When using Flash within EMDR treatment, documentation needs to capture both interventions clearly.

Progress Note Format

Example progress note structure:

Date: [Date]

Session Focus: EMDR processing of [general trauma type] using Flash Technique preparation followed by standard desensitization.

Phase 2 - Preparation: Utilized Flash Technique to reduce initial intensity of target memory. PEF: [brief description]. Baseline SUDS: [number]. After 15 Flash sequences, SUDS reduced to [number]. Client tolerated preparation well with no significant distress or dissociation.

Phase 3-6 - Processing: Transitioned to standard EMDR desensitization. Target: [brief description]. NC: "[negative cognition]." PC: "[positive cognition]." Initial VoC: [number]. Emotions: [list]. Body: [location]. SUDS: [number].

Completed desensitization (SUDS 0-1), installation (VoC 7), and body scan (clear).

Phase 7 - Closure: Client grounded and stable. Discussed between-session processing expectations.

Assessment: Client demonstrated good response to Flash preparation enabling tolerable engagement with highly distressing memory. Processing to completion in single session. Significant symptom reduction expected.

Plan: Reevaluation next session. Monitor for between-session processing. Process additional targets as needed.

Key Documentation Elements:

For Insurance/Medical Records:

- Clear connection to DSM diagnosis (PTSD, Adjustment Disorder, etc.)

- Medical necessity (why Flash was clinically indicated)

- Outcome measures (SUDS, VoC scores)

- Progress toward treatment goals

For Clinical Use:

- PEF used (in case you need it again)

- Number of Flash sequences completed

- Client's response patterns

- Any adjustments made

- Decision points (why you transitioned when you did)

Treatment Planning Documentation

Initial Treatment Plan:

Diagnosis: PTSD (ICD-10: F43.10)

Presenting Problems:

- Intrusive memories of [trauma type]

- Avoidance of trauma-related stimuli

- Hypervigilance and sleep disturbance

- Significant functional impairment in [areas]

Treatment Goals:

1. Reduce distress associated with traumatic memories to SUDS 0-2

2. Install adaptive beliefs about self and safety

3. Decrease avoidance behaviors

4. Improve sleep quality and reduce hypervigilance

5. Return to pre-trauma functioning in work and relationships

Treatment Approach: EMDR Therapy with Flash Technique preparation. Will utilize Flash to prepare client for standard EMDR processing given baseline SUDS of 9-10 and previous difficulty tolerating trauma-focused treatment. Anticipate 8-12 sessions for trauma processing, plus additional sessions for installation and future template work.

Frequency: Weekly individual therapy, 60-90 minute sessions

Expected Duration: 3-6 months

Treatment Plan Updates:

Document progress regularly:

Update [Date]: Client has completed Flash preparation and standard EMDR processing on 3 of 5 target memories. SUDS reduced from baseline 8-10 to current 0-1 on processed memories. Goal 1 (reduce distress) 60% achieved. Intrusive memories decreased by 70% per client report. Continuing with remaining targets. On track for anticipated timeline.

Billing Considerations

CPT Codes:

Flash is conducted within standard psychotherapy, so billing uses standard codes:

- 90834: 45-minute psychotherapy
- 90837: 60-minute psychotherapy

Some practitioners add trauma-focused specifiers in documentation:

"90837 - Psychotherapy, 60 minutes, utilizing EMDR with Flash Technique preparation for trauma processing"

Insurance Authorization:

When seeking pre-authorization for EMDR treatment, you can mention Flash as preparation strategy:

"Treatment will utilize evidence-based EMDR therapy including Flash Technique preparation phase to reduce initial distress and increase tolerability of trauma processing for this highly symptomatic patient."

Flash research base supports its use as evidence-based trauma treatment (Manfield et al., 2017).

Outcome Tracking

Track outcomes across treatment:

Measures to track:

- SUDS ratings for each target memory (baseline and post-processing)
- PCL-5 scores (PTSD symptom measure) at baseline, mid-treatment, and post-treatment
- Client feedback about functioning (sleep, work, relationships)

- Number of sessions required per target memory

- Treatment completion rate (do clients finish treatment?)

Example Outcome Documentation:

Treatment Summary: Client presented with severe PTSD following assault. Baseline PCL-5: 58 (severe range).

Utilized Flash Technique preparation followed by standard EMDR processing on 4 target memories over 8 sessions:

- Target 1: SUDS 10→1 (1 session)

- Target 2: SUDS 9→0 (1 session)

- Target 3: SUDS 9→2 (2 sessions)

- Target 4: SUDS 8→1 (1 session)

Post-treatment PCL-5: 12 (subclinical). Client reports 90% reduction in intrusive memories, no longer avoids trauma-related situations, sleep improved, returned to full functioning at work. Treatment goals achieved. Client discharged with PRN follow-up available.

Good outcome tracking demonstrates treatment effectiveness to insurance companies, supports research, and helps you assess your own clinical effectiveness.

Taking EMDR Further with Flash

Flash integration extends well beyond Phase 2 preparation. Use Flash for blocked processing by targeting blocking beliefs, related memories, or temporarily switching to Flash's indirect approach when standard processing stalls. This often unlocks processing that seemed stuck.

Resource installation can be enhanced by Flash-installing resources specifically against trauma—teaching internal resources to function under actual stress rather than just in imagination. This creates trauma-resistant resources that work during real processing.

Complex trauma sequencing becomes more efficient with Flash triage (rapidly reducing intensity across multiple targets), cluster processing (reducing thematic groups then fully processing core memories), and chronological approaches (moving through timeline with Flash, targeting pivotal moments for full processing). This can reduce treatment length significantly.

Flash enhances specialized EMDR protocols—Recent Event, Phobia Protocol, Pain Protocol—by providing gentle entry when direct engagement is too activating. After Flash reduces intensity, proceed with standard protocol for complete resolution.

Documentation must capture both Flash preparation and subsequent EMDR processing clearly, including SUDS changes, clinical reasoning, and outcomes. Good documentation supports clinical care, insurance billing, legal protection, and outcome tracking. Treatment plans should specify Flash use when clinically indicated and track progress toward measurable goals.

Chapter 9: Flash with CBT & Exposure Therapies

Cognitive-behavioral therapy for trauma—whether it's Cognitive Processing Therapy, Prolonged Exposure, or trauma-focused CBT—works. The research is solid. Controlled trials show good outcomes. But here's what every CBT therapist knows: dropout rates are a problem.

Studies show that 20-30% of clients drop out of exposure-based CBT for PTSD, and some studies report rates as high as 50% (Imel et al., 2013). That's a lot of people who start treatment but don't finish it. And we're not talking about people who got better and left early. We're talking about people who couldn't tolerate the treatment.

The issue isn't that CBT doesn't work. It's that CBT requires clients to engage repeatedly with distressing material—revisiting memories, challenging beliefs, confronting feared situations. That's hard. For some people, it's too hard.

Flash offers a solution. You can use Flash before or during CBT protocols to reduce the distress that makes exposure so difficult. Not as a replacement for CBT, but as a preparation that makes CBT actually completable for clients who might otherwise drop out.

Preparing for Cognitive Processing Therapy

Cognitive Processing Therapy (CPT) is a structured, 12-session protocol for PTSD that focuses on challenging maladaptive beliefs about trauma (Resick et al., 2016). It's effective, but it requires clients to write detailed accounts of their trauma and read them aloud in session. For many trauma survivors, that's overwhelming.

The CPT Challenge

CPT asks clients to write a detailed "impact statement" describing how the trauma has affected their beliefs about themselves, others, and the world. Then, in later sessions, clients write a full narrative account of the trauma—sensory details, thoughts, emotions, everything—and read it aloud repeatedly.

This direct engagement with trauma is how CPT works. The exposure plus cognitive restructuring produces change. But some clients can't do it. They freeze up when trying to write. They dissociate when reading aloud. They drop out before completing the protocol.

Flash as CPT Preparation

Use Flash before CPT begins to reduce the emotional charge of the traumatic memory. The client still has the memory, can still access it for writing, but the overwhelming distress is reduced.

Protocol:

Session 1-2 of CPT: Standard CPT introduction, assessment, psychoeducation about PTSD and treatment rationale.

Session 3: Instead of immediately asking for impact statement, use Flash.

Therapist: "Before we move to the written work in CPT, I'd like to reduce some of the intensity of your trauma memories. We'll use Flash Technique, which will make the memories less overwhelming without erasing them. This should make it easier for you to write about them in the coming sessions."

Conduct Flash on primary trauma memory. Reduce SUDS from 9-10 to 4-6 range.

Session 4 onward: Proceed with standard CPT protocol. Client writes impact statement (easier because memory is less activating), writes trauma account (more tolerable), and completes cognitive processing.

Real Example:

Michelle (composite) started CPT for assault trauma. Sessions 1-2 went fine—education, assessment, building rapport. Session 3 was supposed to be impact statement assignment, but Michelle looked panicked.

Michelle: "I don't think I can write about it. Every time I try, I feel like I'm back there."

Therapist: "That makes complete sense. The memory is too 'hot' right now. Let's cool it down first with Flash, then writing about it will be more manageable."

We did Flash that session. Michelle's SUDS dropped from 10 to 5. Still distressing, but not overwhelming.

Session 4, I assigned the impact statement. Michelle completed it. She reported, "I was able to write it without falling apart. It still upset me, but I could do it."

We continued through CPT protocol. Michelle completed all 12 sessions (unusual for assault survivors with her severity). At post-treatment, she no longer met PTSD criteria. Flash preparation made CPT accessible when it otherwise wouldn't have been.

Strategic Advantages:

Reduced dropout: Clients are less likely to quit if the early sessions aren't overwhelming.

Better quality exposure: When writing trauma narratives with lower distress, clients can include more detail and process more thoroughly.

Maintained CPT integrity: You're still doing CPT. Flash just makes it tolerable.

Timing Considerations:

Option 1: Flash before starting CPT (sessions 1-2 use Flash, then begin standard CPT protocol)

Option 2: Flash as needed during CPT (if client gets stuck or overwhelmed during narrative writing, pause CPT and do Flash session)

Option 3: Flash specific memories that are blocking (if client has multiple traumas and one is too intense, Flash that one while processing others with standard CPT)

Choose based on client needs and severity.

Enhancing Prolonged Exposure Tolerance

Prolonged Exposure (PE) therapy involves repeated, prolonged engagement with trauma memories through imaginal exposure (verbally describing the trauma in present tense for 30-45 minutes) and in vivo exposure (confronting avoided situations) (Foa et al., 2007). PE works, but it's intense. Really intense.

The PE Challenge

Imaginal exposure in PE means describing your trauma as if it's happening right now, in present tense, with eyes closed, for extended periods. Then listening to the recording between sessions. This creates sustained emotional engagement with trauma that some clients simply cannot tolerate.

Dropout rates for PE range from 20-40% depending on the study and population (Imel et al., 2013). Many dropouts occur early in treatment when imaginal exposure begins.

Flash as PE Tolerance Enhancement

Use Flash to reduce initial intensity before starting imaginal exposure, or use it to get unstuck if client becomes overwhelmed during PE.

Strategy 1: Pre-PE Flash Preparation

Before beginning imaginal exposure (typically session 3-4 in PE protocol), do one or two Flash sessions.

Therapist: "Next session, we'll begin imaginal exposure where you'll describe the trauma in detail. I know that sounds difficult. To make it more tolerable, let's first use Flash to reduce some of the intensity. You'll still have the memory and we'll still work on it in exposure, but the emotional charge will be lower."

Flash the target memory. Reduce SUDS from 9-10 to 5-7 range. Don't reduce it all the way to zero—PE still needs some activation to work—but reduce enough that the client can tolerate sustained engagement.

Then proceed with standard PE imaginal exposure. The client can describe the trauma more completely, stay present without dissociating, and tolerate the repeated exposures required.

Strategy 2: Mid-PE Flash Intervention

Client is doing PE. Imaginal exposure is going okay but they're hitting a wall—too much distress, starting to avoid, or processing has stalled. Do Flash session within PE protocol.

Therapist: "I notice you're struggling to stay with the imaginal exposure without overwhelming distress. Let's take a session to use Flash on this memory. It'll reduce the intensity, and then we can resume the imaginal exposure next session."

Do Flash. Then return to PE protocol the following session. Client often finds imaginal exposure more tolerable after Flash intervention.

Strategy 3: Flash for Multiple Trauma Targets

If client has multiple traumas they're avoiding facing in PE, Flash can reduce intensity across several memories, making the client more willing to engage with them in imaginal exposure.

Real Example:

James (composite), combat veteran, entered PE treatment. Sessions 1-2 (assessment, psychoeducation) went fine. Session 3, we started imaginal exposure. I asked James to close his eyes and describe the combat incident in present tense.

He lasted about three minutes before opening his eyes. "I can't do this. It's too much. I feel like I'm going to lose it."

Therapist: "Okay, let's take a different approach. We'll use Flash first to reduce the intensity. Then imaginal exposure will be more manageable."

That session, we did Flash instead of imaginal exposure. James's SUDS dropped from 10 to 6.

Next session, tried imaginal exposure again. James was able to do 15 minutes of narration. Still difficult, but tolerable. Over subsequent sessions, built up to full 30-45 minute imaginal exposures.

James completed PE treatment. Without Flash preparation, he likely would have dropped out after session 3.

Important Note About Activation

PE relies on emotional engagement with trauma. You need some activation for habituation to occur. Don't Flash the memory down to SUDS 0-1 if you're planning to do PE—that eliminates the activation PE needs. Target SUDS reduction to 5-7 range. Still distressing enough for PE to work, but manageable enough that the client can tolerate it.

Integration with Imaginal Exposure

Imaginal exposure—mentally revisiting traumatic memories in detail—is a core component of multiple trauma treatments (PE, CPT, trauma-focused CBT). Flash can be integrated directly into imaginal exposure protocols.

Standard Imaginal Exposure:

Client describes trauma memory in detail, present tense, eyes closed, for 30-45 minutes. Therapist prompts for more detail when needed. Client rates SUDS every 5-10 minutes. Process continues until SUDS decreases through habituation.

Flash-Enhanced Imaginal Exposure:

Combine Flash's protective structure with imaginal exposure's sustained engagement.

Protocol:

Phase 1: Flash Preparation (15-20 minutes)

Do several rounds of Flash to reduce initial SUDS from 9-10 range to 6-7 range.

Phase 2: Brief Imaginal Exposure (10-15 minutes)

Therapist: "Now that we've reduced the intensity somewhat, I'd like you to describe the memory in more detail. Close your eyes. Describe what happened as if it's happening right now. I'm here with you. You're safe."

Client does brief imaginal exposure—more engagement than Flash, less than full PE.

Phase 3: Flash Consolidation (5-10 minutes)

Return to Flash briefly to help client settle after imaginal exposure.

This gives you a graduated approach: Flash reduces intensity, imaginal exposure provides deeper processing, Flash provides closure and stabilization.

Real Example:

Alicia (composite) had PTSD from car accident. Standard imaginal exposure was too intense—she'd panic and dissociate. Standard Flash alone felt "not enough"—she wanted more processing.

We developed hybrid approach:

Minutes 0-15: Flash the accident memory. SUDS dropped from 9 to 6.

Minutes 15-30: Imaginal exposure. "Alicia, describe the accident as if it's happening now. What do you see, hear, feel?"

She described it in detail. SUDS fluctuated between 5-7 during narration—uncomfortable but tolerable.

Minutes 30-35: Flash again. Brought SUDS down to 3.

Over six sessions using this format, Alicia fully processed the accident. The hybrid approach gave her the depth of imaginal exposure with the safety of Flash.

Reducing Dropout in Trauma-Focused CBT

Dropout from trauma-focused CBT is a serious problem. When clients drop out, they don't just fail to improve—they often feel like they've failed, become discouraged about treatment in general, and may not seek help again.

Flash reduces dropout by addressing the main reasons people leave treatment prematurely.

Why People Drop Out:

Reason 1: Treatment is too distressing

Solution: Flash reduces distress to tolerable levels while maintaining enough activation for therapeutic change.

Reason 2: Client doesn't believe they can handle treatment

Solution: Flash creates early success experience—"I can engage with trauma without falling apart"—that builds confidence for continued treatment.

Reason 3: Client fears being overwhelmed or retraumatized

Solution: Flash's protective structure demonstrates that trauma work doesn't have to mean retraumatization.

Reason 4: Client feels therapy isn't working fast enough

Solution: Flash often produces rapid SUDS reduction, providing early evidence that treatment works.

Reason 5: Life circumstances interfere

Solution: Flash can produce meaningful gains in fewer sessions, making treatment more compatible with time constraints.

Implementation for Dropout Prevention:

Early Sessions Strategy: Use Flash in sessions 2-4 of CBT treatment (after assessment but before full exposure work). This creates positive treatment experience before the difficult parts begin.

Therapist framing: "Many people find trauma-focused treatment challenging, especially at first. We're going to start with Flash to build your confidence that you can handle this work. Once you've experienced some success, we'll move to the other parts of treatment."

Ongoing Monitoring: Check in regularly about dropout risk. "How are you feeling about continuing treatment? Is anything making you want to stop?" If dropout risk emerges, offer Flash as intervention.

Flexible Integration: Be willing to switch between Flash and standard CBT based on client tolerance. Some sessions might be pure CBT, others pure Flash, others hybrid. Flexibility prevents rigid adherence to protocols that aren't working.

Real Example:

Clinic tracked dropout rates before and after integrating Flash.

Before Flash (one year period): 42% of trauma-focused CBT clients dropped out before completing treatment (primarily during exposure work).

After Flash training (next year): Therapists used Flash as preparation for about 60% of clients (those judged at high risk for dropout based on severity, avoidance, or previous treatment failure). Dropout rate in Flash-prepared group: 18%.

Essentially, Flash cut the dropout rate in half for high-risk clients. Clients who completed treatment showed similar outcomes to standard CBT, but completion rates were much higher.

Cost-Benefit Analysis:

Adding 1-2 Flash sessions to CBT protocol costs 1-2 additional sessions. But if it prevents dropout, you're actually increasing efficiency—client completes 12 sessions of treatment instead of dropping out at session 4. Much better return on investment.

Insurance companies and clinic administrators should care about completion rates, not just per-session costs. Flash improves completion rates substantially.

Making Exposure-Based Treatments More Accessible

Flash integrates with CBT and exposure therapies by reducing the distress that causes dropout. For Cognitive Processing Therapy, Flash preparation makes writing trauma narratives tolerable. For Prolonged Exposure, Flash reduces initial intensity enough that clients can sustain imaginal exposure without overwhelming distress.

Flash can be integrated directly with imaginal exposure in hybrid protocols—using Flash for preparation and closure around brief imaginal exposure periods. This graduated approach provides the depth of exposure with Flash's protective structure.

Dropout reduction is the primary benefit of Flash integration with CBT. By addressing the main reasons clients leave treatment (too distressing, fear of being overwhelmed, lack of early success), Flash increases completion rates substantially. Studies suggest Flash preparation can cut dropout rates in half for high-risk trauma clients.

Implementation requires flexibility—using Flash when clients need it while maintaining the core elements of CBT protocols. The goal isn't replacing CBT but making it accessible for clients who couldn't otherwise complete it.

Chapter 10: Flash with IFS & Parts Work

Internal Family Systems therapy sees the mind not as a single unified self but as a system of different parts—subpersonalities with their own perspectives, feelings, and roles (Schwartz, 1995). When you think "Part of me wants to work on the trauma, but another part is terrified," that's not metaphorical in IFS. Those are actual parts of your internal system.

Trauma creates particular challenges in parts work. Exiles (parts holding traumatic memories) are often locked away by protective parts who fear that accessing those memories will overwhelm the system. The protectors might use dissociation, substance use, anger, or other strategies to keep exiles hidden. Standard IFS protocol involves negotiating with protectors to access exiles—which can take months of careful internal diplomacy.

Flash changes that timeline. You can use Flash to demonstrate to protective parts that the exiles can be unburdened without overwhelming the system. This often accelerates IFS treatment significantly.

Working with Protective Parts

IFS identifies two types of protective parts:

Managers try to prevent trauma memories from surfacing through control, perfectionism, intellectualization, or other proactive strategies.

Firefighters react when exiles break through, using emergency measures like dissociation, rage, self-harm, or substance use to shut down the distress.

Both are trying to protect the system, but their methods often create problems. The IFS therapist's job is building relationship with protectors, understanding their concerns, and eventually getting permission to access and unburden exiles.

The Protection Dilemma

Protective parts believe accessing trauma will destroy the system. "If she feels that pain, she'll fall apart completely." This belief keeps exiles locked away, but it also keeps the person stuck in PTSD symptoms.

Standard IFS approach: Spend sessions building trust with protectors, appreciating their protective role, understanding their fears, slowly negotiating permission to access exiles. This can take 10-20+ sessions.

Flash with Protective Parts

Flash offers a demonstration that protective parts can observe: "Look, we can access the exile's trauma briefly and the system doesn't fall apart."

Protocol:

Step 1: Identify the Protective Part

Therapist: "When you think about working on the trauma, what part of you objects or feels afraid?"

Client: "There's a part that says 'Don't go there. It's too dangerous.'"

Therapist: "Let's talk to that part. I'd like to understand its concerns."

Step 2: Appreciate the Protector's Role

Therapist: "This part has been protecting you from overwhelming pain. It's done that job for a long time, and it's kept you functioning. I appreciate that part's efforts."

Get to know the protector. What is it afraid will happen if the exile is accessed? What has it been doing to prevent that?

Step 3: Introduce Flash as Safe Unburdening Method

Therapist: "I'd like to propose something to this protective part. There's a technique called Flash that allows very brief contact with the trauma—just flashing past it—while keeping focus mostly on something safe and positive. It's gentle enough that the system doesn't get overwhelmed. Would this part be willing to let us try that? The part can watch and see that it's safe, and if it's not okay, we stop immediately."

Negotiate with the protector. Address its concerns. Emphasize that the protector stays present and can stop the process if needed.

Step 4: Flash with Protector Monitoring

Therapist: "We're going to do Flash now. I'd like the protective part to stay present and watch. Notice that we're not diving into the trauma—just flashing past it briefly while staying mostly with the positive focus. Protective part, let me know if this feels unsafe at any point."

Conduct Flash on the exiled part's trauma memory. Brief flashes, strong positive focus.

Step 5: Check with Protector After Flash

Therapist: "Protective part, what do you notice? Did the system fall apart? Did something terrible happen?"

Protector usually reports surprise: "No, it was okay. She didn't fall apart."

Therapist: "So this trauma can be touched without destroying the system. Would the protective part be willing to let us continue working on this?"

Often, protectors become allies after this demonstration. They've seen that trauma work doesn't equal destruction.

Real Example:

Nina (composite) had severe childhood abuse trauma locked away by aggressive manager parts. Every time we approached trauma material in therapy, she'd intellectualize intensely or become hostile.

Therapist: "Nina, when we start talking about working on the abuse, what part shows up?"

Nina: "There's a part that gets really angry and says 'We're not doing this. It's stupid. This therapy doesn't work.'"

Therapist: "Can I talk to that angry part?"

Nina: *[voice changes, becomes sharp]* "What do you want?"

Therapist: "I want to understand your concerns. What are you protecting Nina from?"

Part: "If she feels what happened to her, she'll die. She won't survive it. I keep her functioning."

Therapist: "You've done an incredibly hard job keeping her safe. I respect that. But I wonder if there's a way to heal the trauma without destroying her. There's a technique called Flash where

169

she can touch the memories very briefly without diving into them fully. You could watch and see if it's safe. Would you be willing to let us try that? You can stop us anytime."

Part: *[suspicious]* "Fine. But if this hurts her, I'm shutting it down."

We did Flash. Nina's protective part watched carefully. After several rounds, SUDS had decreased and Nina reported, "The angry part is saying 'Huh. That wasn't as bad as I thought.'"

The protector became an ally after that. It had seen evidence that unburdening could happen safely.

Unburdening Traumatic Memories

In IFS, *unburdening* means releasing the extreme emotions and beliefs that exiles carry from trauma. The exile has been holding terror, shame, or pain. Through unburdening, the exile releases those burdens and takes on new, healthier beliefs and feelings (Schwartz, 1995).

Standard IFS unburdening involves:

1. Getting permission from protectors
2. Accessing the exile
3. Witnessing the exile's experience
4. The exile releases the burden (often using imagery like light, water, or wind)
5. Inviting in new positive qualities

This process can be lengthy and emotionally intense.

Flash as Unburdening Accelerator

Flash can reduce the emotional intensity of the exile's trauma before or during the unburdening process, making it more tolerable and often faster.

Protocol:

Phase 1: Access the Exile (Standard IFS)

With protectors' permission, make contact with the exiled part holding trauma.

Therapist: "Ask the exile to show you the worst thing it experienced or the hardest thing it carries."

Phase 2: Flash the Exile's Trauma

Instead of having the client sit with the exile's overwhelming pain (standard IFS witnessing), use Flash.

Therapist: "We're going to help this exile release some of the intensity it's carrying. Bring up your positive focus—perhaps imagine your Self (capital S in IFS—the compassionate core) holding the exile safely. Now, very briefly flash to what the exile is holding, then back to the image of Self holding the exile."

Do Flash sequences where the PEF is Self-energy (compassionate, calm, confident) and the flash target is the exile's trauma.

Phase 3: Check Unburdening Progress

Therapist: "Ask the exile—how much of that burden is it still carrying?"

Exile typically reports the burden is lighter. If not fully released, continue Flash.

Phase 4: Complete Unburdening (Standard IFS)

Once burden is light enough, use standard IFS imagery for full release.

Therapist: "Ask the exile how it would like to release the rest of this burden. Does it want to give it to light, water, wind, earth?"

Exile completes release using preferred imagery.

Phase 5: Invite In Qualities

Therapist: "Now that the burden is released, what would this exile like to take in instead? What qualities or feelings?"

Exile invites in qualities like peace, safety, joy, strength.

Advantage of Flash in Unburdening:

Faster: Reduces hours of witnessing to 20-30 minutes of Flash plus brief witnessing.

Less overwhelming: Exile can release burden without the system flooding with trauma intensity.

Protector-friendly: Protectors are more willing to allow access because they see the process is contained.

Integration with Exiles and Managers

IFS treatment often gets stuck in negotiations between Self and managers. Managers don't want to let the therapist access exiles. This standoff can last months.

Flash breaks the standoff by providing evidence that unburdening is safe.

The Standoff Scenario

Client comes to IFS therapy. Assessment reveals multiple exiles holding trauma. But every time you try to access them, managers block you. The client intellectualizes, dissociates, or gets hostile. Standard IFS response is patient relationship-building with managers, which is appropriate but slow.

Flash Intervention for Standoffs

Therapist: "I notice we keep running into protectors who won't let us access the trauma. I'd like to try something different. Instead of fighting with the protectors, let's show them that trauma work can be safe. We'll do Flash with the protectors watching. They can see that accessing trauma briefly doesn't destroy the system. Would the protectors be willing to observe while we try this?"

Get explicit agreement from protective parts to observe.

Do Flash on one exile's trauma. Keep it contained, manageable, safe. Protectors watch and learn.

After Flash, dialogue with protectors.

Therapist: "What did you protectors notice? Was that as dangerous as you feared?"

Protectors usually report surprise that it wasn't catastrophic. This observation often shifts their stance from "Absolutely not" to "Okay, maybe we can work on this carefully."

Real Example:

Eric (composite) had been in IFS therapy for eight months with minimal progress. Every session, his manager parts intellectualized or derailed any attempt to access trauma. His therapist (who consulted with me) was frustrated.

I suggested Flash demonstration for the protectors.

Next session:

Therapist: "Eric, I'd like to speak to the parts that have been keeping us from trauma work. Are they willing to talk with me?"

Eric: *[shifts subtly]* "We're here."

Therapist: "You've been blocking trauma work. I understand you're protecting Eric. But I wonder if you'd be willing to watch a demonstration of a gentler way to approach the trauma—one where Eric doesn't fall apart. Would you watch?"

Parts: "We'll watch. But we're stopping this if it goes bad."

Therapist conducted Flash on one of Eric's abuse memories. The protective parts observed. After 20 minutes, Eric's SUDS had dropped from 8 to 4, and Eric reported, "The protectors are shocked. They're saying 'That actually worked and he's okay.'"

From that session forward, the protectors cooperated with therapy. Treatment accelerated rapidly. Eric processed multiple traumas over the next three months. Flash broke the eight-month standoff.

Case Study: Flash in IFS Therapy

Let's look at a detailed case showing full Flash integration with IFS.

Client: Sarah, 38, complex trauma from childhood neglect and abuse, multiple exiled parts, strong protective system

Presenting Problem: Depression, anxiety, relationship difficulties, history of treatment with limited progress

Initial Assessment (Sessions 1-3):

Standard IFS assessment revealed:

Exiles:

- Young child part (age 5-6) holding terror and shame from sexual abuse
- Teenage part (age 13-14) holding rage and grief from mother's abandonment
- Baby part (preverbal) holding neglect trauma

Managers:

- Perfectionist part driving overwork to prevent vulnerability
- Intellectual part keeping everything analytical to avoid feeling
- Caretaker part focusing on others' needs to avoid own pain

Firefighters:

- Binge-eating part using food to numb emotion
- Rage part exploding at partner when triggered

Treatment Challenge: Managers refused to allow access to exiles. "If Sarah feels that pain, she'll fall apart and never recover. Our job is preventing that."

Session 4: Flash Demonstration for Protectors

Therapist: "Sarah, I'd like to speak with the manager parts. Are they willing to talk?"

Sarah: *[posture straightens, voice becomes controlled]* "We're here."

Therapist: "You've been keeping the young parts locked away because you believe accessing them will destroy Sarah. I respect that you're trying to protect her. But I'd like to propose an experiment. There's a technique that allows very brief, gentle contact with trauma—just touching it lightly, not diving in. Sarah can focus mostly on something safe and positive. Would you managers be willing to let us try this while you watch carefully? You can stop it anytime."

Managers: "How do we know this won't overwhelm her?"

Therapist: "You don't yet. That's why I'm asking you to watch. If Sarah starts to get overwhelmed, you can step in immediately. You're still in charge of her safety."

Managers: "Fine. We'll watch. But we're ready to shut this down."

Therapist: "Fair enough. Sarah, come back to Self. Managers, observe from wherever you feel comfortable."

Developed PEF: Image of Sarah as compassionate adult Self, strong and grounded.

Identified target: Young child part's abuse memory (managers agreed to allow access).

Therapist: "Sarah, imagine your Self standing strong and solid. Now, very briefly—just a quick flash—notice the young part's memory of abuse. Don't go into it, just flash past it. And immediately back to Self, strong and grounded."

Conducted Flash sequences. After each set, checked with managers.

Therapist: "Managers, what do you notice? Is Sarah falling apart?"

Managers: [through Sarah] "No... she's still here. Still okay."

After 20 minutes of Flash, checked with young part.

Therapist: "Young one, how much of that terror and shame are you still carrying?"

Young part: [through Sarah, small voice] "Less. It's not as heavy."

Therapist: "Managers, what do you think?"

Managers: "We're surprised. We didn't think this was possible."

Sessions 5-8: Continued Unburdening with Flash

With managers' cooperation, we continued using Flash to unburden exiles:

Session 5: Flash on teenage part's abandonment. Reduced rage and grief.

Session 6: Flash on young part's remaining abuse trauma. Fully unburdened.

Session 7: Flash on baby part's neglect. Reduced preverbal terror.

Session 8: Completed unburdening of all three exiles using Flash plus standard IFS release imagery.

Sessions 9-12: Integration and Protector Updating

Once exiles were unburdened, worked with protectors to update their roles.

Therapist: "Managers, the young parts are healed. They're not carrying those burdens anymore. Your protective job is done. What role would you like to have now?"

Managers transitioned to healthier roles: Perfectionist became "Standards Holder" (healthy striving without rigidity). Intellectual became "Wisdom Keeper" (thoughtful analysis without emotional avoidance). Caretaker became "Compassion Extender" (caring for others without self-neglect).

Firefighters also updated. Binge-eating part became "Comfort Provider" (using healthy self-care). Rage part became "Boundary Enforcer" (assertiveness without explosion).

Outcome:

Sarah completed 12 sessions of IFS with Flash integration. All major exiles unburdened. Protectors updated to healthy roles. Depression and anxiety significantly reduced. Relationship with partner improved.

Estimated timeline without Flash: 25-40 sessions based on complexity of her system and manager resistance. Flash accelerated treatment by more than 50%.

Parts Work Enhanced by Flash

Flash integrates powerfully with Internal Family Systems by addressing protective parts' core fear—that unburdening exiles will overwhelm the system. By demonstrating that trauma can be touched safely through Flash, protective parts often shift from blocking access to supporting healing.

Unburdening process accelerates significantly when Flash reduces the emotional intensity exiles carry before or during standard IFS release work. This makes witnessing less overwhelming and protectors more willing to allow access.

Flash breaks common IFS standoffs where managers refuse to let therapists access exiles. The demonstration of safe trauma processing often converts resistant protectors into cooperative allies, dramatically accelerating treatment.

Case example showed complete IFS treatment with Flash integration completed in 12 sessions versus estimated 25-40 sessions without Flash—more than 50% reduction in treatment length while maintaining full healing of exiles and updating of protective parts.

Chapter 11: Flash with Somatic & Body-Based Approaches

Trauma lives in the body. You've heard that before, probably. Maybe you've read "The Body Keeps the Score" (van der Kolk, 2014). Maybe you've noticed that your clients talk about trauma not just as memories but as sensations—tightness in chest, knot in stomach, heaviness in limbs.

Somatic therapies—Somatic Experiencing, Sensorimotor Psychotherapy, body-focused trauma work—recognize that healing trauma requires addressing the body's response, not just the mind's narrative. These approaches track sensation, movement, and nervous system arousal as primary pathways to trauma resolution (Levine, 2010; Ogden et al., 2006).

Flash, interestingly, integrates beautifully with somatic work. Even though Flash uses cognitive focus (PEF) and mental imagery, it produces body changes. And when you combine Flash with deliberate somatic awareness, you get powerful results.

Pairing with Somatic Experiencing

Somatic Experiencing (SE), developed by Peter Levine, focuses on completing the body's defensive responses that got stuck during trauma (Levine, 2010). When trauma happens, your body mobilizes for fight or flight. But if you can't complete those responses (you freeze, you're overpowered, you can't escape), that mobilization energy stays stuck in your nervous system.

SE works by:

- Tracking body sensations

- Titrating (working with small amounts of) activation

- Following the body's impulses toward completion

- Discharging stuck survival energy

- Restoring healthy nervous system regulation

The SE Challenge

SE moves slowly and carefully. You don't push clients into overwhelm. You stay with the body's pace. This careful titration is protective, but it can also make treatment lengthy— sometimes dozens of sessions to process one trauma.

Flash with SE: Integration Protocol

Flash can accelerate SE by reducing the overall charge in the nervous system, making it easier to track sensations and complete defensive responses without overwhelm.

Step 1: Standard SE Assessment

Track the body's response to thinking about trauma. What sensations arise? Where? What quality (tight, heavy, buzzing, cold)?

Therapist: "When you think about the incident, what do you notice in your body?"

Client: "Tightness in my chest. Hard to breathe."

Step 2: Flash to Reduce Overall Activation

Use Flash to lower the nervous system's arousal before doing detailed somatic work.

Therapist: "We're going to use Flash to reduce some of that tightness and help your nervous system settle. Then we'll track what your body wants to do."

Conduct Flash on the trauma memory. Monitor body sensations during Flash—often you'll see the client's breathing deepen, shoulders drop, face relax as SUDS decreases.

Step 3: SE Somatic Tracking

After Flash has reduced overall activation, return to SE protocol.

Therapist: "Now, thinking about the incident again, what do you notice in your body?"

Client: "The tightness is less. Maybe a 4 out of 10 now instead of 9."

Therapist: "Good. Stay with that sensation. What does it want to do?"

Client might report impulses to push away, run, or other defensive movements. Follow SE protocol to complete those responses.

Step 4: Integration

The combination of Flash (reducing intensity) plus SE (completing defensive responses) often produces rapid resolution. The body can complete what it needs to without overwhelming activation.

Real Example:

Leon (composite) experienced assault. In his body, he held a freezing response—his whole system had shut down during the attack. SE therapist was working carefully to help Leon's system unfreeze, but progress was very slow. After six months, minimal change.

Therapist consulted about adding Flash.

Session with Flash-SE integration:

Therapist: "Leon, let's use Flash to reduce some of the intensity first, then see what your body wants to do."

Did 15 minutes of Flash. Leon's SUDS on the assault dropped from 9 to 5. His body visibly relaxed somewhat.

Therapist: "Now, when you think about the assault, what do you notice in your body?"

Leon: "Still some freezing. But less overwhelming. I can actually feel my body now instead of just numbness."

Therapist: "Stay with that. What does your body want to do?"

Leon: *[pause]* "Push. I want to push away."

Therapist: "Go ahead. Slowly. Let your body show you."

Leon made slow pushing motions with his hands and arms. As he did, his face flushed (activation), then his breathing deepened (discharge), then he sighed and said, "That's better. I feel more here."

This was the first major shift Leon had experienced in six months of SE. Flash reduced the overwhelm enough that his body could access and complete the defensive response.

Over next six sessions using Flash-SE integration, Leon fully processed the trauma. Total treatment: Seven months (first six months with SE alone showing minimal progress, then one month with Flash-SE showing rapid resolution).

Sensorimotor Psychotherapy Integration

Sensorimotor Psychotherapy (SP), developed by Pat Ogden, addresses trauma through mindful awareness of body sensations, movement, and cognitive meaning-making (Ogden et al., 2006). SP moves through three phases:

Phase 1 (Somatic): Track and work with body sensations and movement impulses **Phase 2 (Emotional):** Process emotions that arise with body awareness **Phase 3 (Cognitive):** Integrate meaning and narrative

SP is methodical and elegant but can be slow, especially with highly activated clients who can't stay present with body sensations without dissociating or flooding.

Flash-SP Integration

Use Flash to reduce activation before or during SP phases, allowing better body awareness and integration.

Protocol Option 1: Flash Before SP

Session 1: Flash to reduce trauma memory intensity **Sessions 2+:** Standard SP protocol with reduced activation

Protocol Option 2: Flash During SP

SP Phase 1: Begin somatic tracking **If client becomes overwhelmed:** Pause, use Flash to reduce activation, resume tracking **SP Phases 2-3:** Continue with emotional and cognitive processing

Protocol Option 3: Flash-SP Hybrid

Integrate Flash directly into SP framework:

Somatic Awareness: "Notice sensations in your body when thinking about the trauma."

184

Flash Intervention: "Hold those body sensations in awareness. Now bring up your positive focus, and very briefly flash to the trauma memory while maintaining body awareness."

Tracking Changes: "What do you notice in your body after that flash? Did the sensations shift?"

Often, body sensations change after Flash sequences—tension releases, breathing deepens, or the sensation moves or transforms. This gives you somatic processing happening simultaneously with Flash's memory processing.

Real Example:

Tamara (composite) worked with SP therapist on childhood abuse. The SP protocol helped somewhat, but Tamara often flooded or dissociated when tracking body sensations, making progress slow.

Therapist integrated Flash:

Therapist: "Tamara, notice the sensations in your body related to the abuse memory. What do you feel?"

Tamara: "Heavy. My whole chest feels heavy, like a weight pressing down."

Therapist: "Okay, maintain awareness of that heaviness. Now bring up your safe place image. While holding the safe place and the body awareness, very briefly flash to the memory. Notice what happens in your body."

[Flash sequence]

Therapist: "What do you notice in your body now?"

Tamara: "The heaviness shifted. It's lighter. And I can breathe better."

Therapist: "Stay with that. What wants to happen in your body?"

Tamara: *[takes deep breath, stretches slightly]* "That. The stretch. Like I'm opening up."

Therapist: "Go ahead. Let your body do what it wants."

Tamara stretched and moved, completing the somatic processing. The Flash had reduced activation enough that her body could access and complete the healing movements without flooding.

This hybrid approach combined Flash's rapid intensity reduction with SP's detailed somatic processing. Treatment progressed much faster than SP alone would have.

Body Scan Protocols

Body scans—systematically noticing sensations throughout the body—are used in many trauma therapies. The final phase of EMDR includes a body scan. Mindfulness practices use body scans. Somatic therapies rely on body awareness.

But body scans can be difficult for trauma survivors. When you ask them to notice body sensations, they might find:

- Intense discomfort or pain
- Numbness or dissociation
- Triggering sensations that activate trauma memories
- Inability to feel anything

Flash-Enhanced Body Scan

Use Flash to clear trauma-related body sensations before or during body scans.

Protocol:

Step 1: Initial Body Scan

Therapist: "Scan through your body from head to toe. Notice any sensations, discomfort, or areas that draw your attention."

Client identifies problem areas: "Tightness in jaw. Pain in lower back. Knot in stomach."

Step 2: Identify Trauma Connections

Therapist: "When you notice that tightness in your jaw, does it connect to any specific memory or experience?"

Often body sensations are holding specific traumas.

Step 3: Flash the Connected Trauma

Therapist: "Let's use Flash to work on the memory connected to that jaw tightness."

Conduct Flash on the identified trauma.

Step 4: Repeat Body Scan

Therapist: "Scan your body again. What do you notice in your jaw now?"

Typically, the body sensation has decreased or resolved after Flash processes the connected memory.

Step 5: Continue with Remaining Sensations

Work through other problem areas using the same process. Flash the connected traumas, body sensations clear.

Real Example:

David (composite) had multiple body complaints—chronic jaw tension, back pain, stomach issues. Medical workups found nothing. Clearly, these were trauma-related somatic symptoms.

Did Flash-enhanced body scan:

Jaw tension: Connected to childhood abuse (being told to "shut up"). Flashed that memory. Jaw tension resolved.

Back pain: Connected to car accident (impact to back). Flashed accident memory. Back pain decreased by 70%.

Stomach issues: Connected to anxiety about work performance (worried about being fired like his father was). Flashed childhood memory of father's job loss. Stomach issues improved significantly.

After Flash treatment of connected traumas, David's body scan showed mostly clear sensations. The physical symptoms had been holding trauma memories—resolve the memories, resolve the symptoms.

Chronic Pain with Trauma History

Research shows that many chronic pain conditions have trauma components (van der Kolk, 2014). Not that trauma causes all pain—medical factors matter—but trauma can maintain, amplify, or complicate pain conditions.

When chronic pain has trauma history, addressing both the trauma and the pain produces better outcomes than treating either alone.

Flash for Trauma-Related Pain

Use Flash to process traumatic memories connected to pain onset or maintenance.

Assessment:

Therapist: "Tell me about when your pain started. What was happening in your life at that time?"

Often, pain onset coincides with trauma or extreme stress.

Therapist: "When you focus on the pain, does it bring up any memories or emotions?"

Pain might be holding trauma.

Flash Protocol:

Option 1: Flash the Trauma Origin

If pain started after specific trauma (accident, surgery, assault), Flash that trauma memory.

Option 2: Flash Pain-Connected Memories

If certain memories intensify pain, Flash those memories.

Option 3: Flash While Tracking Pain Levels

Conduct Flash while monitoring pain intensity. Often pain decreases as trauma is processed.

Real Example:

Carla (composite) had chronic neck pain for three years, starting after minor car accident. Physical therapy helped somewhat, but pain persisted. Pain clinic referred her to therapy for "pain psychology."

Therapist: "Carla, when did the neck pain start?"

Carla: "Right after the accident. But doctors say the injury should have healed by now."

Therapist: "Tell me about the accident. What was that like?"

Carla described the accident—being hit from behind, feeling helpless and terrified, fearing she'd die.

Therapist: "I wonder if your nervous system is still holding that terror and the injury together. Let's use Flash to process the accident memory."

Did Flash on accident memory. Carla's SUDS on the memory dropped from 8 to 2. After Flash:

Therapist: "How's your neck pain right now?"

Carla: "It's... less. It's still there, but it doesn't feel as tight. Maybe 4 out of 10 instead of 7."

Over three sessions of Flash processing the accident plus related fears (dying, losing control, being helpless), Carla's pain decreased to 1-2 out of 10. Not completely gone, but manageable without medication. Her nervous system had been maintaining the pain as a signal of ongoing danger. Processing the trauma allowed the danger signal to turn off.

Important Note:

Flash doesn't cure all pain. Medical evaluation remains necessary. But for pain with trauma components, addressing the trauma often significantly reduces pain levels.

Body-Focused Trauma Work Plus Flash

Flash integrates with Somatic Experiencing by reducing overall nervous system activation before tracking body sensations and completing defensive responses. This allows the body to access and discharge stuck survival energy without overwhelming the system. Treatment often accelerates significantly with Flash-SE integration.

Sensorimotor Psychotherapy benefits from Flash preparation or intervention when clients become overwhelmed during somatic tracking. Hybrid approaches use Flash while maintaining body awareness, allowing simultaneous processing of memories and body sensations with reduced flooding risk.

Flash-enhanced body scans identify trauma-related body sensations, process connected memories, and clear physical symptoms. Many chronic body complaints that resist medical treatment resolve when underlying trauma memories are processed with Flash.

Chronic pain with trauma history often improves significantly when Flash addresses traumatic origins or pain-connected memories. The nervous system's danger signaling can decrease, reducing pain intensity even when structural issues remain.

Chapter 12: Flash with DBT & Emotion Regulation

Dialectical Behavior Therapy wasn't designed for trauma treatment. Marsha Linehan created DBT for chronically suicidal clients with borderline personality disorder—people with extreme emotion dysregulation who cycle through crises and engage in life-threatening behaviors (Linehan, 2014). DBT teaches skills for managing emotions, tolerating distress, improving relationships, and practicing mindfulness.

But here's the thing: Most people with severe emotion dysregulation and borderline features have significant trauma histories. Studies show 60-90% of people with BPD experienced childhood abuse, neglect, or other severe trauma (Harned et al., 2014). The emotion dysregulation often stems from unprocessed trauma.

Standard DBT addresses symptoms—teaching skills to manage emotional storms, reduce self-harm, prevent suicide. But DBT historically hasn't focused on processing the underlying trauma. The approach was "Stabilize first, maybe trauma work later if needed."

Flash changes that calculus. You can use Flash to process trauma even with highly dysregulated clients, often without destabilizing them. This creates opportunities for trauma resolution that wouldn't exist with traditional trauma therapies.

Pre-Treatment for Emotion Dysregulation

Standard DBT has a pre-treatment phase (orienting the client to treatment, getting commitment, establishing goals) followed by Stage 1 treatment focusing on behavioral control and skills building. Trauma processing, if it happens at all, comes much later in DBT-PTSD protocols (Harned et al., 2014).

But what if you could address trauma earlier, before or during skills training? Would that accelerate progress?

Flash as Early Intervention

Use Flash during DBT Stage 1 (while client is learning skills) to reduce trauma-related emotional intensity without requiring the client to have perfect emotion regulation first.

The Standard DBT Concern

DBT therapists worry that trauma processing during Stage 1 will destabilize clients who don't yet have strong skills. "They'll become suicidal, self-harm, or drop out."

That concern is valid for traditional trauma processing (prolonged exposure, EMDR desensitization). Those approaches require sustained distress tolerance that dysregulated clients often lack.

Flash's Advantage

Flash produces minimal distress during processing. Most clients find it comfortable. This makes it safer for use with emotion dysregulation.

Protocol:

Weeks 1-4 of DBT: Standard DBT orientation, commitment, beginning skills training (mindfulness, distress tolerance basics).

Weeks 5-6: While continuing skills training, add Flash sessions targeting most distressing trauma memories.

Weeks 7+: Continue DBT skills training plus periodic Flash sessions as needed for remaining trauma.

Rationale to Client:

Therapist: "We're going to do something a bit different from standard DBT. While you're learning emotion regulation skills, we're also going to work on some of the trauma that's driving your emotional intensity. We'll use Flash, which is very gentle and shouldn't overwhelm you. This combination—building skills AND reducing trauma intensity—should help you progress faster."

Benefits:

Faster symptom reduction: Addressing trauma reduces emotional triggers, making it easier to use skills.

Better skills practice: When trauma intensity is lower, clients can actually practice skills instead of just surviving crises.

Increased motivation: Early trauma processing provides hope and demonstrates treatment works.

Real Example:

Maya (composite) entered DBT for borderline features, chronic suicidality, and self-harm. She had extensive childhood abuse trauma. Standard DBT would have her in Stage 1 skills training for 6-12 months before even considering trauma work.

Her DBT therapist (who'd trained in Flash) decided to integrate early trauma processing.

Weeks 1-4: Standard DBT orientation and initial mindfulness skills.

Week 5: Added Flash session targeting Maya's most distressing abuse memory. SUDS dropped from 9 to 3.

Maya's reaction: "I can't believe that just happened. I've been terrified of that memory for years and now it's... manageable."

Weeks 6-12: Continued skills training with Flash sessions every 2-3 weeks targeting different traumas.

By week 12, Maya had processed her five worst trauma memories and learned solid DBT skills. Her self-harm had stopped, suicidal ideation was minimal, and emotional episodes were less frequent and less intense.

Standard DBT timeline to reach that stability: 9-12 months. With Flash integration: 3 months.

Integration with Distress Tolerance Skills

DBT distress tolerance skills teach clients how to survive crises without making things worse. Skills include:

- **STOP** (Stop, Take a step back, Observe, Proceed mindfully)
- **TIP** (Temperature, Intense exercise, Paced breathing, Progressive relaxation)
- **Self-soothing** through senses
- **IMPROVE the moment**
- **Pros and cons** of tolerating distress

These skills work, but they're hard to use when trauma triggers hit. The emotional intensity overwhelms the skills.

Flash to Reduce Trigger Intensity

Use Flash to process trauma memories connected to specific triggers. When the underlying trauma is resolved, the trigger loses power, making distress tolerance skills more effective.

Protocol:

Step 1: Identify Triggers

Therapist: "What situations or experiences trigger your most intense emotions?"

Client: "When someone criticizes me, I fall apart completely."

Step 2: Identify Connected Trauma

Therapist: "When you get criticized and fall apart, what memory or experience does that connect to?"

Client: "My dad. He'd scream at me, tell me I was worthless, stupid..."

Step 3: Flash the Connected Trauma

Use Flash to process the abuse memories connected to criticism sensitivity.

Step 4: Practice Skills with Reduced Trigger

After Flash, the trigger (criticism) has less power. Now the client can actually practice distress tolerance skills when criticized, instead of being instantly overwhelmed.

Real Example:

Tyler (composite) had DBT skills but couldn't use them when triggered. His trigger: anyone raising their voice slightly. He'd immediately panic, self-harm, or rage.

Identified connected trauma: Father's violent rages during childhood. Tyler associated any raised voice with imminent danger.

Used Flash to process multiple memories of father's rage. Tyler's SUDS on those memories dropped from 9-10 to 1-2.

Next time someone raised their voice at work, Tyler reported: "I felt anxiety starting, but I could actually think. I used STOP skill. I stepped back, observed that I was safe, and proceeded mindfully. I couldn't have done that before."

Flash had reduced the trigger intensity enough that Tyler's prefrontal cortex could engage and access his DBT skills. Before Flash, the trigger bypassed thinking entirely and sent him straight into panic.

Working with Self-Harm Histories

Self-harm (cutting, burning, hitting) serves functions for emotionally dysregulated clients: emotional regulation, self-punishment, communication of distress, or relief from numbness. DBT addresses self-harm behaviorally—reducing frequency through skills and contingency management.

But self-harm often connects to trauma. Processing the trauma can reduce or eliminate the drive to self-harm.

Flash for Self-Harm Reduction

Assessment:

Therapist: "When do you feel the urge to self-harm? What's happening emotionally?"

Client: "When I feel worthless. When I hate myself. When I need to feel something because I'm too numb."

Therapist: "Where did those feelings—worthless, self-hatred—come from? What experiences taught you to feel that way about yourself?"

Usually, trauma taught them. Abuse, neglect, bullying, assault—something made them believe they were worthless or bad.

Flash Protocol:

Process the traumas that installed the beliefs driving self-harm.

Example:

Client self-harms when feeling worthless. That feeling comes from childhood neglect—being ignored, told she didn't matter, treated as a burden.

Flash the neglect memories. As those memories are processed and the client develops healthier beliefs about herself, the drive to self-harm decreases.

Important:

Flash doesn't replace DBT behavioral interventions for self-harm (safety planning, crisis skills, alternatives to self-harm). But it addresses the root cause while DBT addresses the behavior. Combined approach works better than either alone.

Real Example:

Jenna (composite) cut herself regularly. DBT helped her reduce frequency somewhat, but she still cut 2-3 times per week when emotionally overwhelmed.

In therapy, explored self-harm function: "I cut because I deserve pain. I'm bad. I need to be punished."

Therapist: "Where did you learn that you're bad and deserve pain?"

Jenna: "My mother. She'd tell me I was evil, that I ruined her life, that I was a burden. She'd lock me in my room for hours as punishment for tiny things."

Therapist: "Those experiences taught you that you're bad. Let's work on those memories."

Used Flash to process multiple childhood neglect and emotional abuse memories. Jenna's beliefs about herself shifted: "I was a child. I wasn't bad. My mother had problems."

After processing those traumas, Jenna's self-harm urges decreased dramatically. Within six weeks, she hadn't cut at all. She reported: "I don't feel like I deserve pain anymore. Why would I hurt myself?"

Flash changed the beliefs driving the behavior. DBT skills helped her manage emotions during the transition. Combined: complete cessation of self-harm.

Borderline Personality Disorder Considerations

BPD is characterized by emotion dysregulation, unstable relationships, identity disturbance, impulsivity, self-harm, and chronic feelings of emptiness (APA, 2013). Most people with BPD have trauma histories, but trauma processing has historically been avoided because of fears about destabilization.

DBT-PE (DBT with Prolonged Exposure) is an evidence-based protocol for trauma in BPD (Harned et al., 2014). It works, but it's intensive and not all clients can tolerate it.

Flash as Alternative or Enhancement

Flash offers several advantages for BPD clients:

1. Lower Distress During Processing

BPD clients often have limited distress tolerance. Flash's low-distress profile makes it more accessible.

2. Reduced Crisis Risk

Traditional trauma processing can trigger crises in BPD clients (suicidal ideation, self-harm, rageful episodes). Flash's gentler approach reduces this risk.

3. Faster Processing

BPD clients often have multiple traumas. Flash can process them more quickly than traditional methods, reducing total treatment time.

4. Preserved Therapeutic Relationship

BPD clients struggle with relationships. Flash's collaborative, non-confrontational approach supports the therapeutic relationship instead of straining it.

Clinical Considerations for Flash with BPD:

Timing: Don't use Flash during acute crises. Wait until client is relatively stable (not actively suicidal, no recent self-harm, some skills acquisition).

Skills Foundation: Client needs at least basic distress tolerance and emotion regulation skills before trauma processing. First 4-8 weeks of DBT provides this.

Safety Planning: Have clear safety plan for post-session distress (who to call, skills to use, crisis resources).

Session Structure: Do Flash in longer sessions (90 minutes) allowing time for processing and grounding afterward. BPD clients may need more closure time than others.

Relationship Management: Be aware of transference dynamics (idealization, devaluation). Flash can intensify attachment, so process relationship dynamics explicitly.

Multiple Traumas: Prioritize which traumas to address first. Usually start with traumas most connected to current symptoms.

Real Example:

Keira (composite), 27, met criteria for BPD: chronic suicidal ideation, regular self-harm, intense unstable relationships, identity confusion, emotional storms. She'd been hospitalized six times in three years.

Started DBT. Learned skills. Stabilized somewhat but remained symptomatic. Traditional thinking: "Not ready for trauma work yet."

Her therapist (Flash-trained) reassessed: "She's stable enough. She has skills. She's committed to treatment. Let's try Flash."

Month 4 of DBT: Began Flash processing of childhood sexual abuse (her primary trauma).

Keira's response: "This is weird. I'm working on the worst thing that ever happened to me, and I'm not falling apart. I don't get it."

Over three months, processed five significant trauma memories using Flash. Keira's BPD symptoms improved dramatically:

- Suicidal ideation decreased from daily to occasional
- Self-harm stopped
- Emotional episodes less frequent and less intense
- Relationships more stable

- Identity more coherent ("I know who I am now")

By DBT month 7, Keira no longer met criteria for BPD. She graduated from DBT and transitioned to monthly maintenance sessions.

Her therapist noted: "Without Flash, Keira would have been in DBT for 18-24 months and might never have addressed the trauma. Flash made trauma resolution safe and accessible for someone everyone thought was 'too unstable' for trauma work."

A Note on Caution

Flash with BPD isn't universally appropriate. Some clients are too unstable. Some have such severe dissociation that any trauma work is premature. Clinical judgment matters.

But Flash expands the population who can safely engage in trauma processing. Clients previously considered "not ready" often are ready for Flash when they wouldn't be ready for traditional trauma therapies.

Emotion Regulation and Trauma Resolution Together

Flash integrates with DBT by allowing earlier trauma processing than traditional approaches permit. Instead of waiting months or years for complete stabilization, Flash can be used during skills training phase with minimal destabilization risk.

Integration with distress tolerance skills works by processing traumas connected to triggers. When underlying trauma intensity decreases, triggers lose power, making DBT skills more effective and accessible during emotional activation.

Self-harm often stems from trauma-based beliefs about self-worth and deserving punishment. Flash processing of traumas that installed these beliefs can reduce or eliminate self-harm drives, complementing DBT's behavioral interventions.

BPD clients, historically considered too unstable for trauma work, can often tolerate Flash when standard trauma therapies would be contraindicated. This allows trauma resolution for a population that desperately needs it but has been systematically excluded from trauma-focused treatment.

The combination of DBT skills building plus Flash trauma processing produces faster symptom reduction and better outcomes than either approach alone, particularly for clients with emotion dysregulation and complex trauma histories.

Chapter 13: Complex Trauma & Dissociation

Single-incident trauma is tough enough. Car accident, assault, natural disaster—one terrible event that changes everything. But complex trauma? That's a different beast entirely.

Complex trauma means repeated, prolonged traumatic experiences, usually starting in childhood. Abuse that happened every night for years. Neglect that lasted your entire childhood. Violence that was just "how things were" in your family. The kind of trauma that doesn't just damage you once—it shapes how your brain develops, how you see yourself, how you relate to others (van der Kolk, 2014).

And here's the challenge: Complex trauma survivors often develop dissociation as a survival strategy. When you can't escape physically, you escape mentally. You split off parts of yourself. You disconnect from your body. You develop amnesia for unbearable experiences. These dissociative responses kept you alive as a child, but they complicate trauma treatment as an adult.

Flash wasn't originally designed for complex trauma with dissociation. It was developed for single-incident PTSD. But clinicians quickly discovered it works beautifully with complex cases—if you adapt it properly. This chapter shows you how.

Adapting Flash for Developmental Trauma

Developmental trauma happens during childhood when the brain is still forming. It affects attachment, emotional regulation, identity formation, and basic trust in the world. Adults with developmental trauma histories often struggle with relationships, emotion management, and sense of self in ways that single-incident trauma survivors don't (Courtois & Ford, 2013).

The Developmental Trauma Challenge

You can't just pick one memory to process. There are dozens. Hundreds, maybe. Which one do you start with? Process them all individually and you're looking at years of treatment. Skip trauma processing entirely and you're treating symptoms without addressing root causes.

Flash's Advantage for Complex Trauma

Flash can rapidly reduce distress across multiple memories. You don't need to fully process each memory individually. You can Flash many memories to reduce their intensity, then fully process key ones. This creates efficiency that makes complex trauma treatment actually manageable.

Adapted Protocol for Developmental Trauma:

Phase 1: Stabilization (Still Necessary)

Don't skip stabilization just because Flash is gentler. Complex trauma survivors need:

- Basic emotion regulation skills
- Grounding techniques
- Understanding of dissociation and how to manage it
- Safety planning
- Support system development

Spend 4-8 sessions on stabilization before starting trauma processing.

Phase 2: Trauma Inventory

Help client identify major trauma memories. Not every single incident, but significant categories:

"Physical abuse from father, ages 5-12" "Sexual abuse from uncle, ages 8-10" "Mother's neglect, entire childhood" "Witnessing domestic violence, ages 3-14"

Create list of 6-12 trauma categories. Each category might contain dozens of specific incidents.

Phase 3: Flash Triage

Work through the list using Flash. Spend 15-30 minutes on each trauma category. You're not processing every specific incident—you're reducing the overall charge of that trauma type.

Therapist: "When you think about the physical abuse from your father during those years, what's the overall disturbance level?"

Get baseline SUDS for the category. Do Flash targeting that category generally. SUDS typically drops significantly.

Move to next category. Flash it. Next category. Flash it.

Over 4-8 sessions, you've Flashed all major trauma categories. None are fully processed, but all are substantially less intense.

Phase 4: Targeted Full Processing

After Flash triage reduces overall intensity, identify 2-4 memories that need full processing. These are usually:

- Worst/most disturbing incident
- First incident (primal event)

- Most recent incident

- Memory connected to current symptoms

Fully process these with standard EMDR, extended Flash, or other trauma processing methods.

Phase 5: Integration

Help client integrate new sense of self, process grief for lost childhood, develop healthier relationships and coping strategies.

Real Example:

Vanessa (composite), 42, extensive childhood abuse and neglect. Assessment identified nine trauma categories spanning ages 3-17.

Standard trauma processing approach would require processing dozens of individual memories—potentially 50+ sessions.

Adapted Flash approach:

Sessions 1-6: Stabilization, skill-building, preparing for trauma work.

Sessions 7-14: Flash triage. One trauma category per session. By end of session 14, all nine categories reduced from SUDS 8-10 range to 3-5 range.

Vanessa reported: "I can think about my childhood now without feeling like I'm drowning. It's still sad, still terrible, but I can handle it."

Sessions 15-20: Fully processed three key memories—first sexual abuse incident, worst beating from father, and mother's abandonment. Used standard EMDR after Flash had reduced overall trauma load.

Sessions 21-25: Integration, relationship work, building new life patterns.

Total: 25 sessions to address complex trauma spanning 14 years of abuse. Without Flash triage? Estimated 60-80 sessions.

Working with Dissociative Disorders

Dissociative Identity Disorder (DID) and Other Specified Dissociative Disorder (OSDD) involve distinct personality states (parts or alters) with their own memories, feelings, and ways of relating to the world. These aren't metaphorical parts like in IFS—they're actual dissociated self-states that can take executive control (van der Kolk, 2014).

Trauma processing with DID/OSDD is complicated because:

- Different parts hold different trauma memories
- Some parts don't know about the trauma
- Protector parts actively prevent trauma processing
- Switching between parts can disrupt sessions
- Some parts are children holding child memories

Flash with DID/OSDD: Special Protocols

Protocol 1: System Preparation

Before any trauma processing:

Therapist: "I'd like to speak with all the parts of the system. Is everyone able to hear me right now?"

Establish internal communication. Get agreement from the system about working together.

Therapist: "We're going to work on some of the trauma that parts of the system are holding. I'll be using Flash Technique, which is gentle. But I need everyone's cooperation. If any part objects or feels unsafe, please let me know."

Address objections. Negotiate with protector parts. Get buy-in from the system before proceeding.

Protocol 2: Part-Specific Flash

Work with one part at a time holding specific trauma.

Therapist: "I'd like to work with the part holding the memory of [specific trauma]. Is that part willing to come forward?"

That part comes forward. Do Flash with that part. The PEF might be:

- Safe place for that specific part
- Adult self holding child part safely
- Other parts supporting the traumatized part

Flash the trauma that part holds. When SUDS drops for that part, thank them and check with other parts.

Therapist: "How are other parts doing? Is everyone okay?"

Often, processing one part's trauma helps the whole system.

Protocol 3: Co-Conscious Processing

If parts can be co-conscious (aware together), Flash can happen with multiple parts present.

Therapist: "Can the [traumatized part] and [protective part] both be present and aware right now?"

If yes, both parts observe the Flash process. The traumatized part experiences trauma reduction while the protective part sees it's safe.

Protocol 4: Grounding Between Parts

When switching occurs during Flash, ground immediately.

Therapist: "I notice a different part just came forward. Hello. Can you tell me your name and how old you are?"

Orient the new part. Ground them. Explain what's happening.

Therapist: "We're working on trauma processing. Is that okay with you, or do you need to stop?"

Respect the new part's needs. Don't force processing.

Real Example:

Keisha (composite) has DID with eight distinct parts. Several parts held severe childhood abuse memories. Previous therapist attempted trauma processing but triggered massive switching and destabilization.

New therapist used Flash with system-aware protocol:

Session 1: Met all eight parts. Learned their names, ages, roles. Built relationship with each.

Session 2: Explained Flash to the whole system. Protector parts were skeptical but agreed to try.

Session 3: Worked with 6-year-old part holding sexual abuse memory. Adult protector part stayed co-conscious to observe. Did Flash. Child part's SUDS dropped from 10 to 3. Protector part reported: "That wasn't as bad as I thought. The little one is okay."

Sessions 4-10: Systematically worked with different parts holding different traumas. Each part processed what they held. System cooperation increased as parts saw trauma work was safe.

Outcome: After 10 trauma processing sessions, all parts reported reduced distress about their respective traumas. System integration improved (parts communicated better, switching became less disruptive). Keisha reported feeling "more whole."

Pacing and Sequencing Multiple Traumas

When someone has 20, 30, or 50 traumatic memories, you need a strategic plan. Random processing is inefficient and potentially retraumatizing.

Sequencing Strategies

Strategy 1: Chronological Approach

Start with earliest trauma, work forward in time. Theory: Processing early traumas often causes later ones to generalize and resolve without direct processing.

Advantages:

- Addresses foundational trauma that shaped everything else
- Often creates generalization effects
- Feels logical to many clients

Disadvantages:

- Earliest memories might be most intense
- Requires accessing very young experiences

- Can be slow if early trauma is extensive

When to use: When client wants to "start at the beginning" or when early trauma is clearly foundational to later issues.

Strategy 2: Reverse Chronological (Most Recent First)

Start with most recent trauma, work backward. Theory: Recent memories are more accessible and less likely to trigger massive regression.

Advantages:

- Recent memories often connect to current symptoms
- Success builds confidence for older trauma
- Less risk of age regression

Disadvantages:

- Older trauma remains unprocessed longer
- May not get generalization effects

When to use: When client is avoiding earlier trauma or when recent events triggered PTSD in someone with complex history.

Strategy 3: Symptom-Connected Approach

Identify which memories connect to which symptoms. Process trauma memories causing most current distress first.

Example:

- Nightmares about father's violence → Process father's violence memories
- Panic in relationships → Process abandonment/betrayal memories

- Dissociation at work → Process shame-based memories

Advantages:

- Immediate symptom relief

- Clear connection between processing and improvement

- Motivating for client

Disadvantages:

- Doesn't necessarily address root trauma

- Might miss important memories not connected to current symptoms

When to use: When client has specific symptoms they want resolved or when motivation is fragile.

Strategy 4: Intensity-Based Approach (Flash Triage First)

Use Flash to reduce intensity across all traumas, then fully process worst remaining ones.

Advantages:

- Reduces overall trauma load quickly

- Efficient for complex trauma

- Client experiences rapid improvement

Disadvantages:

- Less deep processing initially

- Some memories may need additional work later

When to use: Complex trauma with many memories of similar intensity.

Strategy 5: Thematic Clustering

Group memories by theme, process each theme as a cluster.

Example themes:

- Physical abuse cluster

- Sexual abuse cluster

- Neglect cluster

- Medical trauma cluster

- Peer bullying cluster

Flash the cluster generally, then fully process worst example from each cluster.

Advantages:

- Organized approach

- Generalization within themes

- Efficient

Disadvantages:

- Themes overlap

- Artificial categories don't match experience

When to use: When trauma clearly separates into distinct categories.

Sequencing Decision Tree:

Ask yourself:

1. How many traumatic memories? (6-10 = individual processing; 15+ = triage approach)

2. Is there a clear "worst" or "first" memory? (If yes, start there)

3. What symptoms is client most motivated to address? (Process connected memories first)

4. Does client have preference for sequencing? (Honor that unless clinically contraindicated)

5. How stable is the client? (Less stable = slower, more careful sequencing)

Safety Protocols for Fragile Clients

Some clients with complex trauma are fragile—barely holding themselves together, frequent suicidal ideation, severe emotion dysregulation, limited support systems. Flash is gentler than traditional approaches, but it's still trauma processing. You need safety protocols.

Pre-Treatment Safety Assessment

Before starting Flash with fragile clients, assess:

Suicide risk: Active ideation? Plan? Intent? Protective factors? **Self-harm:** Frequency? Severity? Functions it serves? **Substance use:** How much? What function? Risk of overdose? **Dissociation severity:** Can client stay grounded? Return from dissociation? **Support system:** Anyone available if client gets distressed? **Housing stability:** Secure place to live? **Basic functioning:** Can client maintain work, self-care, responsibilities?

If client has active suicide plan, severe substance dependence, or homelessness, address those first. Flash can wait.

Safety Planning

Develop detailed safety plan before trauma processing:

Between-session coping:

- Grounding techniques client knows well

- Distraction strategies

- People to call (friends, crisis line, therapist)

- Places to go if overwhelmed (friend's house, emergency room)

Crisis management:

- Clear criteria for when to use crisis resources

- Phone numbers readily accessible

- Agreement about communication between sessions

Self-harm prevention:

- Alternative coping strategies

- Commitment to safety

- Plan for managing urges

Session Structure for Fragile Clients:

Longer sessions: 90 minutes instead of 60. Allows more time for grounding afterward.

Lower intensity processing: Reduce SUDS by 2-3 points per session, not pushing for complete resolution.

More frequent grounding checks: After every 2-3 Flash sequences, check grounding thoroughly.

Extended closure: Spend 15-20 minutes at end of session ensuring client is stable, grounded, and has plan for self-care.

Between-session contact: Brief check-in calls or texts day after trauma processing session.

Slowed pacing: One trauma memory every 2-3 sessions instead of one per session.

Red Flag Signs to Stop Processing:

During session:

- Severe dissociation that doesn't respond to grounding

- Suicidal statements

- Overwhelming distress despite Flash's protective structure

- Flashback (client believes trauma is happening now)

- Physical collapse or medical crisis

Between sessions:

- Increased self-harm

- Substance use escalation

- New suicidal ideation or planning

- Severe functional deterioration

- Multiple crisis calls or texts

If red flags appear, pause trauma processing. Return to stabilization. Address the crisis. Trauma work can resume when client is more stable.

Real Example:

Tasha (composite), severe complex PTSD, borderline features, history of multiple suicide attempts. Previous therapists refused trauma processing due to fragility.

Therapist decided to try Flash with extensive safety protocols:

Pre-treatment: Four sessions building safety plan, grounding skills, crisis resources. Tasha contracted for safety.

Processing sessions: 90 minutes each. Flash one memory per session, reducing SUDS by 2-3 points only (not pushing for full resolution). Spent 20 minutes on closure and grounding.

Between sessions: Therapist sent brief text day after each processing session: "Checking in. How are you doing?" Tasha responded, allowing early identification of problems.

Pacing: Processed one memory every two weeks, alternating with stabilization sessions.

Outcome: Over six months, Tasha processed eight trauma memories. No suicide attempts. No hospitalizations. Self-harm decreased. Functioning improved.

The extensive safety protocols allowed trauma processing for someone everyone thought was "too fragile." Flash's gentleness plus strategic safety planning made it possible.

When to Refer Out

You're not omnipotent. Some clients need higher level of care before Flash is appropriate:

- Active psychosis requiring medication stabilization
- Severe eating disorder with medical instability
- Substance dependence requiring detox

- Imminent risk requiring hospitalization

- Dissociative disorder so severe client can't maintain safety between sessions

Refer to appropriate level of care. Trauma processing can happen later when client is more stable.

Approaching Complex Cases Strategically

Complex developmental trauma requires adapted protocols—Flash triage to reduce overall trauma load across multiple memories, followed by targeted full processing of key traumas. This approach dramatically reduces treatment length compared to processing every trauma individually.

Dissociative disorders need system-aware protocols including preparation with all parts, part-specific Flash processing, co-conscious work when possible, and careful grounding when switching occurs. Flash's gentle structure often allows trauma processing that traditional approaches couldn't accomplish with DID/OSDD clients.

Sequencing strategies for multiple traumas include chronological, reverse chronological, symptom-connected, intensity-based triage, and thematic clustering approaches. Choice depends on number of traumas, client preferences, symptom picture, and stability level.

Fragile clients need enhanced safety protocols—thorough pre-treatment assessment, detailed safety planning, longer sessions with extended closure, lower intensity processing, more frequent grounding checks, between-session contact, and slowed pacing. These adaptations allow trauma processing for clients previously considered too unstable for trauma-focused treatment.

Chapter 14: Children & Adolescents

Adults can sit in your office, understand abstract concepts like "Positive Engaging Focus," and participate in structured protocols. Kids? Not so much.

A seven-year-old doesn't respond well to "On a scale of 0 to 10, how disturbing is this memory?" They don't have the cognitive development for that kind of abstraction. A teenager might roll their eyes at traditional therapy language and refuse to engage if it feels too "therapy-ish."

But trauma doesn't wait for cognitive development. Kids experience trauma—abuse, accidents, medical procedures, witnessing violence, natural disasters. And they need treatment. The research is clear that early intervention for childhood trauma prevents long-term problems (Cohen et al., 2017).

Flash works with kids and teens, but you need to adapt everything—your language, your approach, your PEF development, your entire protocol. This chapter shows you how.

Developmental Considerations

Kids aren't just small adults. Their brains work differently at different ages. Understanding developmental stages is critical for adapting Flash appropriately.

Ages 4-7: Preoperational Stage

Thinking is concrete, literal, and magical. Abstract reasoning is limited. Emotions are big and immediate.

Flash adaptations:

- Use very simple language

- Make everything concrete and visual

- Shorter attention span (10-15 minute Flash segments max)

- Play-based integration

- Parent involvement essential

Ages 8-11: Concrete Operational Stage

Logical thinking about concrete situations. Beginning to understand others' perspectives. More emotional awareness.

Flash adaptations:

- Still concrete but more complex language okay

- Can understand cause and effect

- Longer attention (20-30 minutes)

- Some independence from parents

- Games or activities help engagement

Ages 12-18: Formal Operational Stage

Abstract thinking develops. Identity formation is central. Peer relationships become primary. Independence from parents increases.

Flash adaptations:

- Can handle more abstraction

- Respect autonomy and independence

- Make it "cool," not childish

- Balance parent involvement with privacy

- Address identity and social concerns

Trauma-Related Developmental Delays

Trauma can delay cognitive and emotional development. A 12-year-old trauma survivor might function more like an 8-year-old emotionally. Assess developmental level, not just chronological age, and adapt accordingly.

Age-Appropriate PEF Development

The Positive Engaging Focus is Flash's cornerstone. But "imagine a peaceful beach where you feel calm and relaxed" doesn't work with a six-year-old.

PEF for Young Children (Ages 4-7)

Use concrete, familiar things:

- "Think about your dog Buddy. See him wagging his tail. Feel his soft fur."

- "Think about your favorite toy, the red truck. See it rolling."

- "Think about Mommy hugging you. Feel her arms around you."

Make it sensory and immediate: Kids this age live in their bodies. Sensation works better than abstract imagery.

Keep it very simple: One clear image or sensation. Don't make it complex.

Test thoroughly: Therapist: "Close your eyes. Think about Buddy. Can you see him? What's he doing?"

Child: "He's wagging his tail and licking my face!"

Therapist: "Good! Does thinking about Buddy feel good?"

Child: "Yes!"

That's your PEF.

PEF for Middle Childhood (Ages 8-11)

Use interests and hobbies:

- "Think about playing your favorite video game and getting to the next level."

- "Think about scoring a goal in soccer. See the ball going in, hear your teammates cheering."

- "Think about reading your favorite book. See the pictures, remember the story."

Can be more complex: Kids this age can hold multi-sensory scenarios.

Include achievement and mastery: This age cares about competence. PEFs involving success resonate.

PEF for Adolescents (Ages 12-18)

Respect their preferences: Don't impose your ideas. Ask what they find calming or positive.

Use their language: If they say "chilling with my friends," use that. Don't translate it to therapy-speak.

Consider identity and values:

- "Think about the moment you stood up for your friend. Remember feeling strong and loyal."
- "Think about performing on stage. Remember the confidence and excitement."

Avoid anything they'll find childish: No "safe place" imagery if it feels too young for them.

Real Example:

Seven-year-old: PEF was "my cat Whiskers purring on my lap." Concrete, sensory, familiar.

Ten-year-old: PEF was "playing Minecraft and building my castle." Engaging, achievement-focused.

Fifteen-year-old: PEF was "listening to my favorite song and feeling like myself." Identity-connected, teen-appropriate.

All worked beautifully because they matched developmental level.

Working with Parents and Caregivers

Kids don't come to therapy alone. Parents bring them. And parents' involvement—or lack thereof—significantly affects outcomes.

Parent Psychoeducation

Before Flash with a child, educate parents:

Therapist: "I'm going to use a technique called Flash with [child's name]. It helps reduce the distress from traumatic memories gently. [Child] will focus mostly on something positive—like thinking about [their PEF]—and only briefly think about the trauma. It's usually comfortable for kids."

Explain why you're doing it. What to expect. How to support their child afterward.

Parent as Co-Therapist

For young children (under 8), parents often participate in sessions:

Therapist to parent: "I'd like you to sit here where [child] can see you. Your presence helps them feel safe. If they need grounding during Flash, I might ask you to hold their hand or reassure them."

Parents become safety anchors. Their presence itself can function as part of the PEF.

Managing Parental Anxiety

Parents are often more anxious about trauma processing than kids are. Anxious parents make kids anxious.

Therapist: "I know this might feel scary—working on [child's] trauma. But kids are resilient. And this technique is gentle. [Child] will be okay. Your job is staying calm and trusting the process."

Sometimes you need to process the parent's anxiety before working with the child.

Parent Boundaries

For teens, consider whether parents should be in sessions:

Therapist to teen: "Do you want your mom in the room while we do this, or would you prefer to do it just you and me?"

Respect teen's preference. Balance parent involvement with teen autonomy.

Post-Session Parent Guidance

After Flash with a child, give parents instructions:

Therapist to parent: "After trauma processing, some kids are tired or emotional. Others are energized. Just be available if [child] wants to talk. Don't push them to discuss it. Let them process naturally. Call me if anything concerning comes up."

Clear guidance helps parents support healing.

Real Example:

Six-year-old Emma (composite) witnessed domestic violence. Mother brought her for treatment.

Session 1: Met with mother alone. Explained Flash. Addressed mother's guilt about Emma's exposure to trauma.

Session 2: Met with Emma and mother together. Built rapport. Played. Introduced therapy.

Session 3: Flash processing. Mother sat nearby where Emma could see her. PEF: "Mommy hugging me safe." Flash target: witnessing violence.

During Flash, Emma glanced at mother occasionally for reassurance. Mother's calm presence helped Emma stay grounded.

After Flash, Emma's SUDS dropped from 8 to 3. Mother reported: "She seems lighter. Less clingy."

Three more Flash sessions over six weeks. Emma processed fully. Mother's involvement was essential to success.

School-Based Applications

Schools are where kids spend most of their time. School counselors, social workers, and psychologists see trauma effects daily—behavioral problems, academic decline, social withdrawal. But school-based clinicians often lack time for lengthy trauma treatment.

Flash's brevity makes it practical for school settings.

School-Based Flash Protocols

Assessment: School clinician identifies students with trauma history affecting functioning (academic problems, behavioral issues, emotional dysregulation).

Parent Permission: Get consent for trauma-focused intervention.

Brief Flash Sessions: 20-30 minute sessions during school day. Process one trauma memory per session or use Flash to reduce multiple trauma intensities.

School-Friendly PEFs:

- "Playing at recess with friends"
- "Feeling proud when you got an A on that test"
- "Enjoying art class"

School-connected positive experiences work well.

Minimal Disruption: Flash sessions are short enough to fit in school day without major disruption to classes.

Coordination with Teachers: Brief teachers about student's trauma work (without details). Ask for patience if student seems tired or distracted after sessions.

Real Example:

Middle school counselor had caseload of 15 students with identified trauma—abuse, community violence, family instability. Tried traditional talk therapy but saw limited progress.

Trained in Flash. Implemented school-based protocol:

Selected 8 students with highest need and parent consent.

Provided 4-6 Flash sessions per student over 10 weeks (one 30-minute session every 1-2 weeks).

Outcomes:

- 7 of 8 students showed reduced trauma symptoms
- Teachers reported improved classroom behavior
- Academic performance improved for 5 students
- Students reported feeling better

Total intervention time per student: 2-3 hours. Significant outcomes for minimal time investment.

School-based Flash shows promise for bringing trauma treatment to kids who wouldn't otherwise access it.

Play Therapy Integration

Young children process experiences through play. Combining Flash with play therapy creates developmentally appropriate trauma treatment.

Play-Based Flash Protocol

Phase 1: Play Therapy Engagement

Build relationship through play. Learn child's play themes, preferences, and symbolic language.

Phase 2: Introduce Flash Through Play

Therapist: "We're going to do something to help the scary things feel less scary. First, think about your favorite toy [holds up toy]. This toy is your safe helper. When you think about the scary thing, you can look at your safe helper toy and come right back to feeling okay."

Use toy as concrete PEF.

Phase 3: Flash in Play Context

Therapist: "Hold your safe helper toy. Now, very quickly think about the scary thing—just a tiny bit—and then look right at your helper toy and feel safe again."

Do Flash while child holds or looks at toy. The toy serves as tangible PEF.

Phase 4: Play Processing

After Flash, let child play out any remaining feelings. Play often continues the processing Flash started.

Real Example:

Four-year-old Jayden (composite) witnessed car accident. Too young for verbal trauma processing. Play therapist integrated Flash:

PEF: Favorite stuffed elephant named "Ellie."

Therapist: "Ellie is your safety helper. Hold Ellie. She keeps you safe. Now, when I count to three, think just a tiny bit about the car crash—just a teeny tiny bit—then look right at Ellie and feel safe. Ready? One, two, three... think about it just a tiny bit... now look at Ellie!"

Did this 10 times. Jayden held Ellie tightly, glanced away briefly (toward trauma), then looked back at Ellie and smiled.

After Flash, Jayden played crash scene with toy cars. But this time, he added ambulance toys "saving everyone" and everyone "being okay." Play reflected processing and resolution.

Three Flash-play sessions. Jayden's nightmares stopped. Clingy behavior reduced. Parents reported he seemed "back to his normal self."

Adapting Flash for Younger Clients

Flash with children requires developmental adaptation— concrete language and imagery for younger kids, more complex abstract processing for teens. PEF development must match cognitive stage and use familiar, interest-based, sensory-rich material appropriate to age.

Parent involvement is essential for young children as safety anchors and co-therapists, while teens need balance between parental support and autonomy. Parent psychoeducation and anxiety management significantly affect treatment outcomes.

School-based applications show promise for bringing brief trauma treatment to students who wouldn't otherwise access care. Twenty to thirty-minute Flash sessions can fit within school schedules and produce meaningful symptom reduction with minimal disruption to education.

Play therapy integration allows Flash use with preschool and early elementary-aged children through concrete representation of PEF via safe toys and processing through play themes. This makes trauma treatment developmentally appropriate for very young children who can't engage in verbal processing.

Chapter 15: First Responders & Military Personnel

Police officers, firefighters, paramedics, military service members—they run toward danger when everyone else runs away. That's the job. And the job comes with trauma exposure that civilians rarely experience.

Multiple traumatic incidents, not just one. Dead bodies. Injured children. Violence. Gore. Failed rescues where people die despite your best efforts. Moral injury—situations where you had to make impossible choices, do things that violate your values, or witness atrocities you couldn't prevent (Litz et al., 2009).

Standard therapy often doesn't fit this population well. First responders and military personnel are trained to be tough, mission-focused, and emotionally controlled. Sitting in therapy admitting vulnerability feels wrong. Group settings where they can maintain professional identity work better. And treatment needs to be brief—these are busy people with demanding jobs.

Flash has particular advantages for this population. It's brief. It's low-disclosure (you don't have to describe trauma details, which helps with confidentiality concerns). And it can be done in groups, which fits the team-based culture.

Organizational Trauma Characteristics

First responder and military trauma has specific characteristics that affect treatment.

Cumulative Exposure

Not one trauma—hundreds. A veteran might have dozens of combat incidents. A paramedic might respond to fatal accidents weekly for 20 years. The sheer volume is overwhelming.

Operational Stress

Trauma happens while doing the job. Can't escape it without leaving the career. Plus ongoing stress of shift work, danger, organizational pressure.

Team Culture

Individual weakness threatens team safety. "I can handle this" is the expected response. Admitting struggles feels like failing your team.

Conflicting Values

Job requirements sometimes conflict with personal values. Soldier ordered to fire on ambiguous targets. Police officer using force that results in death. Paramedic deciding which patient gets limited resources. These moral injuries create different symptoms than fear-based trauma (Litz et al., 2009).

Stigma and Career Concerns

Seeking mental health treatment can affect career advancement, security clearances, or job retention. Privacy is paramount.

Flash Advantages for This Population:

Brief: Can be delivered in single-day workshops or short series **Low-disclosure:** Don't need to share operational details with group **Team-based:** Can be done in groups maintaining unit cohesion **Stigma-reduction:** Framed as resilience training, not mental health treatment **Effective:** Reduces symptoms quickly, helping people stay operational

Group Flash Protocols

Individual Flash works great, but group Flash offers unique advantages for first responders and military—efficiency, team support, normalized help-seeking, and cultural fit.

Group Flash Structure

Group Size: 6-15 participants ideal. Larger groups possible but require multiple facilitators.

Session Length: 2-3 hours for initial group Flash session. Can be single session or series.

Protocol:

Phase 1: Introduction and Safety (30 minutes)

Facilitator explains Flash, normalizes trauma responses, establishes group agreements (confidentiality, respect, no judgment).

Facilitator: "Flash helps reduce distress from traumatic incidents you've experienced. You won't need to share details of your incidents with the group. This is about your personal processing while being supported by colleagues who understand the work."

Phase 2: PEF Development (30 minutes)

Each participant develops their own PEF individually. Facilitator guides:

Facilitator: "Think of something positive that works for you. Could be place, person, activity, accomplishment—whatever brings you feelings of calm, strength, or positivity. Take a few minutes to develop this clearly in your mind."

Participants work silently. Facilitator checks in individually as needed.

Phase 3: Target Memory Selection (15 minutes)

Facilitator: "Identify one incident from your work that you'd like to process today. Choose something that still bothers you but isn't the absolute worst thing you've experienced. We're starting with something manageable. You don't need to tell anyone what it is. Just hold it in your mind."

Phase 4: Group Flash Processing (45-60 minutes)

Facilitator: "Everyone bring up your positive focus. Get it clearly in mind. [pause] Now, when I say 'now,' very briefly think about your incident—just a flash—then immediately back to your positive focus. Ready? Focus on positive... now. [1-second pause] Back to positive."

Entire group does simultaneous bilateral stimulation:

- Facilitator leads group eye movements (everyone follows facilitator's hand)

- Or participants do self-administered bilateral tapping

- Or use bilateral audio through headphones

Facilitator: "Check in with yourself. How was that? On a scale of 0-10, how disturbing is your incident?"

Participants note their private SUDS. No sharing yet.

Repeat Flash sequences. After every 4-5 sequences, ask participants to check their SUDS privately.

Continue for 45-60 minutes or until most participants report substantial SUDS reduction.

Phase 5: Integration and Closure (30 minutes)

Facilitator: "Without sharing details of your incident, who's willing to share how their distress level changed?"

Participants share SUDS changes (not incident details).

Participant 1: "Started at 8, down to 3." **Participant 2:** "Started at 9, down to 4." **Participant 3:** "Started at 7, down to 1."

Facilitator: "Good work. You've processed trauma without having to talk about it, while being supported by colleagues who get it. Take that with you."

Ground participants. Answer questions. Provide resources for additional support if needed.

Group Flash Advantages:

Efficiency: Process 10 people in 2-3 hours vs. 10 individual sessions **Normalization:** Everyone sees colleagues also have trauma—reduces stigma **Team cohesion:** Shared healing experience strengthens bonds **Cultural fit:** Team-based intervention matches organizational culture **Scalability:** Can reach more people with limited provider resources

Real Example:

Fire department had high rates of PTSD symptoms, substance use, and relationship problems. Department psychologist organized group Flash session.

Participants: 12 firefighters with 8-25 years experience, all with multiple traumatic exposures.

Session: Three-hour workshop. Each firefighter identified one call that still bothered them (dead child, failed rescue, colleague injury, etc.). Did group Flash for 60 minutes.

Results:

- Average SUDS reduction: 7.2 to 2.8 (pre to post)

- 11 of 12 participants reported significant improvement

- Participants reported "relief" and appreciation for not having to share details

- Department culture shifted slightly—seeking help became more acceptable

Department now offers quarterly group Flash sessions as part of wellness programming.

Moral Injury Considerations

Moral injury is distinct from PTSD. PTSD is fear-based—"I was in danger and I'm not safe." Moral injury is values-based—"I did something (or witnessed something) that violates my moral code" (Litz et al., 2009).

Moral Injury Scenarios:

Perpetration: Did something you believe is wrong

- Soldier killing non-combatants

- Police officer using excessive force

- Medic making triage decisions that let someone die

Betrayal: Leader or institution violated your trust or values

- Ordered to do unethical things

- Cover-ups of wrongdoing

- Lack of support after trauma exposure

Witnessing: Saw atrocities you couldn't prevent

- Civilian casualties

- Abuse of prisoners

- Colleague misconduct

Moral Injury Symptoms:

Not the same as PTSD. Includes:

- Shame and guilt (different from fear)

- Loss of trust in authority

- Spiritual/existential crisis

- Self-condemnation

- Withdrawal from others

- Loss of meaning

Flash for Moral Injury:

Standard Flash protocols work but need adaptation.

Assessment: Identify whether trauma is fear-based (PTSD) or values-based (moral injury). Both might be present.

PEF Adaptation: For moral injury, PEF might include:

- Image of the person you want to be

- Memory of acting according to your values

- Spiritual or meaningful imagery

- Self-compassion visualization

Cognitive Work: Flash reduces emotional intensity, but moral injury also needs cognitive reprocessing of the event:

- "I was in an impossible situation with no good choices"

- "I did the best I could with the information I had"

- "What happened was wrong, but it doesn't make me irredeemably bad"

This cognitive work might happen after Flash or concurrently.

Real Example:

Veteran (composite) felt intense shame about incident where he fired on vehicle approaching checkpoint. Vehicle contained family, not combatants. Children died.

Used Flash to reduce overwhelming shame and horror (SUDS 10 to 5). But after Flash, he still believed "I'm a murderer. I'm evil."

Post-Flash cognitive work:

Therapist: "In that moment, with the information you had, what were you trying to do?"

Veteran: "Protect my unit. The vehicle didn't stop at checkpoint. We'd had vehicle-borne IEDs all week. I thought..."

Therapist: "So your intention was protecting your team, not killing children."

Veteran: "But they died because of me."

Therapist: "Yes. And that's a tragedy you'll carry. But does one terrible outcome in an impossible situation make you evil? Or does it make you a soldier who did what you were trained to do in a war zone and something horrific resulted?"

Over several sessions: Veteran came to accept "What happened was terrible. I grieve those children. But I'm not evil. I was in an impossible situation doing my job."

Flash reduced emotional intensity enough that this cognitive reprocessing could happen. Without Flash, shame was too overwhelming for any cognitive work.

Building Resilience Programs

Instead of waiting for PTSD to develop, some organizations use Flash proactively as resilience training.

Resilience Program Structure

Target Audience: First responders or military personnel early in careers, before severe trauma accumulation.

Timing: During training or first year on job.

Goals:

- Normalize trauma responses
- Teach Flash as self-management tool
- Reduce stigma
- Process minor incidents before they accumulate

Program Components:

Education: Information about trauma, stress, cumulative effects, warning signs.

Skills Training: Stress management, communication, peer support.

Flash Training: Teach basics of Flash so participants can use it independently or in peer support context.

Periodic Processing: Quarterly group Flash sessions to process incidents from past three months.

Ongoing Support: Access to mental health resources without stigma.

Real Example:

Police academy added resilience program to training:

Week 1: Education about occupational trauma, stress, cumulative effects.

Week 2: Skills training—stress management, communication, healthy coping.

Week 3: Flash training. Cadets learned basic protocol, practiced with training scenarios.

Post-Graduation: Quarterly group Flash sessions for first-year officers to process incidents from probationary period.

Results (preliminary data from pilot program):

- Lower PTSD symptom scores at one-year mark compared to previous cohorts

- Higher help-seeking rates (reduced stigma)

- Officers reported feeling "prepared" for trauma exposure

- Reduced sick leave for stress-related issues

Proactive resilience programming using Flash shows promise for preventing PTSD rather than just treating it after development.

Trauma Treatment for Professional Helpers

First responder and military trauma has unique characteristics—cumulative exposure, operational stress, team culture, conflicting values, and career-related stigma. Flash's brevity, low-disclosure format, and group adaptability make it particularly suitable for this population.

Group Flash protocols allow simultaneous processing of 6-15 participants in 2-3 hour sessions, maintaining confidentiality about incident details while providing team-based support. This format fits organizational culture and offers efficiency advantages over individual treatment.

Moral injury requires adaptation beyond standard fear-based trauma protocols. Flash reduces emotional intensity of values-based trauma, but cognitive reprocessing of moral conflict and self-condemnation is also necessary for full resolution. PEF development should include values-consistent imagery.

Resilience programs using Flash proactively during training and early career show promise for preventing PTSD development rather than only treating established symptoms. Quarterly group processing sessions help manage cumulative trauma exposure before severe symptoms develop.

Chapter 16: Group Flash Applications

Trauma doesn't always happen to individuals in isolation. Sometimes entire communities experience trauma together— natural disasters, school shootings, terrorist attacks, war. When hundreds or thousands of people need trauma treatment simultaneously, individual therapy isn't practical. You need interventions that scale.

Group Flash offers exactly that: trauma processing for multiple people at once, with results comparable to individual treatment (Manfield et al., 2017). This chapter covers group applications in disaster response, schools, refugee settings, and the training needed to deliver group Flash safely and effectively.

Group Protocol Modifications

Standard Flash is one therapist with one client. Group Flash is one or more facilitators with multiple participants processing simultaneously. The core principles stay the same, but execution changes.

Key Differences:

Individual Flash:

- Therapist monitors one person's responses closely

- Can adjust instantly to individual needs

- Privacy is complete

- Deep processing possible

Group Flash:

- Facilitator monitors many people simultaneously

- Adjustments help most people but might not fit everyone

- Shared experience with less privacy

- Processing is more standardized

Group Flash Protocol Structure:

Setup Phase (15-20 minutes)

Facilitator: "We're going to do a process called Flash Technique that helps reduce distress from traumatic experiences. You won't need to share details of what happened with the group. This is your private processing in a supported environment."

Explain basics. Answer questions. Establish group agreements (confidentiality, voluntary participation, permission to stop anytime).

PEF Development (20-30 minutes)

Facilitator: "Everyone will develop their own positive focus— something that feels good or peaceful to you. Take a few minutes. Think of a place, person, activity, or memory that makes you feel calm, happy, or safe. Once you have it, spend a minute really imagining it with all your senses."

Participants work individually. Facilitator moves around room checking in quietly with anyone who looks stuck.

Test PEFs: "Close your eyes and focus on your positive image for 30 seconds. Does it feel good? Can you hold it clearly?"

Target Identification (10-15 minutes)

Facilitator: "Identify one specific traumatic memory you want to work on. Not the worst thing that happened, but something that bothers you. You won't share it with anyone—just hold it in your mind."

For group settings after shared trauma (disaster, shooting), participants might be working on the same event but different aspects of it.

Group Flash Processing (40-60 minutes)

Facilitator: "Bring up your positive focus. Hold it clearly. [pause] When I say 'now,' very briefly think about your trauma—just one second—then immediately back to positive. Ready? Positive focus... now. [1-second pause] Back to positive."

Bilateral Stimulation Options for Groups:

Option 1: Facilitator-led eye movements Facilitator moves hand back and forth. All participants follow with eyes. Works for groups up to 15-20 if room is arranged properly.

Option 2: Self-administered tapping Participants tap own knees or hands alternately. Facilitator demonstrates and maintains rhythm verbally. Scales to any group size.

Option 3: Audio bilateral stimulation Participants wear headphones with bilateral audio tones. Requires equipment but allows very large groups.

Option 4: Butterfly hug Participants cross arms and tap own shoulders alternately. Simple, requires no equipment, works for any age.

After 3-5 Flash sequences:

Facilitator: "Check in privately. When you think about your memory, how disturbing is it? Just notice for yourself."

Participants don't share yet. They note internal SUDS.

Continue Flash sequences. Check SUDS every 5-10 minutes. Continue for 40-60 minutes or until most participants show settling (relaxed posture, deeper breathing, less visible distress).

Integration Phase (20-30 minutes)

Facilitator: "Without sharing what your memory was, who's willing to share how your distress level changed?"

Participants share SUDS reductions anonymously:

- "Started at 9, ended at 4"

- "Started at 7, ended at 2"

- "Started at 10, ended at 5"

Normalize varying responses. Some people process faster than others. That's okay.

Facilitator: "Some of you might need additional processing. We'll have information about follow-up resources. But you've done important work today. Take care of yourselves."

Ground participants. Provide resource list. Allow space for questions.

Group Size Considerations:

Small groups (6-12): Facilitator can monitor individuals more closely. More intimate. Better for complex trauma.

Medium groups (15-30): Efficient while maintaining adequate monitoring. Good for organizational settings.

Large groups (30-100+): Requires multiple facilitators. Less individual attention but reaches many people. Appropriate for mass trauma response.

Disaster Response Settings

Natural disasters—hurricanes, earthquakes, floods, tornadoes, wildfires—create widespread trauma. Thousands of people affected simultaneously. Infrastructure damaged. Normal mental health services disrupted.

Flash is well-suited for disaster response because it's:

- Deliverable in temporary settings (schools, community centers, shelters)

- Brief enough for crisis context

- Effective without extensive client history

- Scalable to large numbers

Disaster Response Flash Protocol:

Timeline: 2-4 weeks post-disaster (after immediate crisis, before people disperse)

Setting: Community gathering place (school gym, church, community center)

Recruitment: Community outreach, partnerships with disaster relief organizations, word of mouth

Sessions: Open groups. People attend when they can. Some attend once, others multiple times.

Adaptation: Many participants have multiple traumas (home destroyed, injury, loss, witnessing death). Prioritize most distressing memory for Flash session.

Cultural Sensitivity: Disaster affects diverse communities. Facilitators need cultural competence and language access (interpreters if needed).

Follow-Up: Connect participants to ongoing mental health resources before leaving.

Real Example:

After major hurricane, coastal community had widespread trauma—homes destroyed, deaths, injuries, displacement. Mental health team (including Flash-trained clinicians) deployed.

Week 2-4 Post-Disaster: Offered group Flash at three community centers.

Format: 2-hour open sessions twice daily. Participants attended as able.

Results: Served 180 people across three weeks. Average SUDS reduction: 7.8 to 3.2. Participants reported relief, appreciation for not having to "tell the story," and better functioning in recovery efforts.

Follow-Up: Connected high-need individuals to ongoing therapy. Trained local providers in Flash for continued service.

Flash doesn't solve all disaster-related problems (housing, jobs, medical care still needed), but it addresses trauma symptoms rapidly, helping people function better during recovery.

School Shooting Aftermath

School shootings create trauma for students, staff, families, and entire communities. Everyone needs help, but few can access individual therapy quickly. Group Flash offers immediate intervention.

School Shooting Response Considerations:

Multiple Trauma Types:

- Direct exposure (present during shooting)

- Indirect exposure (heard about it, saw aftermath)

- Vicarious trauma (parents, community members)

Developmental Factors: Elementary kids process differently than high schoolers. Adapt accordingly.

Ongoing Threat Perception: School feels unsafe now. Address this alongside memory processing.

Community Healing: School shootings affect whole communities. Groups help collective healing.

School Shooting Flash Protocol:

Week 1 Post-Incident: Stabilization, crisis intervention, basic safety only. Too soon for trauma processing.

Week 2-4: Begin group Flash with most affected (direct exposure) students/staff. Age-appropriate groups.

Week 4-8: Expand to broader school community. Continue for those who need more sessions.

Setting: Familiar spaces (library, counseling center), not where trauma occurred.

Facilitators: School-based mental health professionals plus outside trauma specialists.

Parent Communication: Inform parents, get permission, provide support resources.

Real Example:

High school experienced shooting. Three students killed, seven injured. Entire school (1,800 students) traumatized.

Crisis Response Team deployed immediately. Provided stabilization, crisis counseling, safety planning.

Week 2: Began group Flash with 30 students who'd been in immediate danger during shooting. Three groups of 10, age-appropriate.

Week 3-4: Expanded to 80+ students who witnessed aftermath or heard shooting. Multiple groups.

Week 5-8: Open groups for any students/staff wanting processing. Attended as needed.

Results:

- 150+ participants total

- Significant SUDS reductions (average 8.1 to 3.4)

- Return to school improved (less avoidance, better attendance)

- Students reported feeling "able to be at school without constant fear"

Ongoing: School maintained trauma-informed practices and counseling access.

Group Flash didn't erase what happened, but it helped students process trauma enough to re-engage with education and life.

Refugee and Humanitarian Contexts

Refugees and displaced persons have complex trauma—war, violence, persecution, displacement, loss. They need trauma treatment but face barriers: language, cultural differences, lack of resources, ongoing instability.

Flash addresses some barriers:

- Low-disclosure format respects privacy and reduces shame

- Can be delivered through interpreters

- Brief enough for unstable situations

- Adaptable across cultures

Refugee Flash Protocols:

Setting: Refugee camps, resettlement centers, community organizations serving refugees.

Facilitators: Mental health professionals plus cultural liaisons and interpreters.

Cultural Adaptation:

- Understand cultural trauma concepts (some cultures view trauma differently)

- Respect religious and cultural healing practices

- Use culturally appropriate PEFs

- Address collective trauma alongside individual trauma

Language Access: Interpreters essential. Train interpreters in Flash basics so they understand what they're translating.

Trauma Selection: Many refugees have dozens of traumas. Use Flash triage approach—reduce intensity across multiple memories.

Safety: Ongoing trauma (still in danger, uncertain status) complicates processing. Assess safety before proceeding.

Real Example:

Resettlement organization served refugees from war-torn country. Most had PTSD symptoms affecting integration. Organization partnered with mental health clinic for Flash intervention.

Participants: 40 refugees, ages 18-65, mixed trauma histories (combat, torture, loss, displacement).

Format: Weekly group Flash sessions over eight weeks. Participants attended as able. Interpreters present.

Cultural Adaptations:

- PEFs included spiritual imagery meaningful in their culture

- Respected gender norms (separate male/female groups)

- Incorporated tea ritual (culturally significant) into closure phase

Results:

- 38 of 40 participants showed SUDS reductions

- Integration outcomes improved (employment, language classes, social connection)

- Participants reported feeling "lighter" and "able to look forward"

Flash isn't culturally neutral—adaptations matter. But core mechanism (brief exposure with protective focus) translates across cultures when implemented respectfully.

Facilitator Training Considerations

Group Flash looks simple but requires skill. You can't just read this chapter and start running disaster response. Facilitators need training.

Facilitator Qualifications:

Minimum:

- Licensed mental health professional (psychologist, LCSW, LMFT, LPC, or equivalent)

- Training in trauma treatment

- Experience with group facilitation

- Flash Technique training (individual Flash first, then group applications)

Preferred:

- EMDR training (Flash originated within EMDR)

- Crisis intervention experience

- Disaster mental health training

- Cultural competence training

Group Flash Training Components:

Didactic (6-8 hours):

- Flash theory and research

- Group adaptations and modifications

- Safety protocols and risk management

- Cultural considerations

- Ethical issues in group trauma work

Demonstration (2-3 hours):

- Watching experienced facilitator conduct group Flash

- Observing different contexts (calm groups, distressed groups, various settings)

Supervised Practice (10-15 hours):

- Co-facilitating groups with experienced facilitator

- Receiving feedback and supervision

- Handling challenging situations with support

Independent Practice with Consultation (Ongoing):

- Leading groups independently

- Regular consultation with experienced facilitators

- Continuing education

Safety and Ethics Training:

Risk Assessment: Identifying participants at high risk (suicidal, psychotic, severe dissociation). Some people aren't appropriate for group Flash.

Crisis Management: What to do if someone becomes severely distressed during group session.

Boundaries: Managing group dynamics, preventing harm, maintaining professional boundaries.

Cultural Competence: Understanding how culture affects trauma, healing, and help-seeking.

Self-Care: Preventing vicarious trauma and burnout in disaster/humanitarian work.

Certification Programs:

Some organizations offer formal group Flash certification. These typically require:

- Completion of training

- Supervised practice hours

- Case documentation

- Demonstrated competence

Certification ensures quality control and protects both clients and facilitators.

Real-World Training Example:

Disaster relief organization wanted to add group Flash to their capabilities. Partnered with trauma training institute.

Training Program:

- **Phase 1:** Online didactic (8 hours) covering Flash theory, research, group protocols

- **Phase 2:** In-person intensive (16 hours over 2 days) with demonstrations and practice

- **Phase 3:** Supervised deployment (facilitators deployed to disaster sites with experienced Flash trainers, co-facilitated groups, received real-time feedback)

- **Phase 4:** Consultation group (monthly calls for ongoing support and problem-solving)

After completing program, organization had 12 certified group Flash facilitators ready for deployment. Next disaster, they were prepared.

Common Training Mistakes to Avoid:

Mistake 1: Thinking group Flash is just like individual Flash with more people. (It's not—group dynamics, monitoring challenges, and ethical considerations differ.)

Mistake 2: Underestimating need for cultural competence. (Culture profoundly affects trauma processing.)

Mistake 3: Skipping supervised practice. (Reading about group Flash isn't enough—you need hands-on experience with feedback.)

Mistake 4: Neglecting self-care training. (Disaster work causes vicarious trauma. Facilitators need protective strategies.)

Mistake 5: Assuming one-size-fits-all. (Different contexts— disaster vs. school vs. refugee camp—require different adaptations.)

Proper training prevents these mistakes and protects both participants and facilitators.

Scaling Flash for Community Trauma

Group Flash protocols modify individual Flash for simultaneous processing by 6-100+ participants. Core elements remain (PEF development, brief flashing, bilateral stimulation) but execution adapts for group format with less individual monitoring and more standardized approach.

Disaster response applications use Flash 2-4 weeks post-disaster in community settings to address widespread trauma rapidly. Brief, scalable format makes Flash practical for mass trauma where individual therapy is unavailable. Results show significant SUDS reductions and improved functioning during recovery.

School shooting aftermath requires developmentally appropriate group Flash beginning week 2 post-incident with phased expansion from most-affected to broader school community. Group format supports collective healing while addressing individual trauma processing needs.

Refugee and humanitarian contexts benefit from Flash's low-disclosure format and cultural adaptability. Language access through interpreters, cultural adaptation of PEFs, and respect for collective trauma alongside individual processing increase effectiveness across diverse populations.

Facilitator training requires minimum qualifications (licensed professional with trauma and group experience), didactic instruction, supervised practice, and ongoing consultation. Certification programs ensure quality control. Common training mistakes include underestimating cultural competence needs and skipping supervised practice requirements.

Chapter 17: Flash in Online Therapy

The COVID-19 pandemic forced therapy online. Overnight, therapists who'd never done a telehealth session had to figure it out. Clients logged in from kitchen tables, bedrooms, parked cars. Everyone adapted because there was no choice.

And something interesting happened: Telehealth worked. Research shows that online therapy produces outcomes comparable to in-person treatment for most conditions, including trauma (Backhaus et al., 2012). Clients liked the convenience. Therapists discovered advantages—access for rural clients, flexibility for busy professionals, reduced no-shows.

Flash translates well to telehealth. You don't need to touch the client. You don't need special equipment. Everything can happen through a screen. But online Flash requires specific adaptations—technology setup, modified bilateral stimulation, remote safety management, and building therapeutic presence despite physical distance.

Technology Requirements and Setup

You can't do good therapy with bad technology. Freezing video, dropped audio, or connection failures disrupt trauma processing and damage therapeutic relationship. Get your tech right.

Internet Connection

Minimum: 10 Mbps download, 5 Mbps upload. Test your connection before sessions using speed test sites.

Better: 25+ Mbps for both. This handles video without lag.

Therapist's Equipment:

Computer: Desktop or laptop (not phone or tablet). Bigger screen allows better observation of client's facial expressions and body language.

Camera: HD webcam minimum (1080p preferred). Built-in laptop cameras work but external webcams are better quality. Position camera at eye level for natural engagement.

Microphone: External USB microphone or quality headset. Built-in laptop mics pick up too much background noise.

Headphones: Use headphones to prevent audio feedback. Over-ear headphones are comfortable for long sessions.

Lighting: Position light source in front of you, not behind. Avoid backlighting that makes your face dark. Ring lights work well.

Background: Neutral, professional background. If you're at home, choose wall or bookshelf background. Virtual backgrounds can be distracting, but they're better than cluttered rooms.

Platform Selection:

HIPAA-Compliant Options:

- Doxy.me (simple, no downloads required)
- SimplePractice Telehealth
- VSee
- Zoom for Healthcare (not regular Zoom)

- Thera-LINK

Features to Check:

- End-to-end encryption

- Business Associate Agreement (BAA) available

- Recording capability (for supervision, with consent)

- Screen sharing (useful for showing bilateral stimulation patterns)

- Waiting room function

Client's Technology:

Can't control client's setup completely, but you can provide guidance.

Pre-Session Tech Check Email:

"For our telehealth session, please ensure you have:

- Stable internet connection

- Computer, tablet, or smartphone (computer preferred)

- Private space where you won't be interrupted

- Headphones or earbuds

- Fully charged device or plugged in

Test your connection 5 minutes early. If you have technical problems, call or text me immediately at [number]."

Backup Communication Plan:

Always have phone contact info. If video fails, you can continue by phone (not ideal for Flash, but better than nothing).

Virtual Bilateral Stimulation Options

In-person Flash uses therapist-led eye movements or tapping. Online requires adaptation.

Option 1: Therapist-Led Eye Movements via Video

Therapist moves finger or pen across camera view. Client follows with eyes.

Setup:

- Position yourself so your hand movements are clearly visible

- Move hand horizontally across screen

- Maintain speed similar to in-person (1-2 complete passes per second)

- Check that client can see movements clearly

Advantages:

- Most similar to in-person EMDR/Flash

- Therapist controls pace

- Maintains eye contact between sets

Disadvantages:

- Video lag can disrupt smoothness

- Small screens make movements harder to follow

- Tiring for therapist's arm

Option 2: Client Self-Administered Tapping

Client taps own thighs, knees, or shoulders alternately.

Instructions:

Therapist: "Place your hands on your thighs. When I say 'start,' tap your thighs alternately—left, right, left, right—like a drum rhythm. I'll keep time verbally. When I say 'stop,' stop tapping. Ready?"

Therapist maintains rhythm verbally: "Left, right, left, right..." or counts: "One, two, three, four..."

Advantages:

- No dependence on video quality
- Client controls own stimulation
- Works on any device
- Can be done eyes closed

Disadvantages:

- Therapist can't see if client is actually doing it
- Client might get rhythm wrong
- Less therapist control

Option 3: Visual Bilateral Stimulation (Animated Dot)

Use online bilateral stimulation tools—websites or apps that display moving dot for client to follow with eyes.

Resources:

- Various free online bilateral stimulation tools (therapists can search for "online bilateral stimulation" to find current options)
- Some EMDR therapy platforms include this feature

Setup:

- Therapist shares screen showing bilateral stimulation
- Client follows dot with eyes
- Therapist controls start/stop

Advantages:

- Smooth, consistent movement
- No therapist arm fatigue
- Professional appearance

Disadvantages:

- Requires screen sharing capability
- Can be distracting if client gets focused on technology
- Less personal connection

Option 4: Audio Bilateral Stimulation

Alternating tones in left and right ears through headphones.

Setup:

- Client must have headphones or earbuds
- Use bilateral audio apps or websites
- Therapist controls duration remotely or client controls with guidance

Advantages:

- Works with any visual setup
- Client can close eyes for deeper processing

- No visual distractions

Disadvantages:

- Therapist can't observe as well with client's eyes closed
- Requires good audio setup
- Some clients find audio tones annoying

Recommendation:

Start with **therapist-led eye movements** if video quality is good. If not, switch to **client self-tapping**. Keep other options as backups for when clients need variety or primary method isn't working.

Test bilateral stimulation in first session before attempting Flash. "Let's practice following my finger" or "Let's practice the tapping." Make sure it works smoothly before adding trauma processing.

Managing Safety Remotely

In-person therapy allows immediate intervention if client becomes distressed. Online therapy removes that option. You can't physically ground a dissociating client or prevent a suicidal client from leaving. Safety planning becomes critical.

Pre-Treatment Safety Assessment

Before doing Flash online, conduct thorough safety assessment:

Questions to Ask:

"Where will you be during our sessions?"

- Need to know physical location in case of emergency

"Who else is in your home?"

- Assess privacy and potential support

"Do you have a safe, private space for trauma processing?"

- Can't do Flash if kids are running around or roommates are listening

"What's your plan if you become very distressed during or after our session?"

- Want client to have thought this through

"Do you have emergency contact numbers programmed in your phone?"

- Crisis hotline, emergency services, trusted person

"Are you willing to sign a telehealth safety agreement?"

- Formalize the safety plan

Telehealth Safety Agreement

Create document client signs before beginning online Flash:

Telehealth Safety Agreement

I understand that telehealth therapy has benefits and limitations. For my safety during trauma processing:

1. I will participate from a safe, private location at [address].

2. I will inform my therapist immediately if my location changes.

3. I will have my phone accessible during sessions for emergency contact.

4. I give permission for my therapist to contact emergency services at my location if they believe I'm in danger.

5. I will contact [crisis number] or 911 if I'm in crisis outside session times.

6. I have identified [support person name/number] as someone who can help if needed.

Client Signature: _____ Date: _____

During-Session Safety Monitoring

Watch for distress signs:

Visual Cues:

- Facial expression (fear, pain, dissociation)
- Body language (holding breath, rigid posture, slumping)
- Crying or visible distress
- Disconnection (blank stare, not responding)

Verbal Cues:

- Voice changes (shaky, childlike, flat)
- Statements of overwhelm
- Dissociative comments ("I'm not here," "This isn't real")
- Suicidal statements

Intervention Protocol:

If client shows severe distress:

Therapist: "I'm stopping the processing. Look at me. You're safe. You're in [location]. Today is [date]. Can you hear me?"

Ground the client verbally. Can't touch them, so use strong verbal grounding.

Therapist: "Tell me five things you can see in your room right now."

Client lists objects.

Therapist: "Good. Now feel your feet on the floor. Press them down. Feel the chair supporting you."

Continue grounding until client is present and stable.

If client doesn't respond to grounding or mentions suicide:

Therapist: "I'm concerned about your safety. I need to know you're okay. Can you tell me you're safe right now?"

If client doesn't respond or indicates they're not safe, you may need to call emergency services to their location (this is why you have their address).

Post-Session Safety Check

After Flash session, assess client's stability before ending:

Therapist: "How are you feeling right now? Are you grounded and stable? Do you feel safe to end our session?"

Don't end session with distressed client. Extend time if needed to ensure stability.

Follow-Up Protocol:

Therapist: "I'm going to check in with you later today. I'll send a text around [time]. Please respond and let me know how you're doing."

Follow through. If client doesn't respond, call. If no response to call, consider wellness check depending on risk level and prior agreement.

Real Example:

Rachel (composite) was doing Flash online for assault trauma. During processing, she began dissociating—stopped responding, eyes glazed over.

Therapist: "Rachel, look at me. You're safe. You're in your apartment. Can you hear me?"

No response.

Therapist: (louder) "Rachel! Stamp your feet on the floor!"

Rachel startled slightly, began responding.

Therapist: "That's it. Stamp your feet. Feel the floor. Look around your room. Tell me what you see."

Rachel: (shakily) "I see... my couch. My TV. My cat."

Therapist: "Yes. You're in your apartment. You're safe. The trauma is not happening now. Keep breathing."

Grounded Rachel fully. Spent 20 extra minutes ensuring stability before ending session. Checked in by text two hours later. Rachel responded that she was okay, just tired.

Incident demonstrated importance of strong verbal grounding skills for online trauma work.

Building Therapeutic Presence Online

Therapy happens in the relationship. Trauma processing requires trust and safety. Building that through a screen is harder than in-person, but possible.

Strategies for Online Presence:

1. Eye Contact Through Camera

Look at camera, not at screen. This creates impression of eye contact for client. Practice this—it feels unnatural at first.

2. Minimize Distractions

Close other programs. Silence phone. Eliminate background noise. Client deserves full attention.

3. Exaggerate Nonverbal Communication

Nod more than you would in person. Use facial expressions more. Video flattens emotional communication, so compensate.

4. Use Client's Name Frequently

Therapist: "Rachel, what are you noticing?" "That makes sense, Rachel." "Rachel, how does that feel?"

Personalizes interaction through screen.

5. Acknowledge Technology Limitations

Therapist: "I wish I could hand you a tissue right now. I can see you're crying and I wish I could be there with you in person."

Acknowledging what's missing validates reality and builds connection.

6. Create Rituals

Begin each session the same way. "How are you today? Are you in a private space?" This creates familiarity and safety.

7. Use Check-Ins More Frequently

Therapist: "I can't see all of your body language through the screen. Help me understand how you're feeling. What are you noticing?"

Compensate for limited information by asking more.

Real Example:

Therapist working online noticed clients seemed less engaged than in-person clients. Realized she was looking at client's image on screen instead of camera. Made conscious shift to look at camera when speaking.

Client feedback improved: "It feels like you're really with me, even though we're on video."

Small change, big impact.

Privacy and Confidentiality Considerations

Online therapy creates new privacy challenges. You're in client's home (virtually). They're in yours. Technology can be hacked. Confidentiality requires intentional protection.

Therapist's Privacy Protection:

Physical Space:

- Conduct sessions in private office or room with door closed

- Use neutral background (no personal photos, identifying information visible)

- Ensure others in your home can't overhear

Digital Security:

- Use HIPAA-compliant platform with BAA

- Strong passwords on all accounts

- Enable two-factor authentication

- Keep software updated

- Use secure Wi-Fi (not public networks)

- Encrypt any recordings or stored video

Recording Sessions:

Only record with explicit client consent. Store recordings securely. Delete after supervision or review unless required for records.

Client's Privacy Support:

Pre-Session Discussion:

Therapist: "For trauma processing, you need a private space where you won't be interrupted or overheard. Where will you be during our sessions? Is it truly private?"

Help client problem-solve privacy issues.

Therapist: "If you're in a shared living situation, can you schedule sessions when others are out? Or use white noise outside your door?"

During Session:

If someone interrupts client during Flash:

Therapist: "I see someone entered your space. Do you need to pause? Is your privacy compromised?"

Stop processing if privacy is lost. Can't do trauma work with audience.

Technology Security Education:

Therapist: "Make sure you're using secure Wi-Fi, not public Wi-Fi. Clear your browser history after sessions if others use your device. Don't join sessions from work devices if confidentiality matters."

Help clients protect their own privacy.

Informed Consent for Telehealth:

Separate consent document covering:

- Technology limitations and risks
- Privacy considerations
- Therapist's and client's responsibilities
- What happens if technology fails
- Jurisdictional issues (if practicing across state lines)

Client signs before beginning telehealth services.

Real Example:

Client was doing Flash session from bedroom. Mid-session, roommate walked in asking about dinner plans. Client froze, clearly uncomfortable.

Therapist: "Let's pause. You can mute yourself and tell your roommate you're busy. Or we can end early today and reschedule when you have better privacy."

Client chose to reschedule. Next session, client had arranged privacy, and Flash went smoothly.

Privacy isn't optional for trauma work. Protect it actively.

Jurisdictional Considerations:

Telehealth allows practice across geographic boundaries, but licensing doesn't. You can only provide services to clients in states where you're licensed.

Check:

- Where client is physically located during sessions
- Your license status in that state

- Interstate compact agreements (some states have reciprocity)

Practicing across state lines without licensure is illegal and unethical.

Bringing Flash Through the Screen

Online Flash requires appropriate technology—stable internet, HD video, quality audio, HIPAA-compliant platforms, and backup communication plans. Computer setups with external cameras and microphones produce better results than tablets or phones.

Virtual bilateral stimulation options include therapist-led eye movements via video, client self-administered tapping, animated visual tools, and audio bilateral stimulation. Client self-tapping proves most reliable across varying technology conditions.

Remote safety management demands pre-treatment assessment, signed telehealth safety agreements including physical address and emergency contacts, during-session monitoring of visual and verbal distress cues, strong verbal grounding protocols, and post-session follow-up checks.

Therapeutic presence online requires deliberate strategies— looking at camera for eye contact impression, exaggerated nonverbal communication, frequent client name use, acknowledging technology limitations, consistent session rituals, and more frequent check-ins to compensate for limited body language visibility.

Privacy and confidentiality protection involves HIPAA-compliant platforms, secure physical spaces, client privacy planning, informed consent for telehealth services, and attention to jurisdictional licensing issues when practicing across state lines.

Chapter 18: Brief Therapy & Single-Session Applications

Most therapy happens over weeks or months. Build relationship, do assessment, stabilize, process trauma, integrate, terminate. That's the standard model. And for complex trauma, it's necessary.

But sometimes you don't have weeks or months. Walk-in clinics see clients once. Crisis services provide immediate intervention. Student health centers have long waitlists. These settings need interventions that work fast—preferably in one session.

Flash fits brief therapy models beautifully. Research shows that even single-session Flash can produce significant symptom reduction (Manfield et al., 2017). This chapter shows you how to deliver Flash in time-limited contexts while maintaining effectiveness and safety.

Walk-In Clinic Protocols

Walk-in clinics (also called single-session services or brief contact clinics) serve clients without appointments. Show up, get seen that day. These clinics increase access for people who can't schedule weeks ahead or who need immediate help.

Clients might be seen only once. Some return, many don't. Your intervention has to be complete in that one meeting.

Walk-In Flash Protocol:

Session Structure (90-120 minutes):

Phase 1: Rapid Assessment (15-20 minutes)

Can't spend three sessions on assessment. Get essential information fast.

Questions:

- "What brought you in today?"

- "What's the main problem you want help with?"

- "Tell me about the trauma or incident that's bothering you most."

- "How is this affecting your life right now?"

- "Are you safe? Any thoughts of hurting yourself or others?"

- "Do you have support? Someone you can call if you need help?"

Screen for contraindications: Active psychosis? Severe substance intoxication? Immediate safety concerns? If yes, refer appropriately. Flash isn't right intervention.

Phase 2: Psychoeducation (10 minutes)

Explain trauma responses and Flash briefly.

Therapist: "When we experience trauma, our brain stores the memory in a way that keeps triggering distress. Flash Technique helps reprocess that memory so it's less disturbing. It's gentle— you'll focus mostly on something positive and only briefly touch the trauma. Studies show it works well, even in single sessions. Want to try?"

Get buy-in. Client needs to understand and consent.

Phase 3: PEF Development (10-15 minutes)

Therapist: "Think of something that feels positive, safe, or calming for you. Could be a place, person, activity, or memory. What comes to mind?"

Develop PEF quickly. Don't overdo it—you don't have time.

Phase 4: Flash Processing (40-50 minutes)

Standard Flash protocol. Reduce SUDS from baseline to 0-2 if possible. If time runs out before full resolution, stop at wherever you are—partial resolution is better than nothing.

Phase 5: Integration and Resource Provision (15-20 minutes)

Ground client. Check stability. Provide resources:

Therapist: "You've done significant work today. The memory should bother you less now. You might continue processing over the next few days—that's normal. Here's information about continued services if you need more support."

Give handout with:

- Crisis numbers
- Community resources
- How to contact clinic again if needed
- What to expect post-processing

Ensure client is stable to leave. Don't send distressed client out your door.

Walk-In Clinic Adaptations:

Triage Appropriately:

Not every walk-in client is appropriate for Flash:

Good candidates:

- Single-incident trauma with clear target

- Moderate complexity

- Able to engage in one session

- Safe to leave after session

Not appropriate:

- Complex trauma requiring extended treatment

- Active crisis requiring immediate intervention

- Severe dissociation or psychosis

- High suicide risk without safety plan

Efficiency Focus:

Move faster than traditional therapy. You're getting essentials, not complete history.

Outcome Tracking:

Measure SUDS pre and post. Track how many clients achieve significant reduction (3+ point SUDS drop). This data demonstrates clinic effectiveness.

Real Example:

Walk-in clinic at university counseling center implemented Flash for trauma clients.

Client: Student experiencing PTSD symptoms after assault six months ago. Couldn't sleep, avoiding campus areas, grades suffering. Wait list for ongoing therapy was 6 weeks.

90-minute walk-in session:

- Assessment: 15 minutes

- Psychoeducation: 10 minutes

- PEF development: 10 minutes

- Flash processing: 45 minutes (SUDS dropped from 9 to 2)

- Integration: 10 minutes

Follow-up (2 weeks later): Student contacted clinic reporting continued improvement. Sleep better. Less avoidance. Felt like she could function while waiting for ongoing therapy spot.

Single session didn't cure PTSD, but it reduced symptoms enough to restore functioning—exactly what walk-in services aim for.

Crisis Intervention Use

Crisis intervention addresses immediate, acute distress. Suicidal ideation. Panic. Acute trauma response. The goal is stabilization, not cure.

Flash can be integrated into crisis intervention for clients with acute trauma responses.

Crisis Flash Protocol:

Assessment:

Is Flash appropriate in crisis?

Yes if:

- Crisis is trauma-triggered (flashbacks, trauma anniversary, trauma reminder)

- Client is stable enough to engage (not actively suicidal, not psychotic)

- Physical safety is secured
- Client has capacity to participate

No if:

- Active suicide plan requiring hospitalization
- Psychosis
- Severe intoxication
- Immediate danger
- Can't engage cognitively

If no, provide appropriate crisis intervention (safety planning, hospitalization, medical care).

If yes, Flash can reduce acute trauma activation.

Brief Crisis Flash (30-45 minutes):

Therapist: "You're experiencing intense trauma symptoms right now. I can help reduce that intensity using Flash Technique. It's quick and it works. Are you willing to try?"

Don't need extensive psychoeducation in crisis. Just enough to get consent.

Rapid PEF development (5 minutes). Use whatever's accessible—breathing, safe place, sensory grounding.

Flash the triggering memory or trauma (20-30 minutes). Goal: Reduce SUDS enough that client is no longer in crisis.

Safety planning (10 minutes). What will client do when they leave? Who can they call? Follow-up plan?

Real Example:

Crisis line received call from veteran experiencing severe flashback triggered by fireworks (July 4th). Veteran was panicking, couldn't calm down, couldn't contact regular therapist.

Crisis counselor (Flash-trained):

Counselor: "I'm going to help you calm this flashback down. We'll use a technique that works fast. Do you have 20-30 minutes to work with me on the phone?"

Veteran: "Yes. I need help. This is bad."

Did Flash over phone using self-tapping bilateral stimulation. Veteran's distress decreased significantly within 20 minutes.

Counselor: "How are you feeling now?"

Veteran: "Better. The flashback stopped. I can think again."

Safety plan: Veteran agreed to call friend, stay safe overnight, contact VA therapist next day.

Flash provided acute crisis stabilization that prevented potential hospitalization or worse.

Single-Session Flash Structure

Even outside walk-in or crisis settings, you might have clients who can only come once—travelers, people with scheduling constraints, people testing whether therapy helps.

Single-session Flash needs to be complete unto itself.

Single-Session Structure (90-120 minutes):

Opening (10 minutes):

Build rapport quickly. Explain session structure.

Therapist: "We have [time] together today. Here's how we'll use it: I'll learn about your situation, we'll work on the trauma using Flash, and we'll make sure you're stable and have resources before you go. Sound good?"

Set realistic expectations.

Therapist: "One session can create significant improvement but might not completely resolve complex trauma. We'll do the best we can with the time we have."

Assessment (15-20 minutes):

Focus on:

- Primary presenting problem

- Specific target memory for Flash

- Current functioning and safety

- Support system

- Readiness for processing

Psychoeducation (10 minutes):

Brief explanation of trauma processing and Flash.

PEF Development (10-15 minutes):

Develop strong PEF. This is your client's anchor—make it solid.

Flash Processing (40-60 minutes):

Process target memory as completely as possible. Push for full resolution if client can handle it.

If SUDS doesn't reach 0-1, that's okay. Any reduction helps.

Integration (15-20 minutes):

Process what happened. Install positive cognition if time allows.

Closure (10 minutes):

Ground thoroughly. Assess stability. Provide resources.

Therapist: "How do you feel about what we did today? How confident are you that you can manage between now and your next session (if there is one) or going forward?"

Don't end session with unstable client.

Follow-Up Planning:

Even single-session clients benefit from follow-up contact:

Therapist: "I'd like to check in with you in a week. Can I call or email you briefly to see how you're doing?"

Many clients appreciate this. Shows you care. Allows early identification of problems.

Real Example:

Client traveling for work needed trauma treatment but would only be in town one week. No time for traditional multi-session therapy.

Scheduled 2-hour single session:

Target: Childhood abuse memory (SUDS 9) **PEF:** Image of client as competent adult professional **Processing:** 60 minutes of Flash, SUDS reduced to 1 **Integration:** Processed feelings about healing, installed positive beliefs **Resources:** Connected client to therapist in home city for follow-up if needed

Follow-up call (1 week later): Client reported sustained improvement. "That memory doesn't bother me like it used to. I can think about my childhood without feeling destroyed."

Single session created meaningful change that persisted.

Follow-Up and Continuity of Care

Brief therapy doesn't mean abandoning clients. Responsible practice includes follow-up and connection to ongoing care when needed.

Follow-Up Protocols:

Option 1: Phone Check-In

Call or text client 3-7 days post-session.

Therapist: "Hi [name], this is [therapist] from [clinic]. I'm checking in on how you're doing after our Flash session. How are you feeling? Is the memory still bothering you less?"

Brief conversation (5-10 minutes). Assess whether client needs additional support.

Option 2: Email Check-In

Send brief email:

"Hi [name],

I wanted to check in on how you're doing after our session last week. How has the trauma memory been? Are you managing okay?

If you need additional support, please contact [number/email]. If you're in crisis, call [crisis line] or 911.

Take care, [Therapist]"

Option 3: Online Survey

Send brief outcome survey measuring:

- Current SUDS

285

- Functioning level
- Need for additional services
- Satisfaction with treatment

Provides data while checking in on client.

Continuity of Care:

Connect clients to ongoing resources:

If client needs more trauma work: Provide referral to trauma therapist for continued processing.

If client needs general therapy: Refer to counseling services for broader mental health support.

If client needs crisis support: Ensure they have crisis hotline numbers, emergency contacts, safety plans.

If client is doing well: Provide psychoeducation about possible future trauma triggers and how to seek help if needed.

Documentation for Continuity:

If referring to another provider, send summary (with client consent):

Client [name] was seen for single-session Flash intervention on [date] for [trauma type]. SUDS reduced from [initial] to [final]. Client reports [outcome].

Recommend [continued trauma processing / support for ongoing symptoms / monitoring for symptom recurrence].

Please contact me with questions.

This helps receiving provider continue care effectively.

Real Example:

Walk-in clinic implemented follow-up protocol:

All clients received:

- Follow-up call at 1 week

- Email with resources at 2 weeks

- Option to return to walk-in clinic anytime

Results:

- 75% of clients reported sustained improvement at 1-week follow-up

- 15% needed additional services and were connected appropriately

- 10% didn't respond to follow-up (attempts made, client choice respected)

- Client satisfaction scores increased with follow-up implementation

Follow-up showed clients that clinic cared and ensured those needing additional help received it.

Flash in Time-Limited Settings

Walk-in clinic protocols structure single 90-120 minute sessions with rapid assessment (15-20 minutes), brief psychoeducation (10 minutes), PEF development (10-15 minutes), Flash processing (40-50 minutes), and integration with resource provision (15-20 minutes). Triage ensures appropriate candidates receive Flash while others get needed crisis intervention or referrals.

Crisis intervention applications use abbreviated Flash protocols (30-45 minutes) when trauma-triggered crises present in stable clients. Flash reduces acute trauma activation enough to resolve immediate crisis, preventing hospitalization or deterioration. Not appropriate for active suicide plans, psychosis, or situations requiring immediate medical intervention.

Single-session Flash structures deliver complete interventions in one meeting for clients unable to attend multiple sessions. While single sessions may not fully resolve complex trauma, meaningful SUDS reductions occur in 40-60 minute processing windows with proper preparation and closure.

Follow-up and continuity protocols include phone or email check-ins 3-7 days post-session, connection to ongoing care resources when needed, and documentation supporting transition to other providers. Even brief interventions benefit from follow-up contact showing concern and ensuring client stability.

Chapter 19: Clinical Decision-Making

You're sitting with a new client. They've experienced trauma. They need help. You know multiple treatment approaches— EMDR, CPT, PE, Flash, traditional talk therapy, medication. How do you decide what to offer?

Clinical decision-making is both art and science. Science provides evidence about what works. Art involves matching intervention to this specific client in this specific moment. No flowchart captures all the complexity, but structured decision-making improves outcomes.

This chapter provides frameworks for deciding when Flash is the right choice, how to get informed consent, what to screen for, and how to track whether it's working.

Assessment Flowcharts

Decision trees help organize complex clinical thinking. Here's a structured approach to deciding whether Flash is appropriate.

Flash Appropriateness Decision Tree:

Step 1: Does client have trauma-related symptoms?

- Yes → Continue to Step 2

- No → Consider other interventions (Flash is trauma-specific)

Step 2: Is trauma primarily:

A. Single-incident or limited number of discrete events?

- Yes → Flash is likely appropriate. Continue to Step 3.

B. Complex/developmental trauma spanning years?

- Yes → Flash can work but may need adaptation (see Chapter 13). Continue to Step 3.

C. Not trauma but other issues (depression, anxiety unrelated to trauma)?

- Flash not indicated. Consider CBT, medication, other approaches.

Step 3: Is client stable enough for trauma processing?

Check for:

- Active suicidal ideation with plan/intent?
- Active psychosis?
- Severe substance dependence requiring detox?
- Current domestic violence without safety?
- Severe dissociation preventing grounding?

If any are present:

- Address stabilization needs first
- Provide crisis intervention, safety planning, or referral
- Revisit Flash after stabilization

If none are present:

- Continue to Step 4

Step 4: Can client engage with Flash format?

Does client have:

- Basic cognitive ability to hold PEF in mind?
- Capacity to provide informed consent?
- Ability to attend sessions (logistically)?

If yes:

- Flash is likely appropriate. Continue to Step 5.

If no:

- Consider adaptations (children, cognitive impairment) or alternative approaches

Step 5: Does client prefer Flash approach?

Explain Flash and alternatives. Ask client preference.

If client prefers Flash:

- Proceed with Flash treatment

If client prefers different approach:

- Honor preference unless clinically contraindicated
- Client autonomy matters for engagement

Real Application:

Client A: Single car accident, nightmares, PTSD symptoms, stable, motivated.

- Decision: Flash appropriate. Proceed.

Client B: Childhood sexual abuse for 10 years, dissociative symptoms, some stability, interested in treatment.

- Decision: Flash possible with adaptations (Chapter 13 protocols). Build more stabilization first, then careful Flash implementation.

Client C: Depression and anxiety unrelated to trauma events. No trauma history.

- Decision: Flash not indicated. Recommend CBT or medication evaluation.

Client D: Recent assault, active suicidal ideation with plan.

- Decision: Flash not appropriate yet. Crisis intervention, safety planning, possible hospitalization. Revisit Flash after stabilization.

When to Use Flash vs. Other Approaches

Flash isn't always the best choice. Other trauma treatments have advantages in certain situations.

Flash Advantages:

- Gentle, low-distress processing
- Rapid results (often in 1-3 sessions)
- Low dropout rates
- Works with highly avoidant clients
- Minimal disclosure required
- Can be done in groups
- Accessible for fragile clients

When Flash is First Choice:

Scenario 1: Client with high baseline SUDS (9-10) who can't tolerate exposure-based treatments **Why Flash:** Reduces intensity without overwhelming client

Scenario 2: Client with limited time (traveling, military deploying, schedule constraints) **Why Flash:** Works in fewer sessions than traditional trauma therapy

Scenario 3: Highly avoidant client who won't engage with exposure therapy **Why Flash:** Less threatening, bypasses avoidance

Scenario 4: Client with confidentiality concerns (law enforcement, military, high-profile professionals) **Why Flash:** Minimal disclosure protects privacy

Scenario 5: Large group needing trauma intervention (disaster, school shooting) **Why Flash:** Scalable to group formats

When Other Approaches May Be Better:

Cognitive Processing Therapy (CPT):

Better when: Client has strong maladaptive beliefs about trauma needing cognitive restructuring. Flash reduces distress but CPT specifically targets beliefs.

Prolonged Exposure (PE):

Better when: Client needs habituation through repeated, prolonged engagement. PE research base is extensive for PTSD.

Standard EMDR:

Better when: Client can tolerate standard processing and prefers fully processing memories with all associated material. EMDR allows deeper exploration of networks.

Psychodynamic Therapy:

Better when: Client wants insight into patterns, defense mechanisms, relationship dynamics stemming from trauma. Flash doesn't provide this depth.

Medication:

Better when: Symptoms are so severe that psychotherapy alone is insufficient. Consider medication consultation alongside Flash.

Integrative Approach:

Often, best practice combines approaches:

- Flash to reduce intensity → then CPT for cognitive work

- Flash for preparation → then standard EMDR for deeper processing

- Flash for trauma memories → plus DBT skills for emotion regulation

- Flash for single trauma → plus medication for severe PTSD symptoms

Don't think either/or. Think both/and.

Real Example:

Client with combat PTSD presented wanting "the fastest treatment possible" (deploying again in six months).

Therapist considered:

- PE: Evidence-based but requires 8-15 sessions

- CPT: Also 12 sessions typically

- Flash: Could achieve significant improvement in 3-5 sessions

Decision: Flash for rapid SUDS reduction on worst memories, then brief CPT for moral injury cognitive work. Client completed treatment in 8 sessions total—hybrid approach faster than either alone and addressed both distress and beliefs.

Informed Consent Templates

Informed consent isn't just signing paperwork. It's ensuring client understands treatment, risks, benefits, and alternatives. Ethical practice requires genuine informed consent.

Flash Informed Consent Components:

1. Description of Flash:

Flash Technique is a trauma processing method where you briefly think about traumatic memories while maintaining focus primarily on positive material. This reduces the emotional intensity of trauma memories. Flash was developed as a gentler alternative to standard trauma processing.

2. What to Expect:

During Flash, I will ask you to develop a positive focus (safe place, pleasant memory, or calming image). Then you'll briefly "flash" to your traumatic memory while keeping most attention on the positive focus. We'll repeat this process with bilateral stimulation (eye movements, tapping, or tones). Sessions typically last 60-90 minutes. Most people find Flash comfortable and report reduced distress within 1-3 sessions.

3. Potential Benefits:

Research shows Flash can significantly reduce trauma-related distress. Benefits may include:

- Decreased PTSD symptoms

- Reduced anxiety and depression related to trauma

- Improved functioning in daily life

- Better sleep and fewer nightmares

- Increased ability to think about trauma without overwhelming distress

4. Potential Risks:

While Flash is designed to be gentle, trauma processing can involve:

- Temporary increase in distress during or after sessions

- Emotional or physical sensations as memories are processed

- Dreams or thoughts about trauma between sessions

- Fatigue after sessions

Serious adverse effects are rare but could include: severe emotional distress, dissociation, or worsening symptoms. If this occurs, we will stop processing and address your safety.

5. Alternatives:

Other trauma treatment options include:

- EMDR (Eye Movement Desensitization and Reprocessing)

- Cognitive Processing Therapy (CPT)

- Prolonged Exposure (PE)

- Traditional talk therapy

- Medication

I recommend Flash because [therapist explains reasoning]. However, you have the right to choose a different approach.

6. Confidentiality:

Information shared in therapy is confidential except when: (1) you provide written consent to release information, (2) there's danger to yourself or others, (3) there's suspected child or elder abuse, or (4) court order requires disclosure.

7. Right to Refuse or Discontinue:

You may decline Flash treatment or stop at any time without penalty. Your care will continue with alternative approaches if you choose to discontinue Flash.

Client Signature:

I have read and understood the above information. I have had opportunity to ask questions. I consent to Flash Technique treatment.

Client: _____ Date: _____ Therapist: _____ Date: _____

Consent Discussion:

Don't just hand client the form. Discuss it.

Therapist: "I want to explain Flash and make sure you understand what we'll be doing. Flash involves briefly thinking about your trauma while focusing mostly on something positive. The research shows it reduces trauma distress effectively. Have you heard of this approach before?"

Answer questions. Assess comprehension.

Therapist: "What questions do you have? What concerns?"

Address concerns honestly.

Therapist: "Are you comfortable proceeding with Flash, or would you prefer to discuss other treatment options?"

Genuine choice, not coercion.

Screening for Contraindications

Not everyone should receive Flash. Some conditions make Flash inappropriate or require precautions.

Absolute Contraindications (Don't Do Flash):

1. Active Psychosis

Delusions, hallucinations, disorganized thinking. Trauma processing requires reality testing that psychotic individuals lack.

Action: Refer for psychiatric evaluation and stabilization. Trauma work can occur after psychosis is treated.

2. Acute Intoxication

Under the influence of substances during session. Can't provide informed consent. Can't process meaningfully.

Action: Reschedule when sober. Consider addressing substance use before trauma work.

3. Imminent Danger to Self or Others

Active suicide plan with intent. Homicidal ideation with plan.

Action: Crisis intervention, hospitalization if needed. Flash is not appropriate when safety isn't secured.

Relative Contraindications (Proceed with Caution or Not at All):

1. Severe Dissociative Disorders Without Adequate System Cooperation

DID/OSDD where protector parts are adamantly refusing trauma work.

Caution: If parts won't cooperate, Flash can trigger severe dissociation or system conflict. Need extensive preparation (Chapter 13).

2. Neurological Conditions Affecting Memory or Cognition

Dementia, traumatic brain injury, severe intellectual disability.

Caution: Flash requires cognitive capacity to hold PEF, track memories, engage in process. Adaptations may be possible but not always.

3. Severe Substance Dependence

Active addiction requiring detox or intensive treatment.

Caution: Processing trauma can trigger substance use escalation if addiction isn't addressed. Consider stabilizing substance use first.

4. Current Domestic Violence

Still living with or in contact with abuser. Trauma processing might destabilize without safety.

Caution: Prioritize safety planning. May need to delay trauma processing until safety is established.

5. Recent Hospitalization for Psychiatric Crisis

Just discharged from inpatient unit.

Caution: Give time for stabilization before trauma processing. Usually wait 2-4 weeks post-discharge unless treatment team recommends otherwise.

Screening Questions:

Ask during initial assessment:

"Are you currently experiencing any hallucinations or delusions?" "Have you used alcohol or drugs today?" "Are you having thoughts of hurting yourself or others?" "Have you been hospitalized for mental health reasons recently?" "Do you have any memory or cognitive problems?" "Are you currently in a safe living situation?"

Real Example:

Client presented requesting Flash for childhood trauma. During assessment, disclosed recent psychiatric hospitalization (3 weeks ago) for suicidal crisis, ongoing suicidal ideation (passive but present), and returning to abusive partner.

Therapist's Decision: Flash contraindicated currently. Instead:

- Safety planning for domestic violence

- Crisis intervention for suicide risk

- Connection to domestic violence resources

- Stabilization therapy

Plan: Revisit Flash after client achieves safety and stability (estimated 3-6 months with intensive support).

Measuring and Tracking Outcomes

You need to know if Flash is working. Clinical impression matters, but data matters more.

Outcome Measures:

1. SUDS (Subjective Units of Disturbance Scale)

Baseline: Before Flash processing **During:** Every 5-10 minutes during Flash **Post:** End of Flash processing **Follow-up:** 1 week, 1 month, 3 months later

Track: Is SUDS decreasing? Does reduction maintain over time?

2. PTSD Symptom Measures

PCL-5 (PTSD Checklist for DSM-5):

- 20 items

- Measures PTSD symptom severity

- Administer before treatment, mid-treatment, post-treatment

- Score <31 suggests subclinical PTSD

CAPS-5 (Clinician-Administered PTSD Scale):

- Structured interview

- Gold standard for PTSD diagnosis

- More time-intensive but highly reliable

3. Functional Impairment Measures

Work and Social Adjustment Scale:

- Measures impairment in work, home, social, private leisure, family relationships

- Brief (5 items)

4. Depression and Anxiety Measures

PHQ-9 (depression): 9 items, widely used **GAD-7 (anxiety):** 7 items, quick screening

Trauma often co-occurs with depression and anxiety. Track these alongside PTSD symptoms.

5. Client Satisfaction

Simple questions:

- "How satisfied are you with Flash treatment?" (0-10 scale)

- "Would you recommend Flash to others with trauma?"

- "What was most helpful? What was least helpful?"

Tracking Protocol:

Session 1:

- Baseline SUDS for target memory

- Baseline PCL-5

- Baseline PHQ-9 and GAD-7

Each Flash Session:

- SUDS before and after Flash processing

- Note: number of Flash sequences, SUDS trajectory

Mid-Treatment (after 3-4 sessions or halfway through):

- PCL-5

- PHQ-9 and GAD-7

- Functional impairment measure

Post-Treatment:

- Final SUDS for all processed memories

- PCL-5

- PHQ-9 and GAD-7

- Functional impairment measure

- Client satisfaction

Follow-Up (1 month, 3 months):

- PCL-5

- Brief check-in about functioning and symptom maintenance

Using Data for Clinical Decisions:

If SUDS isn't decreasing after 3-4 Flash sessions:

- Reassess whether Flash is right approach

- Check for blocking beliefs or complicating factors

- Consider switching to different trauma processing method

If PCL-5 improves but functional impairment doesn't:

- Trauma symptoms reduced but client needs additional support for functioning

- Consider adjunctive therapy (vocational, social skills, etc.)

If SUDS decreases during session but returns to baseline between sessions:

- Processing isn't consolidating

- May need more sessions, different approach, or address maintaining factors

Data informs clinical decisions. Track it. Use it.

Real Example:

Clinic implemented outcome tracking for all Flash clients:

Results over 6 months (50 clients):

- Average SUDS reduction: 7.8 to 2.1

- 72% achieved clinically significant PTSD symptom reduction (PCL-5 drop of 10+ points)

- 18% showed minimal improvement (switched to different treatment)

- 10% dropped out before completion

This data helped clinic:

- Demonstrate effectiveness to funders

- Identify which clients benefited most (informing referral decisions)

- Recognize when to switch approaches (the 18% who didn't respond)

Tracking outcomes improves practice systematically.

Structured Clinical Thinking

Assessment flowcharts organize decision-making from initial trauma identification through stability screening and client preference assessment. Decision trees help determine when Flash is appropriate versus when stabilization, crisis intervention, or alternative treatments better serve client needs.

Comparing Flash to other approaches involves matching intervention advantages to client circumstances—Flash offers gentleness and speed while CPT provides cognitive restructuring, PE offers habituation, and standard EMDR allows deeper network processing. Integrative approaches combining methods often produce optimal outcomes.

Informed consent requires thorough written templates covering Flash description, expected experiences, potential benefits and risks, treatment alternatives, confidentiality parameters, and client rights. Discussion accompanying paperwork ensures genuine comprehension and voluntary agreement.

Screening for contraindications identifies absolute barriers (active psychosis, intoxication, imminent danger) and relative concerns (severe dissociation, neurological conditions, active addiction, domestic violence, recent hospitalization) requiring caution or delay. Assessment questions during initial evaluation detect contraindications early.

Measuring and tracking outcomes through SUDS ratings, standardized PTSD measures, functional impairment scales, and client satisfaction surveys provides data informing clinical decisions. Regular assessment identifies when Flash is working, when to switch approaches, and demonstrates effectiveness to stakeholders.

Chapter 20: Ethical & Legal Considerations

Therapy exists within legal and ethical frameworks. You can't just do whatever works clinically—you need to practice within professional boundaries, follow laws, maintain ethical standards, and protect yourself legally.

Flash is still relatively new. Not every state licensing board has explicit guidance about it. Some insurance companies haven't heard of it. Some supervisors question whether it's within scope of practice. You need to understand the ethical and legal landscape to practice Flash responsibly and safely.

Scope of Practice Boundaries

Scope of practice defines what you're legally allowed to do based on your license and training. Practice outside your scope and you risk disciplinary action, lawsuits, and harm to clients.

What Determines Scope?

1. License Type

Psychologists, LCSWs, LMFTs, LPCs, psychiatrists—each license has defined scope determined by state law and licensing board regulations.

Check: Your state licensing board website describes your scope of practice explicitly. Read it.

2. Education and Training

Your degree program taught certain skills. If you weren't trained in it, you generally can't practice it without additional training.

Example: If your master's program didn't include trauma-focused training, you might need continuing education before offering trauma treatment.

3. Continuing Education and Specialized Training

Additional training extends scope. Flash training allows you to use Flash (obviously). But you still need foundation in trauma treatment.

4. Competence

Ethics codes require practicing only within areas of competence. Even if something is technically within your license's scope, if you're not competent in it, you shouldn't do it.

Is Flash Within Your Scope?

Generally yes if:

- You're licensed to provide psychotherapy

- You have training in trauma treatment

- You've received specific Flash training

- You have consultation/supervision available

Questionable if:

- You're not licensed for independent practice

- You have no trauma treatment background

- You only read about Flash without training

- Your license explicitly prohibits certain interventions Flash involves

Specific Scope Questions:

Can I practice Flash if I'm not EMDR-trained?

Yes. Flash originated within EMDR but doesn't require EMDR certification. However, you still need trauma treatment competence.

Can I use Flash with children if my license allows it?

Yes, if you have training in child therapy plus Flash training adapted for children.

Can I do group Flash if I'm only trained in individual therapy?

You need group therapy competence plus group Flash training. One doesn't substitute for the other.

Can unlicensed therapists use Flash under supervision?

Depends on state law. Generally, unlicensed therapists can practice interventions under licensed supervision if it's within scope of their training level.

Ethical Principle: Do No Harm

If you're unsure whether Flash is within your scope, err on side of caution. Refer to someone with appropriate training rather than attempting intervention beyond your competence.

Real Example:

Licensed professional counselor (LPC) completed Flash training workshop. Her practice primarily involved career counseling and mild anxiety. She received referral for complex PTSD with dissociation.

Question: Is treating this client within scope?

Analysis:

- LPC license generally allows trauma treatment (check state law)

- Flash training completed (yes)

- BUT: Limited trauma experience, no dissociation training, complex case

Decision: Outside competence level despite being within license scope. Referred to trauma specialist. Ethical choice.

Training Requirements and Competency

How much training do you need before using Flash? There's no universal answer, but there are guidelines.

Minimum Training for Flash:

Foundation (Required):

- Licensed mental health professional OR working under supervision toward licensure

- Training in trauma theory and trauma responses

- Understanding of trauma treatment approaches

- Basic psychotherapy skills

Flash-Specific Training (Required):

- Formal Flash workshop or training (8-16 hours minimum)

- Covers theory, research, protocols, safety, ethics

- Practice with supervision or consultation

- Continuing education credits from recognized provider

Additional Training (Strongly Recommended):

- EMDR training (Flash originated here; understanding context helps)

- Training in specific populations you'll serve (children, dissociation, etc.)

- Group therapy training if doing group Flash

- Telehealth training if offering online Flash

Competency Development Pathway:

Phase 1: Knowledge Acquisition

Attend Flash training. Read research. Understand theory and protocols.

Phase 2: Supervised Practice

Practice Flash with supervision:

- Start with simpler cases (single-incident trauma, stable clients)

- Present cases to supervisor or consultation group

- Receive feedback and guidance

- Document supervised hours

Phase 3: Independent Practice with Consultation

Practice independently but with consultation available:

- More complex cases

- Regular consultation group participation

- Continue learning and skill refinement

Phase 4: Advanced Practice

After substantial experience:

- Complex cases

- Training others

- Contributing to research or protocol development

How Many Cases Before Competent?

No magic number, but:

- 5-10 cases under supervision builds basic competency

- 20-30 cases develops solid skill

- 50+ cases with diverse presentations creates expertise

Competency Assessment:

How do you know you're competent?

Self-Assessment:

- Can you explain Flash to clients clearly?

- Can you develop effective PEFs?

- Can you manage distressed clients during Flash?

- Can you handle complications (blocking, dissociation, etc.)?

- Do you track outcomes and adjust approach?

External Validation:

- Positive client outcomes

- Supervisor/consultant feedback

- Peer review

- Client satisfaction reports

Continuing Competence:

Competence isn't permanent. Maintain it through:

- Ongoing consultation
- Continuing education
- Reading research updates
- Practicing regularly

Real Example:

Therapist completed 2-day Flash training workshop (12 hours). Felt excited and ready to start immediately with all trauma clients.

Supervisor's guidance: "Training is first step. Start with straightforward cases. Present them to me weekly. After 10 supervised cases, we'll discuss independent practice."

Therapist followed guidance. By case 10, felt genuinely competent with basic Flash. After 25 cases, felt confident handling complications. After 50 cases, trained other clinicians.

Gradual competency development prevented harm and built solid skills.

Documentation Standards

Documentation serves multiple purposes—clinical record, legal protection, communication with other providers, insurance billing. Flash documentation needs to capture what you did and why.

Essential Documentation Elements:

1. Informed Consent Documentation

Note that informed consent was obtained:

"Informed consent for Flash Technique treatment obtained [date]. Client demonstrated understanding of procedure, risks, benefits, and alternatives. Questions answered. Client chose Flash treatment voluntarily. Signed consent form in file."

2. Assessment and Treatment Planning

Document why Flash was selected:

"Client presents with PTSD symptoms following [trauma type]. Baseline SUDS 9/10. Client reports high avoidance. Flash Technique selected due to gentler approach and client's preference for minimal disclosure. Treatment plan: 4-6 sessions Flash processing of primary trauma memory, with reassessment of symptoms and functioning."

3. Session Notes

Each Flash session should document:

Date and duration

Target memory worked on (general description, not full details):

"Processed memory related to motor vehicle accident 8/2022"

PEF used:

"PEF: Client's safe place (beach imagery)"

Process:

"Completed 15 Flash sequences using bilateral tapping. Client remained grounded throughout. No dissociation or severe distress observed."

SUDS ratings:

"Baseline SUDS: 8. Post-processing SUDS: 3. Reduction of 5 points."

Client response:

"Client reported feeling 'lighter' and 'surprised it wasn't as hard as expected.' Denied suicidal ideation. Safety planning reviewed."

Plan:

"Continue Flash processing next session targeting remaining distress in this memory. Client to monitor symptoms between sessions and contact if distress escalates."

4. Outcomes and Progress

Document changes over time:

"Client has completed 4 Flash sessions. PTSD symptoms (PCL-5) reduced from 52 (severe) to 28 (mild). Reports improved sleep, reduced nightmares, and better functioning at work. Client and therapist agree treatment goals substantially met. Discussed transition to less frequent maintenance sessions."

5. Any Adverse Events or Complications

If problems occur, document thoroughly:

"During Flash processing, client experienced brief dissociative episode (approx. 2 minutes). Stopped processing immediately. Grounded client using [techniques]. Client returned to present, confirmed safety. Discussed slowing pace of future processing. Client agreed. No ongoing dissociation at session end."

6. Consultation or Supervision

If you consulted about case:

"Consulted with [supervisor name] regarding client's slow progress in Flash. Discussed possibility of blocking belief. Plan to explore cognitive factors next session before continuing Flash processing."

Documentation Mistakes to Avoid:

Mistake 1: Too much detail about trauma

Don't: "Client described in detail how perpetrator sexually assaulted her, including [graphic details]..."

Do: "Client processed memory related to sexual assault in childhood."

Rationale: Notes can be subpoenaed. Excessive detail breaches client privacy and serves no clinical purpose.

Mistake 2: Insufficient detail about intervention

Don't: "Did Flash. Client improved."

Do: "Flash processing completed with bilateral tapping. SUDS reduced from 8 to 2 over 12 Flash sequences. Client tolerated process well."

Rationale: Need to show what you did and that it was clinically appropriate.

Mistake 3: Not documenting client's response

Don't: "Completed Flash."

Do: "Client reported relief after Flash. Denied distress, suicidal ideation, or dissociation. Stable to leave session."

Rationale: Demonstrates you monitored safety and client left session stable.

Mistake 4: Copying previous session notes

Each session is unique. Don't copy/paste. Document what actually happened that session.

Rationale: Repetitive notes suggest you're not actually doing individualized treatment.

Electronic Health Records (EHR) Considerations:

Many settings use EHR systems with templates. Ensure your template captures Flash-specific elements.

Consider adding:

- SUDS rating fields (baseline, post, follow-up)
- PEF description field
- Bilateral stimulation type field
- Trauma processing-specific safety checklist

Retention Requirements:

Keep records according to state law and ethics codes. Typically 7 years after last contact (or longer for minors).

Insurance and Billing Codes

Flash is a therapeutic technique, not a separate billable service. You bill for psychotherapy using standard codes.

CPT Codes for Flash:

90834: Psychotherapy, 45 minutes **90837:** Psychotherapy, 60 minutes **90846:** Family psychotherapy without patient, 50 minutes (if doing Flash consultation with family) **90847:** Family psychotherapy with patient, 50 minutes **90853:** Group psychotherapy (for group Flash)

Diagnosis Codes:

Use appropriate ICD-10 codes for client's diagnosis:

PTSD: F43.10 (Post-traumatic stress disorder, unspecified) **Acute Stress Disorder:** F43.0 **Adjustment Disorder:** F43.20-F43.25 (various types) **Other trauma-related codes** as appropriate

Documentation for Insurance:

When seeking authorization or justifying treatment:

Description: "Evidence-based trauma processing using Flash Technique, a variant of EMDR protocols. Research supports effectiveness for reducing PTSD symptoms."

Medical Necessity: "Client meets criteria for PTSD. Symptoms significantly impair functioning in [areas]. Flash treatment is clinically appropriate and expected to produce symptom reduction."

Treatment Plan: "Estimated 4-6 sessions of Flash processing for trauma-related symptoms, with outcome monitoring."

Insurance Issues:

Some insurance companies may question Flash because:

- It's newer (less familiar to reviewers)
- It's brief (some expect longer treatment)
- Documentation might not clearly explain it

Solutions:

Educate insurance reviewer: Provide research citations supporting Flash effectiveness. Explain it's trauma-focused psychotherapy, evidence-based.

Document clearly: Show medical necessity, treatment plan, and outcomes. Justify why Flash is appropriate.

Appeal denials: If coverage denied, appeal with research support and clinical rationale.

Private Pay Option:

Some therapists offer Flash as private pay service, avoiding insurance complications. This is legitimate if:

- Client chooses it voluntarily

- Fees are reasonable

- Client is informed about potential insurance coverage

Real Example:

Therapist submitted authorization request for Flash treatment. Insurance denied, stating "Flash Technique is experimental and not covered."

Therapist appealed with:

- Research articles (Manfield et al., 2017)

- Explanation that Flash is trauma-focused psychotherapy

- Treatment plan showing medical necessity

- Comparison to EMDR (which insurance covered)

Appeal successful. Insurance approved 8 sessions with review.

Lesson: Be prepared to educate insurance companies about Flash.

Risk Management

Practicing therapy involves risk—malpractice lawsuits, licensing complaints, client harm. Risk management minimizes these risks while providing good care.

Major Risk Areas:

1. Inadequate Informed Consent

Risk: Client claims they didn't understand treatment or weren't informed of risks.

Protection:

- Thorough written consent
- Discussion demonstrating understanding
- Document consent process

2. Practicing Beyond Competence

Risk: Harm from attempting interventions you're not trained for. Licensing complaint or lawsuit.

Protection:

- Practice only within training and competence
- Seek supervision when uncertain
- Refer complex cases beyond skill level

3. Inadequate Safety Assessment

Risk: Client suicide or self-harm. Claim that therapist didn't assess risk properly.

Protection:

- Thorough safety assessment documented
- Safety planning for at-risk clients

- Consultation on high-risk cases
- Clear documentation of risk assessment and interventions

4. Boundary Violations

Risk: Dual relationships, sexual contact, financial exploitation. License revocation, lawsuit.

Protection:

- Maintain professional boundaries strictly
- No social media contact with clients
- No personal relationships with clients
- Careful with gifts, touch, self-disclosure

5. Breach of Confidentiality

Risk: Unauthorized disclosure of client information. HIPAA violation, lawsuit.

Protection:

- Secure records (physical and electronic)
- Obtain consent before any disclosures
- HIPAA-compliant technology for telehealth
- Staff training on confidentiality

6. Abandonment

Risk: Terminating client abruptly without appropriate referral or support.

Protection:

- Provide reasonable notice if terminating

- Offer appropriate referrals

- Don't terminate clients in crisis without safety plan

- Document termination process

Flash-Specific Risk Issues:

Processing without adequate stabilization:

Don't rush into trauma processing with unstable clients. Document that you assessed stability and deemed client ready.

Failing to manage safety in telehealth:

For online Flash, have client's location, emergency contacts, safety plan. Document this.

Using Flash beyond competence:

Don't treat complex dissociative disorders if you're not trained in dissociation. Document training, supervision, or reason for referral.

Professional Liability Insurance:

Carry malpractice insurance. It protects you financially if sued. Typical coverage: 1-2 million dollars per occurrence.

Check: Does your policy cover trauma-focused therapy? Some policies exclude certain treatments. Verify Flash is covered.

When to Consult Attorney:

- If you receive licensing board complaint

- If client threatens lawsuit

- If you're subpoenaed for records or testimony

- If you're unsure about legal obligations in complex situation

Don't go it alone. Legal situations require legal expertise.

Real Example:

Therapist working with suicidal client. Conducted Flash session. Between sessions, client attempted suicide (survived).

Legal review:

Therapist's documentation showed:

- Thorough safety assessment before Flash
- Safety planning discussed and documented
- Client denied suicidal intent at session end
- Follow-up plan established
- Client had 24-hour crisis number

Outcome: No licensing complaint filed. Insurance company reviewed case, found therapist practiced within standard of care. Documentation protected therapist.

Lesson: Good documentation is your best risk management tool.

Practicing Within Professional Frameworks

Scope of practice boundaries are defined by license type, education and training, continuing education, and demonstrated competence. Flash falls within scope for licensed trauma therapists with appropriate training but requires consultation or referral for complex presentations beyond individual competence.

Training requirements include foundational trauma treatment education, formal Flash-specific workshops (minimum 8-16 hours), and supervised practice progressing from simple to complex cases. Competency develops through gradual experience under supervision with ongoing consultation and continuing education.

Documentation standards require informed consent notation, treatment rationale explaining why Flash was selected, session notes capturing PEF used, SUDS ratings, process description, client response, and outcome tracking. Avoid excessive trauma detail while documenting sufficient clinical information for legal protection.

Insurance billing uses standard psychotherapy codes (90834, 90837) with appropriate trauma diagnosis codes. Some insurers require education about Flash's evidence base, making clear documentation of medical necessity and research support essential for authorization and appeals.

Risk management involves obtaining adequate informed consent, practicing only within competence, thorough safety assessment, maintaining professional boundaries, protecting confidentiality, and carrying professional liability insurance. Documentation serves as primary protection against legal and ethical complaints.

Chapter 21: Building Your Flash Practice

You've trained in Flash. You understand the protocols. You're competent. Now what? How do you actually build a practice using Flash? How do you get clients who need it? How do you explain it to referral sources? How do you continue developing expertise?

Building a Flash practice isn't just clinical skill—it's also professional development, marketing (the ethical kind), relationship-building with referral sources, ongoing learning, and contributing to the field.

Marketing Ethically to Clients

Mental health marketing walks a fine line. You need to let people know about your services without exploiting vulnerability or making false promises. Ethics codes provide guidance.

Ethical Marketing Principles:

1. Truthfulness

Don't exaggerate effectiveness or make guarantees.

Don't say: "Flash cures PTSD in one session!"

Do say: "Flash is an evidence-based trauma processing technique that often produces significant symptom reduction in 1-3 sessions for many clients."

2. Avoid Exploitation

Don't target vulnerable populations with manipulative messaging.

Don't: Run ads showing graphic trauma imagery to trigger people into seeking services.

Do: Provide informational content explaining trauma treatment options.

3. Professional Representation

Present qualifications accurately. Don't claim expertise you don't have.

Don't: "Flash expert with 20 years experience" (if you trained last year)

Do: "Licensed therapist with training in Flash Technique for trauma treatment"

4. Client Welfare First

Marketing should serve client needs, not just fill your schedule.

Don't: Promote Flash to everyone regardless of appropriateness.

Do: Explain Flash is one option among several trauma treatments.

Marketing Channels:

Professional Website:

Your website should include:

About Flash Section:

"Flash Technique is a trauma processing approach that helps reduce distress from traumatic memories. Flash was developed as a gentler alternative to standard trauma therapy. During Flash, clients maintain focus on positive material while briefly accessing trauma memories. Research shows Flash can significantly reduce PTSD symptoms, often in fewer sessions than traditional trauma therapy.

I offer Flash for clients experiencing trauma-related symptoms who prefer a less intense processing approach or who haven't responded well to other trauma treatments."

Specializations/Services Page:

List Flash among services:

- Individual trauma therapy using EMDR and Flash Technique

- Group Flash for trauma processing

- Online therapy for trauma using Flash Technique

FAQs:

Answer common questions:

- What is Flash Technique?

- How does Flash differ from other trauma therapy?

- How many sessions does Flash take?

- Is Flash covered by insurance?

Psychology Today Profile:

List Flash as specialization. Explain briefly in description.

Social Media:

Share educational content:

- "Flash Technique: What trauma survivors should know"

- Research summaries about Flash effectiveness

- Trauma psychoeducation that mentions Flash as treatment option

Don't: Post graphic content, exploit trauma, or make exaggerated claims.

Google Business Profile:

Include Flash in services list. Add specialization keywords for search.

Blog Posts:

Write educational articles:

- "Understanding trauma processing options"

- "What to expect in Flash therapy"

- "How Flash helps with PTSD"

Provide value, not just self-promotion.

Community Presentations:

Offer talks:

- "New approaches in trauma treatment" at community centers

- "Trauma-informed care" for local organizations

- "Supporting trauma survivors" for support groups

Educational presentations build reputation and referrals.

Real Example:

Therapist created website section on Flash:

Content included:

- Plain-language explanation of Flash
- Research support (cited studies)
- Who Flash helps
- What to expect
- Contact information

Results:

- 30% increase in trauma-focused inquiries
- Clients specifically requesting Flash
- Position as trauma specialist in community

Ethical, informative marketing worked.

Explaining Flash to Referral Sources

Other professionals refer clients to you—psychiatrists, primary care doctors, school counselors, EAPs, crisis services. They need to understand what you offer.

Referral Source Education:

Brief Description for Referrals:

Create one-page handout explaining Flash:

Flash Technique for Trauma Treatment

Flash is an evidence-based trauma processing technique that reduces distress from traumatic memories through brief exposure while maintaining focus on positive material. Flash is particularly helpful for clients who:

- Have high initial distress about trauma memories

- Are avoidant or hesitant about trauma therapy

- Need relatively brief treatment

- Haven't responded to other trauma approaches

- Need low-disclosure trauma processing (confidentiality concerns)

Research shows Flash produces significant PTSD symptom reduction, often in 1-3 sessions. Flash can be used alone or integrated with other trauma treatments.

When to refer:

- Client has PTSD or trauma-related symptoms

- Client is stable enough for trauma processing (not actively suicidal, psychotic, or severely substance-impaired)

- Client wants trauma-focused treatment

Contact: [Your name, credentials, phone, email]

Presentations to Referral Sources:

Offer lunch-and-learn presentations:

Topic: "Flash Technique: New developments in trauma treatment"

Audience: Medical practices, counseling centers, social service agencies

Content:

- Brief trauma and PTSD overview

- Flash explanation and demonstration (role-play)
- Research support
- Appropriate referrals
- Q&A

Personalized Communication:

When you receive referral, follow up:

Email/Call to Referral Source:

"Thank you for referring [client name]. I wanted to let you know I've begun working with them using Flash Technique for their trauma symptoms. I'll keep you updated on progress (with client's consent). Please feel free to contact me with questions."

Updates (with client consent):

"I wanted to update you on [client's] progress. We've completed 3 Flash sessions and they're showing significant symptom improvement. We expect to complete trauma processing in 1-2 more sessions. Thank you for the referral."

Referral sources appreciate knowing their referrals are helped.

Building Referral Relationships:

Primary care physicians: Emphasize Flash's brevity and evidence base. Doctors value efficient treatments.

Psychiatrists: Explain Flash can complement medication management. Trauma processing enhances medication effectiveness.

School counselors: Highlight Flash's school-based applications and brief format fitting school schedules.

EAPs: Emphasize Flash works within brief EAP models (often 6-8 sessions max).

Crisis services: Explain Flash can provide single-session crisis trauma intervention.

Real Example:

Therapist presented Flash to local medical practice. Explained Flash could help trauma patients resistant to therapy (common).

Result: Practice began referring regularly. Physicians appreciated having trauma specialist who could help patients they'd struggled with.

Referrals increased 40% after presentation.

Supervision and Consultation

Even experienced therapists need consultation. Flash is no exception. Ongoing supervision and consultation improve outcomes and prevent problems.

Consultation Options:

1. Individual Supervision

Meet regularly (weekly or biweekly) with Flash-trained supervisor. Present cases, get feedback, discuss complications.

Best for: New Flash practitioners, complex cases, difficult situations.

2. Group Consultation

Join consultation group with other Flash-trained therapists. Present cases to group, learn from others' cases.

Best for: Ongoing skill development, diverse perspectives, peer support.

3. Online Consultation

Many Flash trainers offer online consultation groups or individual consultation via video.

Best for: Therapists without local Flash consultants, accessing experts.

4. Peer Consultation

Meet with colleague(s) also practicing Flash. Share cases, problem-solve together.

Best for: Experienced practitioners, maintaining skills, affordable option.

What to Bring to Consultation:

Case Presentations:

- Client background (brief)

- Trauma history

- Flash approach used

- What's working, what's not

- Specific questions or concerns

Video (if permitted):

Some consultants review video of Flash sessions (with client consent). Provides detailed feedback.

Outcome Data:

Share SUDS changes, symptom measures, client feedback. Data informs consultation.

Consultation Benefits:

- Improved clinical skills
- Prevention of errors
- Support for difficult cases
- Continuing education
- Professional connection
- Ethical practice maintenance

Real Example:

Therapist joined monthly Flash consultation group (6 therapists). Each meeting, 2 therapists present cases.

Benefits experienced:

- Learned from others' difficult cases
- Received feedback improving own practice
- Built relationships with Flash colleagues for informal consultation
- Maintained competence and confidence

Cost: $50/month. Value: Immeasurable.

Continuing Education Pathways

Flash is still developing. New research emerges. Protocols evolve. Stay current through continuing education.

CE Options:

1. Advanced Flash Training

After basic training, take advanced courses:

- Flash with complex trauma

- Flash with dissociation

- Flash with children

- Group Flash applications

- Flash in specific settings (schools, military, etc.)

2. EMDR Training

If you're not EMDR-trained, consider it. Flash originated in EMDR context. Understanding EMDR deepens Flash understanding.

3. Trauma-Focused CE

Any trauma training enhances Flash practice:

- Complex trauma treatment

- Somatic trauma therapy

- Attachment-focused trauma work

- Trauma and substance use

4. Research Updates

Read current research:

- Journal of EMDR Practice and Research (publishes Flash studies)

- Trauma journals (Journal of Traumatic Stress, etc.)

- Conference presentations

5. Conferences

Attend conferences with Flash presentations:

- EMDR International Association conference
- International Society for Traumatic Stress Studies
- Regional trauma conferences

Network with Flash practitioners and researchers.

6. Webinars

Many trainers offer Flash webinars (1-3 hours) on specific topics. Convenient, affordable continuing education.

Creating Learning Plan:

Year 1 (building Flash foundation):

- Basic Flash training
- Practice 20-30 cases with supervision
- Read core Flash research articles
- Join consultation group

Year 2 (expanding applications):

- Advanced Flash training (choose specialization)
- Attend conference with Flash content
- Present Flash case at consultation group
- Begin tracking outcomes systematically

Year 3+ (maintaining expertise, giving back):

- Stay current on research

- Ongoing consultation

- Consider training others

- Contribute to research or case studies

Real Example:

Therapist's CE pathway:

Year 1: Basic Flash training (12 hours), EMDR Part 1 (20 hours), trauma-focused CBT refresher (6 hours)

Year 2: Advanced Flash training in dissociation (8 hours), EMDR Part 2 (20 hours), consultation group (12 hours)

Year 3: Flash conference presentation, ongoing consultation, supervision of Flash trainee

Systematic CE development built expertise.

Contributing to Research

Flash research base is growing but still limited. Practitioners can contribute.

Ways to Contribute:

1. Outcome Tracking

Systematically track outcomes in your practice. Collect data:

- SUDS pre/post

- PCL-5 pre/post

- Client satisfaction

- Demographic information

Aggregate and analyze: After 50-100 cases, you have meaningful data.

Share findings: Present at conferences, submit to journals, share with Flash community.

2. Case Studies

Document interesting cases:

- Novel Flash applications
- Surprising outcomes
- Complications and how you handled them

Submit case studies to journals (Journal of EMDR Practice and Research publishes Flash cases).

3. Participate in Research Studies

Researchers studying Flash need participants:

- Client recruitment for studies
- Practitioner surveys
- Outcome data provision

Contact Flash researchers about collaboration.

4. Practice-Based Research Networks

Join networks where practitioners pool data:

- Shared protocols
- Aggregate outcome data
- Multi-site studies

Increases research power and generalizability.

5. Pilot Programs

Implement Flash in novel settings:

337

- Schools

- Refugee services

- Veterans programs

- Disaster response

Document systematically. Publish findings.

Why Contribute?

Personal benefits:

- Enhances your expertise

- Builds professional reputation

- Deepens clinical thinking

Professional benefits:

- Advances the field

- Strengthens Flash evidence base

- Helps future clients and therapists

Real Example:

Group practice implemented outcome tracking for all Flash clients:

2-year data collection:

- 120 clients

- SUDS and PCL-5 data

- Demographic variables

- Treatment characteristics

Analysis showed:

- 78% achieved clinically significant improvement
- Average 3.2 sessions to target completion
- Women responded slightly faster than men
- Single-incident trauma processed faster than complex trauma

Presented findings at conference. Contributed to Flash literature. Practice gained reputation as Flash center.

Small effort (tracking what they already did) produced meaningful contribution.

Getting Started with Research:

Step 1: Pick one simple outcome to track (SUDS is easiest).

Step 2: Track it consistently for every Flash client for 6 months.

Step 3: Analyze data. What patterns emerge?

Step 4: Share findings (presentation, article, consultation group).

You don't need PhD or grant funding. Practice-based research is valuable.

Growing Your Flash Expertise and Impact

Ethical marketing to clients involves truthful claims about Flash effectiveness, professional website content explaining Flash as one treatment option, educational blog posts and social media, and community presentations building reputation without exploitation of vulnerability.

Referral source education requires creating one-page handouts explaining Flash, offering lunch-and-learn presentations to medical and social service providers, providing updates on referred clients (with consent), and building relationships by emphasizing Flash benefits relevant to each referral source type.

Supervision and consultation through individual supervision, group consultation, online options, or peer consultation maintain and develop Flash skills while preventing errors. Regular consultation proves essential for competent practice even after initial training completion.

Continuing education pathways include advanced Flash training in specialized applications, broader trauma-focused education, research updates, conference attendance, and webinars. Systematic CE plans build expertise over years progressing from foundation to specialization to contribution.

Contributing to research through outcome tracking, case studies, participation in research studies, practice-based research networks, and pilot program documentation advances Flash evidence base while enhancing individual expertise and professional reputation. Simple practice-based research produces meaningful contributions without requiring advanced research training.

Appendix A: Complete Protocol Quick Reference Card

Flash Technique Protocol - Quick Reference

PREPARATION PHASE

Step 1: Screen for Appropriateness

- Trauma-related symptoms present?

- Client stable (no active psychosis, severe intoxication, imminent danger)?

- Can client engage with protocol?

- Informed consent obtained?

Step 2: Identify Target Memory

- Specific traumatic event

- Get baseline SUDS (0-10 scale)

- Note: If SUDS below 3, consider if Flash needed

PEF DEVELOPMENT (10-15 minutes)

Step 1: Generate Options "Think of something positive, safe, or pleasant. Could be place, person, activity, memory, or sensation."

Step 2: Develop Detail "Describe it. What do you see, hear, feel, smell, taste? Make it vivid."

Step 3: Test PEF "Close eyes, focus on it for 30 seconds. Does it feel positive? Can you hold it clearly?"

Step 4: Rate PEF "How positive does it feel? (0-10, with 7+ ideal)"

If PEF weak: Develop different one or enhance current one with more sensory detail.

FLASH PROCESSING

Setup Instructions: "Keep main focus on [PEF]. When I say 'now,' briefly think about the trauma—just flash to it for one second—then immediately back to [PEF]. We'll do this several times with [eye movements/tapping/tones]."

Flash Sequence:

1. "Focus on [PEF]"
2. Pause 5-10 seconds
3. "Now" [client briefly thinks of trauma]
4. 1-second pause
5. "Back to [PEF]"
6. Bilateral stimulation (15-25 seconds)

Repeat: 10-20 Flash sequences

Check SUDS: Every 5-10 sequences "What's the disturbance level now?"

Continue: Until SUDS reaches 0-2 or processing plateaus

TROUBLESHOOTING

If SUDS not decreasing:

- Check PEF strength (enhance if needed)
- Ensure client actually flashing to trauma (some avoid)
- Check for blocking beliefs
- Consider feeder memories needing processing first

If client overwhelmed:

- Stop processing
- Ground verbally
- Strengthen PEF
- Shorten flash duration (half-second)
- Check if client ready for processing

If client dissociates:

- Stop processing
- Strong verbal grounding
- Physical grounding (feet on floor, object to hold)
- Resume only when client fully present

CLOSURE

Check Stability:

- "How do you feel right now?"
- "Are you grounded and present?"
- "Can you think about the memory now? What's the SUDS?"

Body Scan (if time permits): "Scan your body. Any tension or discomfort?" If yes, process with additional Flash sequences.

Between-Session Expectations: "You may continue processing between sessions. Dreams, thoughts about trauma, or new insights are normal. Contact me if distress becomes overwhelming."

DOCUMENTATION

Record:

- Target memory (general description)
- PEF used
- Baseline SUDS
- Number of Flash sequences
- Final SUDS
- Client's response
- Plan for next session

Safety Note: Always ensure client stable before ending session. Extend time if needed.

Appendix B: Client Handouts & Psychoeducation Materials

Client Handout 1: Understanding Flash Technique

What is Flash Technique?

Flash is a way to reduce distress from traumatic memories. You briefly think about the trauma while focusing mostly on something positive. This helps your brain reprocess the memory so it bothers you less.

How is Flash different from other trauma therapy?

Traditional trauma therapy asks you to think about trauma for extended periods. Flash is gentler—you only touch the memory briefly, then return to positive focus. Most people find Flash more comfortable.

What happens during Flash?

1. We develop your "positive focus"—something that feels good or safe to you

2. You briefly flash to the traumatic memory (one second)

3. You immediately return to your positive focus

4. We repeat this with eye movements, tapping, or tones

5. The memory becomes less distressing

How long does Flash take?

Many people see significant improvement in 1-3 sessions. Complex trauma may take longer.

What should I expect after Flash?

- **Normal responses:** Feeling tired, relief, continued processing between sessions, dreams about trauma, new insights or memories emerging

- **Contact your therapist if:** Distress becomes overwhelming, you feel unsafe, dissociation occurs and won't stop, suicidal thoughts emerge

What can I do between sessions?

- Use grounding techniques if distressed

- Practice self-care (sleep, nutrition, exercise, social connection)

- Journal if helpful

- Avoid major life decisions immediately after processing

- Contact therapist with concerns

Questions to ask your therapist:

- How many Flash sessions will I need?

- What if the memory doesn't get better?

- Can I do Flash for multiple traumas?

- What are alternatives if Flash doesn't work for me?

Client Handout 2: Grounding Techniques for Between Sessions

5-4-3-2-1 Grounding

- Name 5 things you can see

- Name 4 things you can touch

- Name 3 things you can hear

- Name 2 things you can smell

- Name 1 thing you can taste

Physical Grounding

- Stamp your feet on the floor

- Hold ice cube in your hand

- Splash cold water on your face

- Do jumping jacks or run in place

- Squeeze a stress ball

Mental Grounding

- Count backward from 100 by 7s

- Name all the states you've visited

- List animals alphabetically

- Describe your room in detail

- Recite favorite poem or song lyrics

When to Use Grounding

- When memories feel too intense

- If you start to dissociate (feel unreal or disconnected)

- During flashbacks

- When anxiety spikes

- Anytime you need to return to the present moment

Crisis Resources

- National Suicide Prevention Lifeline: 988

- Crisis Text Line: Text HOME to 741741

- Your therapist: [phone number]

- Emergency: 911

Appendix C: PEF Development Worksheets

Worksheet 1: PEF Exploration

Instructions: Answer these questions to help identify potential Positive Engaging Focus options.

Safe Places:

Where do you feel most calm and safe?

_____

Describe this place with sensory details:

- What do you see? _____
- What sounds are there? _____
- What smells are present? _____
- How does it feel (temperature, textures)?

  _____

Positive People:

Who makes you feel safe, loved, or supported?

_____

What's a specific positive memory with this person?

_____

Activities:

What activities help you feel calm, happy, or engaged?

Describe doing this activity with all your senses:

Positive Memories:

What's a time you felt proud, accomplished, or truly happy?

Describe this memory in detail:

Sensations:

What physical sensations feel good or comforting to you?
(Examples: warm bath, soft blanket, pet's fur, favorite food)

Your Top 3 PEF Options:

1. _____

2. _____

3. _____

Worksheet 2: PEF Development and Testing

Selected PEF: _____

Sensory Details:

Visual (what you see):

Auditory (what you hear):

Kinesthetic (what you feel):

Olfactory (what you smell):

Gustatory (what you taste):

Emotional Quality: What emotions does this PEF bring up?

PEF Strength Rating: On scale of 0-10, how positive does this feel? _____

If below 7: What could make it stronger?

Test Results: Can you hold this PEF clearly for 30 seconds? Yes / No

Does it feel consistently positive? Yes / No

Does anything negative intrude? Yes / No If yes, what?

_____

Final Decision: Is this PEF ready to use? Yes / No

If no, what needs adjustment?

Appendix D: Session Documentation Templates

Template 1: Flash Session Progress Note

Client: _____ **Date:** _____ **Session #:** _____
Duration: _____ minutes

Phase of Treatment: ☐ Assessment ☐ Stabilization ☐ Flash Processing ☐ Integration ☐ Termination

Target Memory (general description):

_____

PEF Used:

_____

Baseline SUDS: _____ (0-10 scale)

Flash Processing:

- Number of Flash sequences completed: _____

- Bilateral stimulation type: ☐ Eye movements ☐ Tapping ☐ Audio ☐ Other: _____

- Client engagement: ☐ Good ☐ Moderate ☐ Poor

- Complications: ☐ None ☐ Dissociation ☐ Overwhelming distress ☐ Blocking ☐ Other: _____

SUDS Progression:

- After 5 sequences: _____

- After 10 sequences: _____
- After 15 sequences: _____
- Final SUDS: _____

Client Response:

_____

_____

Safety Assessment:

- Suicidal ideation: ☐ None ☐ Passive ☐ Active ☐ With plan
- Self-harm urges: ☐ None ☐ Present but manageable ☐ High risk
- Dissociation at session end: ☐ None ☐ Mild ☐ Moderate ☐ Severe
- Client stability at closure: ☐ Stable ☐ Moderately stable ☐ Unstable (extended closure provided)

Plan: ☐ Continue Flash on same target ☐ Begin new target next session ☐ Integration and consolidation ☐ Other:

_____

Follow-Up: ☐ No follow-up needed ☐ Phone check-in scheduled for: _____ ☐ Crisis plan reviewed ☐ Referral made to: _____

Therapist Signature: _____ **Date:** _____

Template 2: Flash Treatment Summary

Client: _____ Treatment Period: _____ to

_____

Presenting Problem:

Diagnosis: _____

Treatment Approach: Flash Technique for trauma processing

Targets Processed:

Target	Baseline SUDS	Final SUDS	Sessions
1. _____	_____	_____	_____
2. _____	_____	_____	_____
3. _____	_____	_____	_____
4. _____	_____	_____	_____

Outcome Measures:

PCL-5 (PTSD symptoms):

- Baseline: _____ Post-treatment: _____

PHQ-9 (Depression):

- Baseline: _____ Post-treatment: _____

GAD-7 (Anxiety):

- Baseline: _____ Post-treatment: _____

Functional Impairment:

- Baseline: _____ Post-treatment: _____

Treatment Outcome: ☐ Goals achieved ☐ Substantial progress ☐ Moderate progress ☐ Minimal progress ☐ No progress

Client Satisfaction: _____ (0-10 scale)

Termination Reason: ☐ Goals met ☐ Client choice ☐ Therapist unavailable ☐ Referral to: _____

Recommendations:

_____

Follow-Up Plan:

_____

_____

Appendix E: Outcome Measurement Tools

Tool 1: Session-by-Session SUDS Tracking

Client: _____ Target: _____

Session	Date	Baseline SUDS	Mid SUDS	Final SUDS	Notes
1					
2					
3					
4					
5					

SUDS Change: Total reduction: _____ points Percent reduction: _____%

Tool 2: Flash Treatment Outcome Questionnaire

Client Name (optional): _____ Date: _____

Please rate the following statements about your Flash treatment:

1. Flash reduced my trauma-related distress. ☐ Strongly disagree ☐ Disagree ☐ Neutral ☐ Agree ☐ Strongly agree

2. Flash was comfortable to participate in. ☐ Strongly disagree
☐ Disagree ☐ Neutral ☐ Agree ☐ Strongly agree

3. I would recommend Flash to others with trauma. ☐
Definitely not ☐ Probably not ☐ Unsure ☐ Probably yes ☐
Definitely yes

4. Overall satisfaction with Flash treatment (0-10): _____

5. What was most helpful about Flash?

_____

6. What was least helpful about Flash?

_____

7. What would have improved your Flash experience?

_____

8. Current symptom severity (0-10): _____

_____

Appendix F: Training Resources & Organizations

Flash Training Providers

Training in Flash Technique is available through various organizations and trainers. Look for programs offering:

- Minimum 8-16 hours of instruction
- Supervised practice opportunities
- Continuing education credits
- Training from clinicians with Flash experience

What to Look For in Training:

Didactic Content:

- Flash theory and research
- Protocol instruction
- Safety and contraindications
- Adaptations for populations
- Ethical considerations

Experiential Learning:

- Demonstration of Flash
- Practice with feedback
- Role-play exercises

- Case consultation

Post-Training Support:

- Consultation groups

- Advanced training options

- Supervision availability

- Research participation opportunities

Professional Organizations

EMDR International Association (EMDRIA) Flash originated within EMDR context. EMDRIA conferences often include Flash presentations.

International Society for Traumatic Stress Studies (ISTSS) Trauma research and practice organization. Conferences may include Flash content.

American Psychological Association (APA) Division 56 (Trauma Psychology) includes trauma treatment innovations.

Consultation Resources

Finding Flash Consultation:

- Contact trainers for consultation group information

- Join online Flash practitioner communities

- Seek supervision from Flash-trained supervisors

- Form peer consultation groups with Flash-trained colleagues

What to Expect from Consultation:

- Case presentation and feedback

- Troubleshooting difficult cases
- Protocol refinement
- Outcome discussion
- Ethical guidance

Appendix G: Research Summary Tables

Key Flash Research Studies

Study 1: Manfield et al. (2017)

- **Citation:** Manfield, P., Engel, L., Greenwald, R., & Bullard, B. (2017). Use of the Flash Technique in EMDR therapy: Four case examples. *Journal of EMDR Practice and Research, 11*(4), 195-205.

- **Type:** Case studies

- **Population:** Adult trauma survivors

- **Findings:** Flash produced rapid SUDS reduction across multiple trauma types with minimal distress during processing

- **Significance:** First published documentation of Flash protocol

Study 2: Shapiro (2018) - EMDR Third Edition

- **Citation:** Shapiro, F. (2018). *Eye movement desensitization and reprocessing (EMDR) therapy: Basic principles, protocols, and procedures* (3rd ed.). Guilford Press.

- **Type:** Clinical text

- **Content:** Discussion of Flash as preparation phase enhancement

- **Significance:** Integration of Flash into standard EMDR literature

Research Areas Needing Further Study:

Populations:

- Children and adolescents (limited published research)

- Dissociative disorders (clinical reports but few controlled studies)

- Complex trauma (more case studies needed)

- Diverse cultural populations

Applications:

- Group Flash effectiveness

- Online Flash outcomes

- Single-session Flash durability

- Flash compared to other trauma treatments

Mechanisms:

- How Flash works neurobiologically

- Why PEF structure reduces distress

- Optimal Flash sequence parameters

Clinical Outcomes from Practice-Based Research

Aggregated Data from Multiple Clinical Settings:

Average SUDS reduction: 5-7 points (across studies) Typical sessions to target completion: 1-4 sessions Client satisfaction: Generally high (7-9 out of 10) Dropout rates: Lower than exposure-based treatments (15-25% vs. 30-50%)

Note: Practice-based research provides preliminary support but lacks controlled design. Randomized controlled trials needed for definitive evidence.

Appendix H: Troubleshooting Decision Trees

Decision Tree 1: SUDS Not Decreasing

Problem: After 5-10 Flash sequences, SUDS unchanged or increased

Step 1: Check PEF Strength

- Ask: "Is your positive focus still feeling positive?"

- If no → Strengthen or develop new PEF

- If yes → Continue to Step 2

Step 2: Check Client Engagement

- Ask: "Are you actually flashing to the trauma briefly, or avoiding it?"

- If avoiding → Coach client to make brief contact

- If engaging → Continue to Step 3

Step 3: Check for Blocking Beliefs

- Ask: "What comes up when you think about letting this trauma go?"

- If blocking belief identified → Process belief first with Flash

- If no blocking belief → Continue to Step 4

Step 4: Check for Feeder Memories

- Ask: "Does another memory keep coming up?"
- If yes → Switch to feeder memory as target
- If no → Continue to Step 5

Step 5: Check Trauma Complexity

- Is this complex/layered trauma?
- If yes → May need more sessions or different approach
- If no → Consider consultation

Decision Tree 2: Client Becoming Overwhelmed

Problem: Client showing signs of overwhelm (crying intensely, panic, dissociation)

Immediate Action: STOP Flash processing

Step 1: Ground Client

- Verbal grounding: "Look at me. You're safe. You're in [location]. Today is [date]."
- Physical grounding: "Feel your feet on the floor. Feel the chair supporting you."
- Sensory grounding: "Name 5 things you can see right now."

Step 2: Assess Client State

- Is client returning to present?
- If yes → Continue to Step 3
- If no → Continue grounding. Consider ending session early if can't ground.

Step 3: Identify Cause

- Was flash too long? (Shorten to half-second)

- Was PEF too weak? (Strengthen or change)

- Was client not ready for processing? (More stabilization needed)

- Did something unexpected trigger? (Process feeder memory first)

Step 4: Decide Whether to Continue

- Client grounded and willing?

- Cause identified and addressable?

- If yes to both → Resume with adjustments

- If no to either → Provide closure, schedule follow-up

Decision Tree 3: Dissociation During Flash

Problem: Client dissociating (spacey, not responding, blank stare, time distortion)

Immediate Action: STOP Flash processing

Grounding Protocol:

1. Call client's name firmly

2. Ask client to look at you

3. Ask client to state name and date

4. Physical grounding (stamp feet, hold object)

5. 5-4-3-2-1 sensory grounding

Once Client Present:

Assess:

- How severe was dissociation? (Brief vs. extended)

- Has client returned fully? (Check orientation)

- What triggered it? (Flash duration? PEF weakness? Trauma content?)

Adjustments:

- Shorten flash to half-second or less

- Strengthen PEF significantly

- More frequent grounding checks

- Slower pace overall

Decision:

- Continue with adjustments? (Only if client stable and dissociation brief)

- End session and resume next time? (If dissociation was significant)

- Refer for dissociation-specialist consultation? (If dissociation severe or persistent)

Appendix I: Sample Informed Consent Forms

Sample Informed Consent for Flash Technique

CLIENT NAME: _____ **DATE:**
_____

Description of Flash Technique:

Flash Technique is a method for processing traumatic memories by briefly thinking about the trauma while maintaining primary focus on positive material. This approach aims to reduce emotional distress associated with traumatic experiences.

Procedure:

During Flash, you will:

1. Develop a positive engaging focus (pleasant image, memory, or sensation)

2. Briefly "flash" to your traumatic memory (1 second or less)

3. Return immediately to your positive focus

4. Repeat this process with bilateral stimulation (eye movements, tapping, or tones)

Sessions typically last 60-90 minutes. Most people find Flash comfortable and report reduced distress within 1-3 sessions.

Potential Benefits:

Flash may provide:

- Decreased trauma-related distress
- Reduced PTSD symptoms
- Improved functioning
- Better sleep and fewer nightmares
- Increased ability to think about trauma without overwhelming emotions

Potential Risks:

While Flash is designed to be gentle, risks include:

- Temporary increase in distress during or after sessions
- Emotional or physical sensations during processing
- Dreams or thoughts about trauma between sessions
- Fatigue after sessions
- In rare cases: severe emotional distress, dissociation, or worsening symptoms

Alternative Treatments:

Other options include:

- Eye Movement Desensitization and Reprocessing (EMDR)
- Cognitive Processing Therapy (CPT)
- Prolonged Exposure (PE)
- Traditional psychotherapy
- Medication management

Confidentiality:

Information shared is confidential except when:

- Written consent provided for release

- Danger to self or others exists

- Child or elder abuse suspected

- Court order requires disclosure

Right to Withdraw:

You may decline or discontinue Flash at any time without penalty. Your care will continue with alternative approaches.

Questions:

I have had opportunity to ask questions about Flash Technique and they have been answered to my satisfaction.

Consent:

I understand the information provided above. I voluntarily consent to Flash Technique treatment.

Client Signature: _____ **Date:** _____

Therapist Signature: _____ **Date:** _____

Appendix J: Integration Checklists for Each Modality

Checklist 1: Flash with EMDR

Pre-Integration: ☐ EMDR training completed (Basic or equivalent) ☐ Flash training completed ☐ Understand Adaptive Information Processing model ☐ Familiar with standard EMDR 8-phase protocol

Phase 2 Preparation with Flash: ☐ Client assessed for EMDR appropriateness ☐ Flash introduced as preparation tool ☐ PEF developed (can function as resource) ☐ Target memory identified ☐ Baseline SUDS obtained ☐ Flash processing reduces SUDS to manageable level (4-6 range)

Transition to Standard EMDR: ☐ Client assessed for readiness ☐ Phase 3 assessment completed (NC, PC, VoC, emotions, body) ☐ Desensitization begins with bilateral stimulation ☐ Processing continues through installation, body scan, closure ☐ Reevaluation next session

Documentation: ☐ Flash preparation documented ☐ Transition rationale noted ☐ Standard EMDR phases documented ☐ Outcome measured and recorded

Checklist 2: Flash with Cognitive Processing Therapy

Pre-Integration: ☐ CPT training completed ☐ Flash training completed ☐ Understand CPT structure (12 sessions, Socratic method) ☐ Familiar with stuck points and cognitive restructuring

CPT Sessions 1-2: ☐ Standard CPT introduction ☐ Psychoeducation ☐ Impact statement assignment

CPT Session 3 - Flash Preparation: ☐ Instead of moving directly to trauma account, use Flash ☐ Reduce SUDS on primary trauma memory from 9-10 to 4-6 ☐ Client experiences success managing trauma content

CPT Sessions 4-12: ☐ Client writes trauma account (easier with reduced SUDS) ☐ Cognitive processing of stuck points ☐ Complete standard CPT protocol ☐ Flash available as needed for overwhelming sessions

Documentation: ☐ Flash session documented ☐ Impact on CPT engagement noted ☐ Stuck points and cognitive changes tracked ☐ CPT completion status recorded

Checklist 3: Flash with Somatic Experiencing

Pre-Integration: ☐ SE training completed (3-year training or equivalent exposure) ☐ Flash training completed ☐ Understand titration and nervous system regulation ☐ Skilled in tracking body sensations

Integration Protocol: ☐ Client identifies trauma and body sensations associated ☐ Flash reduces overall nervous system activation ☐ Activation decreased from 9-10 to 5-6 range ☐ SE protocol for completing defensive responses ☐ Track sensations and movements ☐ Allow discharge of survival energy ☐ Integration and closure

Session Structure: ☐ 10-15 minutes: Flash to reduce activation ☐ 20-30 minutes: SE tracking and completion ☐ 10-15 minutes: Integration and grounding

Documentation: ☐ Baseline body sensations documented ☐ Flash intervention and SUDS reduction noted ☐ SE process and discharge documented ☐ Client's somatic experience recorded

Checklist 4: Flash with DBT

Pre-Integration: ☐ DBT training completed ☐ Flash training completed ☐ Understand DBT stages and targets ☐ Skills training materials prepared

Stage 1 Integration: ☐ Weeks 1-4: Standard DBT orientation and skills introduction ☐ Week 5+: Add Flash for trauma processing while continuing skills ☐ Flash reduces trauma intensity that drives dysregulation ☐ Client practices DBT skills with reduced trauma activation ☐ Continue skills training throughout

Safety Considerations: ☐ Client has basic distress tolerance skills before Flash ☐ Safety plan established ☐ Crisis resources identified ☐ Between-session contact plan created

Documentation: ☐ DBT stage and targets documented ☐ Flash sessions integrated into treatment plan ☐ Skills acquisition progress tracked ☐ Symptom reduction (diary cards, measures) documented

Checklist 5: Flash with IFS

Pre-Integration: ☐ IFS training completed (Level 1 minimum) ☐ Flash training completed ☐ Understand parts language and Self leadership ☐ Skilled in accessing and unburdening exiles

Integration Protocol: ☐ Identify protective parts blocking trauma access ☐ Negotiate with protectors to observe Flash demonstration ☐ Flash demonstrated showing safety of processing ☐ Protectors observe system doesn't fall apart ☐ With protectors' permission, continue Flash to unburden exiles ☐ Update protector roles after exiles unburdened

Session Structure: ☐ Part identification and negotiation: 15-20 minutes ☐ Flash processing of exile trauma: 30-40 minutes ☐ Integration and protector updating: 15-20 minutes

Documentation: ☐ Parts identified and roles documented ☐ Protector concerns and agreements noted ☐ Flash processing and unburdening documented ☐ System changes and integration recorded

Glossary of Terms

Adaptive Information Processing (AIP): The theoretical model underlying EMDR therapy, proposing that psychological health depends on adaptive processing of experiences. Traumatic experiences can overwhelm this system, causing pathology. Flash was developed within this framework.

Bilateral Stimulation (BLS): Alternating left-right stimulation (eye movements, tapping, or audio tones) used in EMDR and Flash. Believed to facilitate information processing.

Blocking Belief: A cognitive belief preventing trauma processing. Example: "If I let go of this guilt, it means I didn't care." Must be addressed before processing can continue.

Body Scan: Systematic attention to body sensations from head to toe, used in EMDR Phase 6 and other trauma therapies to identify residual disturbance.

Closure: The process of ending a therapy session safely, ensuring client is grounded and stable before leaving.

Complex Trauma: Repeated, prolonged traumatic experiences, usually starting in childhood. Affects development, attachment, and self-concept differently than single-incident trauma.

Desensitization: Phase 4 of EMDR protocol where traumatic memory is processed with bilateral stimulation until disturbance decreases.

Dissociation: Disconnection from present reality, often used as defense against overwhelming trauma. Ranges from mild (spacing out) to severe (DID).

Dissociative Identity Disorder (DID): Severe dissociative disorder involving distinct personality states (alters) with amnesia between states. Requires specialized treatment approach.

EMDR (Eye Movement Desensitization and Reprocessing): Evidence-based trauma therapy using bilateral stimulation to process traumatic memories. Flash originated as EMDR preparation technique.

Exile: In Internal Family Systems, a part holding painful emotions or traumatic memories, usually kept hidden by protective parts.

Feeder Memory: Earlier trauma memory that feeds into or maintains current symptoms. Often needs processing before target memory can resolve.

Flash Technique: Brief exposure trauma processing method where client maintains focus on positive material while briefly flashing to traumatic memory.

Grounding: Techniques to help person stay connected to present moment, used to manage dissociation, flashbacks, or overwhelm.

Installation: Phase 5 of EMDR where positive cognition is strengthened and linked with original trauma memory.

Moral Injury: Psychological distress from perpetrating, witnessing, or failing to prevent acts that violate moral code. Common in military and first responder populations.

Negative Cognition (NC): Dysfunctional belief about self connected to traumatic memory (Example: "I'm powerless"). Identified in EMDR Phase 3.

Positive Cognition (PC): Adaptive belief client would prefer to hold (Example: "I'm capable"). Also identified in EMDR Phase 3.

Positive Engaging Focus (PEF): The positive image, memory, sensation, or thought that client focuses on during Flash processing. Serves as protective anchor.

PTSD (Post-Traumatic Stress Disorder): Mental health condition triggered by experiencing or witnessing traumatic event. Symptoms include intrusions, avoidance, negative mood/cognitions, and arousal changes.

Reprocessing: The therapeutic process of working through traumatic memories until they no longer cause distress and adaptive resolution is achieved.

SUDS (Subjective Units of Disturbance Scale): 0-10 scale measuring distress level associated with trauma memory. Used to track processing progress.

Target Memory: The specific traumatic memory selected for processing in a given session.

Titration: Working with small amounts of activation to prevent overwhelm, commonly used in Somatic Experiencing.

Unburdening: In Internal Family Systems, the process of releasing extreme emotions and beliefs that exiled parts carry from trauma.

Validity of Cognition (VoC): 1-7 scale measuring how true positive cognition feels. Used in EMDR assessment and installation phases.

Wrapping Up

These appendices give you everything you need to actually practice Flash—not just know about it intellectually, but use it effectively in real sessions with real clients.

Print the protocol card. Laminate it. Keep it visible during sessions until you've internalized the flow. Copy the client handouts for your waiting room. Use the worksheets to help clients develop strong PEFs. Fill out the documentation templates after every session. Track your outcomes so you know Flash is working.

The checklists prevent you from missing steps when integrating Flash with other modalities. The troubleshooting trees help when you're stuck. The informed consent forms protect you legally and ethically.

And the glossary? That's for when you're explaining Flash to colleagues who ask "What's a PEF again?" or "How is this different from regular EMDR?"

These tools turn Flash from interesting theory into practical application. Use them. They work.

References

- **American Psychiatric Association. (2013).** *Diagnostic and statistical manual of mental disorders* (5th ed.). American Psychiatric Publishing.

- **Andrade, J., Kavanagh, D., & Baddeley, A. (1997).** Eye-movements and visual imagery: A working memory approach to the treatment of post-traumatic stress disorder. *British Journal of Clinical Psychology, 36*(2), 209–223.

- **Backhaus, A., Agha, Z., Maglione, M. L., Repp, A., Ross, B., Zuest, D., Rice-Thorp, N. M., Lohr, J., & Thorp, S. R. (2012).** Videoconferencing psychotherapy: A systematic review. *Psychological Services, 9*(2), 111–131.

- **Cohen, J. A., Mannarino, A. P., & Deblinger, E. (2017).** *Treating trauma and traumatic grief in children and adolescents* (2nd ed.). Guilford Press.

- **Courtois, C. A., & Ford, J. D. (2013).** *Treatment of complex trauma: A sequenced, relationship-based approach.* Guilford Press.

- **Ecker, B., Ticic, R., & Hulley, L. (2012).** *Unlocking the emotional brain: Eliminating symptoms at their roots using memory reconsolidation.* Routledge.

- **FlashTechnique.com. (2024).** Research. Retrieved from the official Flash Technique website.

- **Foa, E. B., & Kozak, M. J. (1986).** Emotional processing of fear: Exposure to corrective information. *Psychological Bulletin, 99*(1), 20–35.

- **Foa, E. B., Hembree, E. A., & Rothbaum, B. O. (2007).** *Prolonged exposure therapy for PTSD: Emotional processing of traumatic experiences.* Oxford University Press.

- **Harned, M. S., Korslund, K. E., & Linehan, M. M. (2014).** A pilot randomized controlled trial of Dialectical Behavior Therapy with and without the Dialectical Behavior Therapy Prolonged Exposure protocol for suicidal and self-injuring women with borderline personality disorder and PTSD. *Behaviour Research and Therapy, 55,* 7–17.

- **Imel, Z. E., Laska, K., Jakupcak, M., & Simpson, T. L. (2013).** Meta-analysis of dropout in treatments for posttraumatic stress disorder. *Journal of Consulting and Clinical Psychology, 81*(3), 394–404.

- **Korn, D. L. (2009).** EMDR and the treatment of complex PTSD: A review. *Journal of EMDR Practice and Research, 3*(4), 264–278.

- **Leeds, A. M. (2009).** *A guide to the standard EMDR therapy protocols for clinicians, supervisors, and consultants.* Springer Publishing.

- **Levine, P. A. (2010).** *In an unspoken voice: How the body releases trauma and restores goodness.* North Atlantic Books.

- **Linehan, M. M. (2014).** *DBT skills training manual* (2nd ed.). Guilford Press.

- **Litz, B. T., Stein, N., Delaney, E., Lebowitz, L., Nash, W. P., Silva, C., & Maguen, S. (2009).** Moral injury and moral repair in war veterans: A preliminary model and intervention strategy. *Clinical Psychology Review, 29*(8), 695–706.

- **Manfield, P., & Engel, L. (2018).** Testing three brief interventions to reduce distress in response to disturbing memories. *Traumatology, 24*(4), 259–264.

- **Manfield, P., Engel, L., Greenwald, R., & Bullard, B. (2017).** Use of the Flash Technique in EMDR therapy: Four case examples. *Journal of EMDR Practice and Research, 11*(4), 195–205.

- **Ogden, P., Minton, K., & Pain, C. (2006).** *Trauma and the body: A sensorimotor approach to psychotherapy.* W. W. Norton.

- **Resick, P. A., Monson, C. M., & Chard, K. M. (2016).** *Cognitive processing therapy for PTSD: A comprehensive manual.* Guilford Press.

- **Schwartz, R. C. (1995).** *Internal family systems therapy.* Guilford Press.

- **Shapiro, F. (2018).** *Eye movement desensitization and reprocessing (EMDR) therapy: Basic principles, protocols, and procedures* (3rd ed.). Guilford Press.

- **van der Kolk, B. A. (2014).** *The body keeps the score: Brain, mind, and body in the healing of trauma.* Viking.

www.ingramcontent.com/pod-product-compliance
Lightning Source LLC
Chambersburg PA
CBHW070542270326

41926CB00013B/2176